S0-BBY-849

CHURCHES AND CHURCHGOERS

CHURCHES AND CHURCHGOERS

PATTERNS OF CHURCH GROWTH IN THE BRITISH ISLES SINCE 1700

Robert Currie
Alan Gilbert
Lee Horsley

CLARENDON PRESS · OXFORD
1977

Oxford University Press, Walton Street, Oxford OX2 6DP
OXFORD LONDON GLASGOW NEW YORK
TORONTO MELBOURNE WELLINGTON CAPE TOWN
IBADAN NAIROBI DAR ES SALAAM LUSAKA ADDIS ABABA
KUALA LUMPUR SINGAPORE JAKARTA HONG KONG TOKYO
DELHI BOMBAY CALCUTTA MADRAS KARACHI

British Library Cataloguing in Publication Data

Currie, Robert
Churches and churchgoers.
1. Great Britain – Church history
I. Title II. Gilbert, Alan III. Horsley, Lee
301.5'8'0941 BR755

ISBN 0 19 827218 9

*Set by Getset Ltd, Eynsham, Oxford
and printed in Great Britain by
William Clowes, Beccles.*

Preface

Our aim in preparing this study has been twofold: first, to collect and compile hitherto unused and often little-known numerical data on many aspects of church life in Great Britain and Ireland from the eighteenth to the twentieth century; and, secondly, to use these data to test a theory of church growth. We have been primarily concerned with the phases of church growth and with the changing relationship between churches and the population from which they draw their membership as they pass through successive stages of rapid growth, stabilization, and decrease. One of the problems considered is the extent to which a church is able to generate its own growth, for example, by recruitment and church-building programmes; and we conclude, from the available data, that church policy is on the whole of less significance than external influences such as secularization, industrialization, urbanization, trade fluctuations, political changes, and war. In assessing the effects of these exogenous factors, we have also examined the validity of several earlier, non-statistical accounts of church growth, including arguments about the effects of economic or political crises on religious activity.

This is the first study to be based on a comprehensive survey of the quantifiable aspects of church life in the British Isles as a whole. We have therefore attempted to demonstrate the reliability and value of the statistics analysed and to present them in a way that will make them of use to other scholars interested in the study of organized religion. It is hoped that we have thus been able to make a contribution not only to the sociology of religion and to church history, but also to the larger sociological and historical study of British culture and institutions.

This book arises from work by Robert Currie, Alan Gilbert, and Lee Horsley for a 'Statistical Survey of Religion in Britain and Ireland since 1700', which was supported by a grant from the Social Science Research Council, administered by Wadham College, Oxford. The Survey drew on work published by Robert Currie in *Methodism Divided: A Study in the Sociology of Ecumenicalism* (1968); by Robert Currie and Alan Gilbert in the chapter on 'Religion' in A. H. Halsey (ed.), *Trends in British Society* (1970); and by Alan Gilbert in *Religion and Society in Industrial England: Church, Chapel, and Social Change, 1740-1914* (1976).

We would like to express our gratitude to the Social Science Research Council, to Wadham College, to the Oxford Computing Laboratory, and to the many churches and other bodies who have assisted us in our inquiries, and permitted us to publish data, the sources of which are acknowledged in the notes to the tables in the Appendix. We would also like to record our appreciation of the advice and assistance given to us by Robert Bacon, Pamela Currie, Ingrid Gilbert, Anthony Horsley, Michael Surrey, John Walsh, and Bryan Wilson.

ROBERT CURRIE
ALAN GILBERT
LEE HORSLEY

Contents

List of Figures

List of Tables in the Text

For tables in the Appendix see pp. 125-6

Introduction

This book investigates changes over time in certain quantifiable aspects of church life, such as the number of members, communicants, Sunday-school scholars, clergy or ministers, and church buildings attached to the various Christian bodies. These changes provide evidence for many types of inquiry, but they are here used as material for the study of the sociological character of religious organization and religious activity, the relationships between churches and the societies in which they operate, and the effects upon churches of the kind of social and economic changes experienced in Britain since 1700.

We define religion as *the attempt to effect certain ends either in this world or in other worlds by means wholly or partially supernatural,* whether the ends to be effected are, for instance, victory in war, a good harvest, or salvation from sin. This definition follows the work of a number of anthropologists and sociologists who have questioned the validity of any distinction between 'religion', a system involving 'submissiveness to the super-empirical', and 'magic', a system involving 'the instrumental significance of supernature', in Roland Robertson's words. Much of the distinction traditionally drawn between religion and magic rests upon value judgements, and much upon the specific emphases of any particular empirical system. For virtually no form of 'submissiveness to the super-empirical' contains no element of instrumentalism, whether propitiation of the deity or the search for the right mode of existence; while virtually no effort to exploit 'the instrumental significance of supernature' excludes the need to submit to (as well as use) powers greater than those of nature.[1]

This definition interprets religion as a purposive process or as an instrumentality, however reverently handled. The 'point' of religion so defined is, to adapt some well-known words of Marx, not to *interpret* the world but 'to change it'. Religion is therefore associated with, and issues in, activity, because religious people expect their religion to impinge directly upon their own life and goals. Such people will tend to understand religion as a matter of ritual or cult, rather than contemplation, though the cultic cannot altogether displace the contemplative; and religious ritual will be perceived as a means to secure at least the approval, if not the assistance, of the supernatural: the forgiveness of trespass, if not the provision of daily bread.

1. Roland Robertson, *The Sociological Interpretation of Religion,* Oxford, 1972, pp. 47-8; J. Milton Yinger, *The Scientific Study of Religion,* New York, 1970, pp 69-71.

If religion were primarily contemplative, or if the most efficacious rites were held to be necessarily solitary, religion would remain more or less a private matter. In practice, however, religious people tend to form collectivities, organized to conduct a public cult which is held to be most appropriate to the purposes to be realized. 'Although we ought at all times humbly to acknowledge our sins before God,' in the words of the *Book of Common Prayer,* 'yet ought we most chiefly so to do, when we assemble and meet together to render thanks for the great benefits that we have received at his hands, to set forth his most worthy praise, to hear his most holy Word, and to ask those things which are requisite and necessary, as well for the body as the soul.'

Robertson's recent analysis of religious collectivities uses two criteria only: the number of 'valid religious vehicles' perceived by the collectivity's leaders; and the rigour of the 'standards of admission and . . . practice' required for membership of the collectivity. Both criteria can be related to religion as an attempt to use supernatural means. If religious leaders recognize 'vehicles' other than their own as 'valid', they are adopting the *pluralist* position of admitting the effectiveness of more than one religious collectivity's use of supernatural means; but if they only recognize their own 'vehicle' as 'valid', they are adopting the *universalist* position of denying effectiveness to the use of supernatural means by all religious collectivities other than their own. If participants in a religious collectivity must meet high 'standards', their organization accepts an *exclusive* concept of membership, which implies pessimism about the effectuality of a resort to the supernatural by all sorts and conditions of men; but if participants in such a collectivity are obliged to reach only low 'standards' their organization accepts an *inclusive* concept of membership which implies optimism about all men's ability to use supernatural means.[2]

The statistical material published and analysed in this book refers almost entirely to religious collectivities classifiable, by use of these criteria, into four groups. Universalist-exclusive organizations may be categorized as 'sects'; pluralist-exclusive organizations as 'institutionalized sects'; universalist-inclusive organizations as 'churches'; and pluralist-inclusive organizations as 'denominations'. But the collectivities exist in complex historical and social contexts, and their changing relationship to one another and to society requires various modifications of the general typology, different categories of which a single religious organization may, in any event, occupy at successive stages in its history.

Since about 1700 British (and especially English) society has been, by European standards, both secular and tolerant; and since the union between England and Scotland in 1707, the state has contained two coequal established churches, the episcopalian Church of England and the presbyterian Church of Scotland. Furthermore, throughout the period since 1700 there has been an unestablished Episcopal

2. Robertson, op. cit., p. 124.

Church in Scotland in communion and historical continuity with the Church of England; while, since 1876, Scottish and English presbyterian churches in England have been organized in a Presbyterian Church of England (now part of the United Reformed Church) in communion and historical continuity with the Church of Scotland. Finally, the episcopalian state church was disestablished in Ireland and Wales by statutes of 1869 and 1914 respectively. Thus the 'universalism' characteristic of a 'church' in the sociological typology of religious collectivities has, over many years, been modified in the empirical cases of the Church of England and the Church of Scotland.

The legal, political, and cultural advantages nevertheless enjoyed by the two established churches during the last three centuries have been denied to certain other organizations stemming from these churches. The Reformed Presbyterian Church of Scotland, the United Presbyterian Church of Scotland, the Free Church of Scotland, and other bodies separated from, and long continued in rivalry with, the Church of Scotland; but, through a series of reunions, the latter now includes about 98 per cent of all Scottish Presbyterians in its membership. So, too, the Congregationalists, Baptists, Methodists, and Calvinistic Methodists separated from the Church of England, from which, in the absence of any large-scale reunion of English Protestantism, they remain divided, despite the virtual disappearance of their erstwhile bitter rivalry.

These dissenting bodies, both in England and Scotland, exemplify the 'denomination' in the sociologists' typology, precisely because their rivalry with each other and with the establishment is nowadays, and has long been, so muted. But these organizations' inclusive pluralism must be contrasted with the exclusive universalism of some of their early constituents, such as the seventeenth-century Independent congregations and certain of the groups that went to make up the United Presbyterian Church of Scotland. Just as the established churches may be treated as churches turned denominations, the dissenting churches may, therefore, be treated as sects turned denominations.

During the shift toward denominationalism, new generations of 'sects' arose. Some of these, such as the New Church and the Salvation Army, have developed out of, or been organized by members of, the denominations; and, after a period perhaps as short as a generation, the new 'sects', too, have become denominationalized. How far that process has gone in any particular case is a matter of debate. The Churches of Christ, for example, are classified by most sociologists as a 'denomination'. The Salvation Army, on the other hand, tends to be treated as an 'institutionalized sect' because, whilst it maintains what is broadly a pluralist attitude toward other churches, its membership standards are at least in effect exclusive. The classification of the Quakers has also been the subject of some discussion; but certain other bodies, such as the Christian Scientists, the Jehovah's Witnesses, and the Church of Jesus Christ of Latter Day Saints, are widely held among sociologists to remain fairly close to the 'sect' type.[3]

The history and sociology of the Catholic Church in the British Isles raises problems of classification even more difficult than these. The Reformation scarcely affected Catholicism in Ireland but almost extinguished it in Britain where, by 1780, Catholics accounted for less than 1 per cent of the population. Indeed, while Catholicism remained a 'church' in Ireland, it might be said to have become almost an institutionalized sect in Britain by that date, despite the political and legal disabilities of Catholics. Thereafter, however, and especially after 1845, Irish migration to Britain created a large Catholic community which, on some estimates, now amounts to more than 10 per cent of the British population. The collective organization of this community – universalist and inclusive among the Irish population, yet largely 'closed' by ethnic boundaries – presents a typological puzzle to which there is no easy solution.

Typology involves study of organizational detail at one point in time, usually the present. Yet, processes by which sects cease to be sects, how religious bodies come to be what they are in a subject otherwise largely ignored in sociology. *Change* in churches is therefore left to historians who, very properly, concern themselves with the historical modifications of doctrines, politics, and hierarchies, but not with every matter that might be expected to arise in the study of churches as organizations.

Perhaps *the* great missing problem in the sociology of religion is the problem of growth. Historians tell us how churches have evolved; sociologists tell us what churches, and their members, are like and do; but neither historians nor sociologists attempt to explain how and why churches get, keep, and lose their members. A historian wrote in 1963 that, though knowledge of 'the changing incidence of religious practice' in France remains 'terribly imprecise and impressionistic', that knowledge is still 'vast alongside what we know about the situation in England'. A sociologist, writing in 1967, could say no more than that it was 'difficult to decide' whether the current level of church membership and religious practice 'represents a trend from the mid-nineteenth century or . . . from the period of the first world war'.[4]

We try to dispel some of these uncertainties through the statistical data contained in the thirty-four tables of the Appendix to this book, and through the use of this evidence to test a theory of church growth. Obviously this material has many other applications, and part of our purpose is to make it more readily available to scholars with different interests. Nevertheless the problem of growth seems to us to be fundamental to the continued development of the sociology of religion.

3. Bryan R. Wilson (ed.), *Patterns of Sectarianism, Organisation and Ideology in Social and Religious Movements,* London, 1967, *passim.*

4. K. S. Inglis, *Churches and the Working Classes in Victorian England,* London, 1963, pp. 325-6; David Martin, *A Sociology of English Religion,* London, 1967, pp. 43-4.

I
Methods and Materials

A THEORY OF CHURCH GROWTH

An organization's membership usually fluctuates over time and any given change can be considered either in isolation or by comparison with membership at the beginning or end of the period of change. Such a comparison can be made most simply by dividing the difference between membership at the beginning and the end of the period under consideration by membership at the beginning of the period, the quotient being multiplied by a hundred if it is desired to express the change as a percentage. For example, the Wesleyan Methodist Church had 23 110 members in Great Britain in 1767 and 24 641 in 1768. This church's membership growth in the period 1767–8 was, therefore, 1531 (the difference between 24 641 and 23 110) divided by 23 110, or 0·0662. As a percentage, the membership growth of the Wesleyan Methodist Church in 1767–8 was 6·62 per cent.

Such a comparison tells us much more about an organization than can be learnt from simple net change of membership. In this example, a net increase of 1531 over one year represents a very high growth rate (6·62 per cent); but when the Wesleyan Methodist Church increased from 497 487 to 499 285 in 1927–8, this net increase of 1798 over one year represented the low growth rate of 0·36 per cent. Organizations growing at rates so dissimilar exhibit many different characteristics and exist in quite different relationships to the population that they recruit.

But a net membership change, however it be considered, indicates a transfer of persons between the member and non-member categories of the population; and growth rates measured in this way relate net change simply to the size of the organization, and not to the size of the population being recruited. The size of the organization relative to the size of the recruited population is its *density* in that population; and density can be measured simply by dividing the organization's membership by the population's membership. The Wesleyan Methodist Church numbered 484 879 and 498 464 members in 1905 and 1906 respectively. The population aged fifteen and over in Great Britain, that is the population eligible for membership of this church, numbered 26·258 million in 1905 and 26·591 million in 1906, so that the Wesleyans constituted 1·85 and 1·87 per cent of the population in 1905 and 1906 respectively. In other words, while Wesleyan membership grew nearly 3 per cent in 1905–6, it increased only 1 per cent in relation to the population it recruited.[1]

Any large population will display many different degrees of religious practice, awareness, and sensibility; and church membership represents only one part of the continuum of religiosity on which these degrees must be measured. Moreover, religiosity varies sharply from individual to individual. In January 1969 only 22 per cent of British respondents gave 'religious' answers to eight or all of nine questions in a scale devised by Opinion Research Centre to test 'how important religion is to each individual in his. . . daily life', while, at the other extreme, 51 per cent gave 'religious' answers to four or less of these questions. It seems reasonable to argue, therefore, that only a small fraction of the total population is likely either to be church members or to show any significant tendency toward becoming church members.[2]

This fraction of the population does not consist of isolated individuals scattered at random through families and socio-economic groups, though of course any given individual may show a degree of religiosity unusually high by comparison with that of his relatives, friends, and workmates. In general, those persons who are church members, or significantly disposed toward church membership, will be related to each other by familial or other ties. A church's membership is itself a human community, and it recruits new members from the children of existing members and from the families that make up the 'constituency' of persons significantly disposed toward membership through the operation of some psychological or sociological factor. While a church may always recruit some individuals isolated in the population at large, new membership will usually be found in the church-centred community consisting of the church and its constituency. An increase in church membership is not, therefore, simply a transfer from the non-member to the member population. It is, rather, a late stage in a process that begins with a birth in, or a transfer to, the constituency for church membership.

Constituencies can be divided into two sections, the *external* constituency of persons who have as yet made no formal or public affirmation of their disposition toward church membership, and the *internal* constituency of non-member adherents who have made some such affirmation. Different churches' constituencies overlap, but it is the external constituency where this overlapping chiefly occurs. For a church has little control, and generalized socio-economic factors have very considerable control, over the formation of external constituencies which, in consequence, may experience and demonstrate scant loyalty

1. Population aged fifteen and over has been calculated by applying age ratios extrapolated from the Census of Population to the Registrar General's mid-year estimates.

2. Independent Television Authority, *Religion in Britain and Northern Ireland,* London, 1969, pp. 10, 53.

toward any specific religious organization. And in so far as church-membership growth can be attributed to a supply-and-demand relationship, in which membership facilities are supplied by a church and demanded by a recruitable population, the external constituency probably acts on the church to produce demand-induced supply, while the church probably acts upon the internal constituency to produce supply-induced demand.

To effect transfers between these various sections, and especially from external to internal constituency and from internal constituency to membership, a church (or some other agency) must raise the religiosity of the recruitable population. There must be, in other words, a process of religious socialization, for a population low in religiosity cannot be made voluntary members of a church. But during the period under discussion here, the British population has, religiously speaking, been desocialized by the Reformation, by civic tolerance and secularization. In these conditions, churches cannot directly recruit a population already socialized but must engage in a religious socialization quite separate from, and prior to, their recruitment activities proper: and the success or failure of this religious-socialization process is a key determinant of church growth.

If the church is to get, keep, and recruit from a constituency it must have proximity to, congruity with, and utility for that constituency. To begin with, it must bring membership facilities — certainly professionals able to administer the cult, and probably also special buildings where the cult can be conducted — into the vicinity not only of those who are ready for recruitment in the short term, but also those who can, under appropriate influences, be made responsive to recruitment in the longer term. Furthermore, since church growth consists almost entirely of recruitment from a church-centred community, the recruiting church must remain congruous with the community that it recruits; and any change in the social, economic, political, and cultural congruity of constituency and church must reduce church growth.

Yet no church can grow unless its constituency can perceive the utility of church membership; and any such perception must depend upon favourable assessment of the church and its activities or functions. A church's primary function is religious, that is to say, using our definition of religion, it is the attempt to effect ends either in this world or in other worlds by means wholly or partially supernatural. A church's secondary function is the employment of means to stimulate the supernatural into favourable activity: in other words, it is a cultic function relating to the performance of religious rites deemed to be valid and efficacious. A church's tertiary function consists in whatever is necessary to, and consequent on, the introduction, establishment, and maintenance of such rites: it is a function that involves all non-cultic aspects of the church's existence as an organization. Church growth can therefore be separated theoretically, if not empirically, into primary, secondary, and tertiary growth, according to the type of function whose utility attracts persons to membership.

Primary growth arises from individuals' certainty of the need, and the possibility, of employing supernatural means to effect ends important to them; such growth is therefore especially vulnerable to any secularization of the general culture of a population. Secondary growth arises from interest in the cult *in and for itself;* for such growth to occur, the cult must be perceived to have an aesthetic, intellectual, or social value desired by the individual. Tertiary growth arises from interest in the organization *in and for itself:* as an economic or political instrumentality, as a community, and so forth. Perceptions of the logically prior function will of course modify both secondary and tertiary growth. Those who think a church's strictly religious functions futile or otiose will be unlikely to respond favourably to that church's cultic or organizational functions; and those who find a church's cultic functions offensive or oppressive are unlikely to interest themselves in that church's organizational functions.

Church growth can also be classified as autogenous or allogenous, that is, as growth accruing either from the families of church members or from the families of non-church members. Children of church members are more likely to remain members than those whose parents are not church members. But over the last two hundred years the fertility of women members of Protestant churches in Britain has not been significantly greater than that of women non-church members, so that autogenous growth has played only a certain part in the expansion of church membership. Indeed, almost all sharp increases in net church growth can be attributed to increases in allogenous rather than autogenous growth, with important consequences for the rate of membership retention.

Given an increasing population, net change in membership produces in membership density changes which can be grouped into four phases, often of considerable duration: a progressive, a marginal, a recessive, and a residual phase. Each phase arises from a characteristic relationship between the recruiting church and the recruited population, and manifests a characteristic combination of autogenous and allogenous growth.

During the progressive phase, the external and internal constituencies grow rapidly and the church recruits freely. Density increases quickly because membership grows at a high rate. At first, almost all this growth is allogenous. But the stock of member-parents grows, their children reach membership age, and autogenous growth becomes absolutely larger. Moreover, by this time, the special conditions associated with high allogenous growth may no longer obtain; while the increase in autogenous growth begins to give the church community a specificity that reduces its freedom to appeal to all non-members. Throughout this phase, all membership retention is high by comparison with later phases but, given the differential retention rates typical of autogenous and allogenous growth, and the extreme reliance on the latter, the church's net retention of membership is rather low.

In the marginal phase, the external constituency ceases to grow, but probably very largely sustains its numbers. The internal constituency also ceases to expand, and may even begin to shrink. The church has greater difficulty recruiting; membership density is almost stable; growth rate is falling; and, though autogenous growth is still high, allogenous growth is declining. All members' commitment to the church is rather less than in the progressive phase; but since autogenous growth begins to predominate, net retention of membership may rise. During this phase membership fluctuates well-nigh *pari passu* with population.

When a church enters the recessive phase, its external constituency has already begun to dwindle. The internal constituency is depleted and recruitment becomes still more difficult. Density begins to fall, and the downward movement of membership growth rate continues. Autogenous growth decreases slowly, allogenous growth rapidly. Membership retention continues to decline, but a greater reliance on autogenous growth may more than offset this as membership diminishes but comes to contain a larger proportion of more loyal members. The church no longer keeps pace with population but represents an ever-decreasing proportion of the whole.

In the residual phase, the external constituency has virtually ceased to exist, and the internal constituency is fast disappearing. Recruitment is therefore very difficult; density is falling rapidly; and net membership increase becomes net membership decrease. Allogenous growth approximates to zero, but the continued decline in membership retention both among children of non-members and among children of members tends to keep losses high.

This theory of church growth is examined in the following chapters. Verification of the theory must depend on the availability and accuracy of reliable historical statistics: and the existence of such data has often been doubted.

QUANTIFYING RELIGION

'There simply are no reliable historical statistics on church membership', wrote two highly respected American sociologists of religion in 1959; and this scepticism seems to be shared by British scholars. For though sociologists working in the United Kingdom make much use of opinion-poll data on religion – especially on religious attitudes – they seem uninterested in, or even unaware of, the body of religious statistics, collected by various agencies over many years, but hitherto available almost solely in primary sources, which appear to have evaded the attention of the historians also.[3]

3. Charles Y. Glock and Rodney Stark, *Religion and Society in Tension*, Chicago, 1965, p. 82. But see also David O. Moberg, *The Church as a Social Institution, The Sociology of American Religion*, Englewood Cliffs, New Jersey, 1962; and Bryan R. Wilson, *Religion in Secular Society*, London, 1966.

It is true that there is relatively little governmental data on British religion, despite the prevalence and significance of this type of material in other countries. Governments usually undertake or commission statistical inquiries into religion only when the governed population's religious affiliations are divided between different churches, and when those divisions are significant in the conduct of state business. During most of the period when British governments displayed little interest in statistics and had poor statistical techniques, either the population was religiously undivided — that is, all were Catholics — or (as in the era of religious tolerance that began about 1700) divisions in religious affiliations could safely be discounted in affairs of state. And when, during the nineteenth and twentieth centuries, governments developed an interest in statistics and improved their statistical technique, religious divisions were becoming progressively still less important to the state. Hence, there are in Britain few government statistical records on religious affairs.

There are four important exceptions. From time to time the government has investigated the relative strength of different religious groups. The two most famous inquiries are the 'Compton Census' of members of the Established Church, Nonconformists, and Catholics in England in 1676, and the census of religious worship in Britain directed by Horace Mann in 1851. Compton relied largely upon estimates of population made by parish priests of the Established Church. Mann used attendance counts made either by the minister or clergy of the church concerned or by his own enumerators. Compton's returns are complicated by various difficulties of interpretation on which historians are still engaged. A major problem in Mann's returns is the duplication involved in counting *attendances* at different services during the census day, rather than individual *attendants* regardless of the number of times they went to church on that day. Both censuses are, moreover, analyses of religious geography at one point in time, rather than data for the time series by which church growth can be measured.[4]

Secondly, the religious division of Ireland led the United Kingdom government during the years up to 1911, and the Republic of Ireland and Northern Ireland governments since 1921, to inquire into religious affiliations when they have taken a census of the island's population. Although the religious question in the census has been optional since 1970, almost all Irishmen answer it for themselves and their dependants: in 1951, for example, the number of persons claiming, or assigned to, a religious affiliation constituted 98·8 per cent of the total population. But the census is decennial, rather than annual, and has been conducted at irregular intervals since 1920, so that the returns provide a time series of limited value only.[5]

4. A Summary of the Compton Census is to be found in *State Papers Domestic,* 1693, King William's Chest 14, No. 89. Summary data from, and sources for, the census of 1851 are contained in Tables F1 and F2 of the Appendix.
5. The returns are summarized and discussed in Tables G1 and G2 of the Appendix.

Thirdly, the changing relationship between the established and other churches in Britain (which was one factor leading to Mann's census), has caused the United Kingdom government to investigate various matters relating to these bodies. The results of such investigations have been published in parliamentary papers which contain much information collected by the Registrars-General, the Ecclesiastical Commissioners, and inquiries such as the Royal Commission on the Church and other Religious Bodies in Wales, which reported in 1910. Though much of this information is miscellaneous rather than serial, it is often exceedingly useful.[6]

Finally, under legislation of 1836, the Registrars-General have collected and published statistics of marriages by the rite or ceremony according to which they were solemnized. These statistics are available for England and Wales from 1838 onwards; for Wales from 1840; for Ireland from 1845; and for Scotland from 1855. The series have considerable value, but are partly vitiated as indices of religious affiliations by the tendency in Britain of persons of other or no religious commitment to marry according to the rites of the established churches. Moreover, since 1914 the Registrar-General for England and Wales has published returns for only nine years, so that an annual series for the marriage patterns of the greater part of the British population is no longer available.[7]

The deficiencies in governmental data on religion have not been offset by private inquiries. Private individuals made some statistical studies of Nonconformist churches, especially in the eighteenth century in England; and a large but somewhat tendentious literature on the strength of the various Scottish churches appeared during the nineteenth century. Between 1880 and 1900 various individuals and groups published unofficial comparisons with Mann's returns for certain towns; and Booth, Mudie-Smith, and others published detailed local surveys of religious activity after 1900. After the Second World War, a few, chiefly documentary, studies of religious attitudes and practices began to appear: but these, like pre-war inquiries, have contributed little to the formation of time series.[8]

Since 1945 social-survey and opinion-poll techniques have also been applied to the study of religion in Britain. Gallup, National Opinion Polls, Opinion Research Centre, Louis Harris, and other firms have surveyed religious practice and

6. For the Registrar-General's data, see e.g. *Parliamentary Papers,* 1852-3, LXXXVIII; for the Ecclesiastical Commissioners, see *Pp.* 1835, XXII; 1836, XXXVI; and 1847-8, VII; for the Royal Commission, see *Pp.* 1910, XIV-XIX.

7. The returns are summarized and discussed in Tables H1-5 of the Appendix.

8. See the bibliographical details in the notes to Tables A2 (Presbyterians) and A4 (Nonconformists) of the Appendix. For a summary of some private censuses designed to be comparable with the Census of Religion of 1851, see A. Mearns, *The Statistics of Attendance at Public Worship, 1881-2,* London, 1882; and see also the files of local, urban newspapers for the period 1880-1900. For local surveys, see C. Booth, *Life and Labour of the People in London, 3rd Series: Religious Influences,* London, 1902; R. Mudie-Smith (ed.), *The Religious Life of London,* London, 1904. Among more recent local studies, see E. R. Wickham, *Church and People in an Industrial City,* London, 1957. National studies include chiefly documentary works such as G. Gorer, *Exploring English Character,* London, 1955; B. S. Rowntree and G. R. Lavers, *English Life and Leisure,* London, 1957; and more quantitative works, such as John D. Gay, *The Geography of Religion in England,* London, 1971.

attitudes from time to time, and have published some of their findings in newspapers and elsewhere. During the 1960s both ABC Television and the Independent Television Authority brought out in book form the results of polls on religion carried out on their behalf. These inquiries tend to emphasize beliefs, and provide little material for time series.[9]

But religious statistics of the types discussed above are, however useful, of secondary importance compared with those collected by the churches themselves. Just as, for example, it would be impossible to study the growth of trade unions or political parties without reference to their own membership series, it is impossible to study church growth unless the churches' own membership returns are used; and these returns are probably unique among those available for organizations in Britain, both in quantity and in variety.

The collection of church membership and similar data arises in a situation of religious pluralism, for a universalist religious body will tend to treat all persons as members of itself and either decline to count them or be content with some civil measure of population such as a census. Hence the tardiness of the established churches in collecting statistics, and the apparent failure of the Catholic Church in Ireland (but not in Britain) to collect any statistical data whatever. A pluralist religious body, on the contrary, will be concerned with its standing and success in relation to other such bodies, and will tend to resort to membership statistics as a test of this.

The longest, and in many ways the best, British church-membership series are those collected by the Methodists, who published their first complete membership returns in 1767. The first statistical response to the Methodist initiative came from the New Connexion of General Baptists who published a consistent annual membership series from 1772 onwards. The organization of both Baptists and Congregationalists into Unions, a development that accelerated about 1830, prompted an interest in statistics; and both groups began publishing data in the 1840s, although some decades passed before these statistics were put on a satisfactory basis.[10]

The growing bureaucratization of religious bodies from about the 1860s onwards caused both an extension and elaboration of the statistical records of churches long engaged in collecting such data and the commencement of statistical records by churches that had not kept them hitherto. The Wesleyans, for example, added to their basic membership series the number of 'on trial' members (1855 onwards), Sunday-school scholars (1863 onwards), deaths (1864 onwards), new members (1875 onwards), junior members, those who ceased to be members, and membership transfers between circuits (all 1881 onwards), losses through

9. *Television and Religion, A Report Prepared by Social Surveys (Gallup Poll) Ltd. on behalf of ABC Television*, London, 1964; *Religion in Britain and Northern Ireland.* For studies which include data on religion, see e.g. David Butler and Donald Stokes, *Political Change in Britain*, London, 1969.

10. See Tables A3, A4, B6-9, D2, D3, and E of the Appendix.

emigration (1888 onwards), and transfers to and from other churches (1906 onwards). And among those bodies that now *commenced* statistical records were the Presbyterian Church in Ireland (1869 onwards), the Presbyterian Church of England (1876 onwards), the Church of Scotland (1881 onwards), and the Church of England (1891 onwards). When the Baptist and Congregational Unions began consistent annual series in 1891 and 1898 respectively, coverage of the major churches on a year-to-year basis was complete.[12]

Almost all this material is first collected by priests, clergy, or ministers attached to particular churches or groups of churches. The unit for the collection of data in the Church of England, Church of Scotland, and Catholic Church is the parish; in the Congregationalist, Baptist, and unestablished Presbyterian Churches, the chapel; and in the Methodist Church, the circuit of chapels. The local returns, once collected, are forwarded at intervals, which vary from organization to organization, to a central body which publishes all or part of the data in a yearbook, handbook, or directory.[13]

Membership returns can be divided into three categories, according to the principles upon which they are collected, as *demographic, roll,* and *participation* data. Demographic data measure the number of persons admitted to a religious community by birth, infant baptism, or circumcision. Some Catholic material, notably that calculated from baptisms or marriages, falls entirely into this category. But the Catholic parish priests' returns of the estimated Catholic population of their parishes are only semi-demographic: for the priests evidently derive their estimates partly from the number of Catholics known to them, and that total will exclude a varying quantity of inactive or lapsed Catholics who would be included in strictly demographic data. A. E. C. W. Spencer has recently argued that the 'alienated' Catholic population of England and Wales numbers over two million, or (in 1970) about 30 per cent of the estimated baptized Catholic population of England and Wales. These figures have been disputed but both demographic and semi-demographic data are plainly rather insensitive indicators of religious practice. Thus, for example, between 1966 and 1969, according to parish priests' returns, Catholic attendance at mass in England and Wales fell 5·98 per cent, while estimated Catholic population fell only 0·08 per cent.[14]

The term 'roll data' refers to data on the number of duly qualified persons sufficiently active in church life to have their names entered and retained on a membership or communicant roll or in similar church records. The best examples of this type of data are afforded by the Nonconformist membership and Presbyterian communicant series, but the Church of England electoral roll provides

11. See Table B8 of the Appendix.
12. See Tables A1, A2, A4, B1-5, B10, D3 and E of the Appendix.
13. For a more detailed discussion see Gay, *The Geography of Religion in England.*
14. See Table A5 of the Appendix; and A. Spencer, 'Demography of Catholicism', *The Month,* April 1975.

similar material. Obviously religious practice is measured more closely by roll data than by demographic or semi-demographic data. But there is no doubt of the still greater sensitivity of participation data – such as the Church of England Easter Day communicant series, the Church of Scotland series on the number of communicants receiving the sacrament at least once a year, and Catholic actual mass attendance figures – which measure active participation in a specific rite. Thus, in the Church of Scotland, for instance, between 1938 and 1945, the number on the communicant roll fell 2·07 per cent, while the number of those who received the sacrament at least once a year fell 20·48 per cent.[15]

THE RELIABILITY OF STATISTICS OF RELIGION

There is, then, much statistical evidence both on church membership and on many other aspects of religious activity in the British Isles. But Glock and Stark's complaint is against the *reliability* rather than the *availability* of such statistics. In other words, these authors, and those who think with them, doubt the accuracy with which the statistical evidence enumerates those items that it purports to enumerate, whether because of error or falsification or inadequacy of definition and consistency.

One type of data discussed above may be immune from these criticisms. Registrars-General count the number of marriages conducted according to particular rites; and the churches count the number of their church buildings and their clergy or ministers. In these series, the items enumerated can be specified quite precisely and each item can be verified independently by reference to relatively accessible documents, such as marriage certificates, rentals, or title-deeds and lists of names. Both the data and the supporting documentation could be falsified, but at considerable cost, and without any very obvious benefit being achieved. Moreover, falsification would be attended not merely by legal penalties for fraud but by all the administrative difficulties which must beset a rational bureaucratic organization, such as a church, which has incorrect records of its own personnel and property. It would seem reasonable to argue, therefore, that this type of data is reliable in the sense that what is said to be counted is counted, and that the count is, if not error-free, at least accurate enough for use in most statistical procedures.

Another important category of data includes material relating to certain utterances. The B.B.C., for example, estimates from answers to questionnaires the number of persons who listen to, or watch, B.B.C. programmes, including religious programmes; the Irish Censuses count the number of persons who assign themselves, or are assigned, to a particular religious denomination; and scholars and

15. See Table A2 of the Appendix.

opinion-poll firms have conducted surveys of religious beliefs, attitudes, and practices, as affirmed by respondents to their inquiries. Among those who have used this latter type of material are Glock and Stark.

Certain difficulties do arise in the handling of such data however. Either there are no independently verifiable documents, or, where such documents (for example, original census returns) do exist, they are not available for consultation. Nor is any confirmation available from an independent observer. Thus, for instance, respondents to opinion polls who claim to go to church 'most Sundays', are unlikely never to go to church at all; but it might appear to an observer able to count the occasions on which these respondents enter the church doors that they go to church 'some Sundays' rather than 'most Sundays'. Yet the social-survey method finds no place for independent observations such as this.

This difficulty is rendered the more serious by the operation of extraneous pressures that tend to distort statements about religious practices. Even in a highly secularized society such as present-day southern England, to believe in God and to go to church is still (if decreasingly) respectable, and not to do so not respectable, if in ever smaller degree. Respondents to questionnaires and opinion polls may well, through influences such as these, overstate both the intensity of their religious convictions and the frequency of their religious practices; and this difficulty seems most serious when questions are asked about private religious practices, such as private prayer.

Finally, many of the topics raised by investigators who resort to social-survey techniques are both highly complex and entirely intangible. Thus, we may know that so many persons told an interviewer from an opion-poll firm that 'Jesus Christ is the Son of God'. But this is an exceedingly complex statement not merely semantically but culturally, since even if the meanings of these words could be specified, their attitudinal context would need to be elucidated by the use of subtle (if imprecise) historical and critical methods not usually applied to social-survey material.

We wish to rely very largely on membership data drawn from church records. For all social-survey material counts *statements* about thoughts and behaviour, but almost all church-membership returns count the *actions* necessary to get and keep membership; and, while the former may be as good evidence of thoughts as the latter, it is difficult to see how the latter can be inferior to the former as evidence of behaviour. Moreover, though the statements in question are no more than the unverified utterances of the subjects of the inquiry, the actions under consideration are enumerated not by the actors themselves but by observers, proceeding in a more or less uniform way according to well-known criteria; and just as an opinion-poll interviewer is very probably a better witness of the interviewee's statements (say, about church-membership) than is the interviewee himself, so church leaders are better witnesses of the reality of the interviewee's church-membership than are either the interviewer or the interviewee. In short, the essence of church-membership records is that they count not individuals' utterances but their observed actions.

The element of observation is of course most significant in participation data and least significant in demographic data. But most of the statistical material used here is roll data, to which certain criticisms must attach themselves. Of such criticisms, the most basic is that 'true', 'real', or 'active' membership is either under or overstated by roll data, because such data will always understate 'true' membership in the sense that it will distinguish in a somewhat arbitrary way between persons of equal commitment to (and even activity in) the organization, by including persons just entered, and excluding persons just about to be entered, at the moment when the roll is counted. And on the other hand, the data will always overstate 'true' membership by including persons who have ceased membership but not yet been struck off the roll at the moment it is counted.

A further complaint against all church-membership data is that those who collect or handle the data tendentiously alter the figures from ulterior motives. Some critics have claimed that the original collectors of church-membership data understate the numbers in their church or parish in order to evade some inconvenience, such as a centrally administered capitation levy; while others have claimed that the collectors or compilers of the data inflate the returns in order to produce more impressive totals. But the *mores* of church leaders probably minimize, if they do not remove, the likelihood of such falsification; while the requirements of successful policies of manpower deployment, school and church building, and so on, also do tend to militate against falsified records.

The character of the statistics also suggests that error and distortion, if present, are not present in sufficient degree to inhibit their use. One possible consequence of error or distortion would be series the values of which either remained unchanged or grew at a steady rate from year to year, as those who prepared the series left them alone or added conventional quantities to allow for assumed or desired increases. But most of the series published here vary quite widely from year to year. Changes in the Wesleyan Methodist membership series, for example, range between +13·52 (1793-4) and –15·65 per cent per annum (1850-1). Moreover, as this example shows, not merely do the series vary, they also show decreases as well as increases: a characteristic incompatible with the publication of the data for propaganda purposes only.

The series might nevertheless be manipulated or distorted in a rather random way by the addition or subtraction of different quantities from year to year. Such alterations to the data, which could not be immediately detected, may indeed occur, since it is unlikely that all the many individuals who have shared in collecting and compiling the data over several generations have been entirely consistent and uniformly accurate in their work. In an extreme case, such random manipulations and errors would produce data with which most other data would correlate only at or near zero. This extreme case, at least, does not obtain here because, taking the years 1900-70 inclusive (that is, the years for which most churches publish membership data), nearly all the series presented in Tables A1-6 of the Appendix correlate with each other positively or negatively at or above the level at which there is a probability of only one in a hundred of the result arising by chance. Given the number of items in each series, the level is represented in this case by a correlation coefficient of + or – 0·3, while nearly half the series correlate with each other positively or negatively at between 0·4 and 0·8.

Of course, we cannot be certain that, were unknown errors removed from the data, the series would not yield still higher correlation coefficients. Moreover, a significant correlation of whatever level, whether positive or negative, does not of course prove, in the absence of other evidence, either that the series do refer to what they purport to refer to, or that they do measure what they appear to measure. Nevertheless, if a number of independently collected statistical series, which purport to refer to rather similar things (in this case the membership of churches), correlate among themselves at levels as high as those observed here, it is reasonable to attribute those correlations to the similarity in the things referred to, and to conclude that the statistics – though they might indeed be more accurate – are as they stand a sufficiently accurate measurement to reproduce this similarity.

These inferences are strengthened by the tendency of each series to correlate most closely with the series published by the churches historically and sociologically nearest to them. Taking year-to-year fluctuations, the Church of England Easter Day communicant series and the Church of Scotland communicant-roll series correlate at 0·4; the Church of England series correlates with the Baptist and Methodist membership series at just under 0·4; the Church of Scotland series correlates with the Baptist, Congregationalist, Methodist, and Presbyterian Church of Wales series at between 0·4 and 0·6; and the latter series correlate among themselves at between 0·7 and 0·8. Finally, the Church of Jesus Christ of Latter Day Saints, Jehovah's Witnesses, and Seventh Day Adventist series, which correlate negatively with the church and denominational series about or above the level at which there is a probability of only one in twenty of the result arising by chance, correlate positively among themselves at or well above that level.

Such correlations do suggest that, even if the figures do not provide a precise measure of the *magnitude* of church membership, they do at least indicate with reasonable accuracy *changes* in magnitude. In other words, even if we cannot be certain that, at any one time, a church does have exactly as many members as its records indicate, we can be reasonably certain that, when those records show an increase or decrease in membership, such a change does occur. And that certainty is strengthened by the considerations that the membership of most churches appears to increase and decrease at the same time; that, since the churches compile their membership series independently, this simultaneity can scarcely be contrived; and that the pattern of these increases and decreases does seem to bear a consistent, significant historical relationship to such vicissitudes as war and peace, boom and slump.

It is possible to allow that church-membership statistics are 'reliable' in the sense that they do measure changes in church membership, while arguing that these statistics are too 'formal' to be of interest or use to scholars concerned with the 'reality' of religion. Arguments of this type fall into two groups. Some critics claim that, even if changes in membership are accurately measured by the data, comparative magnitudes of membership are seriously obscured by variations in the character and requirements of membership over time and between different churches. Other critics claim that, even if membership data measured both changes in and magnitudes of church membership with perfect accuracy, such data would take no account of the facts that, on the one hand, some church members are not really religious while, on the other, some really religious people are not church members. And this latter argument appears also in the claim that 'religion' is not unitary but rather divisible into certain elements (of which church membership is but one); and that individuals may be really religious in respect of one or some but not all of these elements.

The first of these arguments is, in substance, difficult to gainsay. Different churches do make different demands on their members – hence the distinction between 'inclusive' and 'exclusive' churches – and the same church can vary its demands upon its members over time – and hence the transition from sect to denomination. But these differences, which recur *mutatis mutandis* in the membership data of almost any category of organization, should not preclude the quantitative study of churches, because such differences are rarely so serious (and so little known) that they cannot be allowed for by care in use of the material.

For despite the variety of membership types, fluctuations in membership do tend toward one general historical pattern; while adequate comparisons can be made between the magnitude of the memberships of religious bodies, and especially between sociologically similar religious bodies, provided these comparisons are made with due caution. Thus, for example, fluctuations in Church of England Easter Day communicants and Jehovah's Witnesses' publishers do form broadly similar curves, and some significance does reside in the 30:1 ratio of communicants and publishers, despite the extreme differences between those two bodies' demands on their members. Furthermore, though membership of a church does mean different things from period to period, transitions between periods occur gradually enough to allow generalizations to be made about widely distant points in time. To be a Methodist does mean something different in 1770, 1870, and 1970, but it would be far-fetched to argue that statistical comparisons of

Methodist membership at those dates are any less possible – given due caution – than the comparisons of polity or doctrine that form the staple of historical scholarship.

Arguments about the relationship between church membership and 'real' religion are perhaps more complex than arguments about disparities between different kinds of church membership. One form of this argument appears in N. J. Demerath's claim that church membership 'need not connote a commitment to religion. It may make a status claim or serve as a vehicle for mobility . . . It may be a prerequisite for . . . credit or a job. . . . Or it may simply represent a penchant for formal associations'. Demerath distinguishes between what is here termed a church's primary or religious functions and its tertiary or organizational functions, and wishes to argue that, since church growth includes tertiary as well as primary growth, only part of any church's total growth can be treated as the product of a 'commitment to religion'.[16]

Demerath's objection must be valid, in the sense that fluctuations in church membership arise from a multiplicity of motives. Yet the objection is not such as to deprive church-membership statistics of interest or use. For tertiary growth still remains *church* growth, and not the growth of another organization. Moreover, any society that affords a church tertiary growth – for example, by linking status, credit, or employment with church membership – displays a higher level of religiosity than one that does not; while any individual willing to use church membership as a means to those ends is less hostile to religion than one who is not so willing. In any event, once inside a church persons motivated in this way are more exposed to, and more likely to respond to, influences toward a 'commitment to religion', than persons outside any church, whatever their motivation. Hence the phenomenon, observed by J. W. Pickett in his classic study *Christian Mass Movements in India,* that, in the Indian churches, whether recruits were moved to become Christians by 'spiritual' or by purely 'secular' concerns had little bearing upon the subsequent intensity and quality of their 'commitment to religion'.[17]

Another form of the argument about church membership and 'real' religion is that presented most influentially by Glock and Stark. These authors distinguish several 'dimensions of religiosity' – such as belief, participation in religious practices, and religious knowledge – and claim that 'several recent studies strongly suggest that being religious on one dimension does not necessarily imply religiosity on other dimensions'. In particular, they cite Gerhard Lenski's *The Religious Factor,* a study of religious and other attitudes among the population of Detroit. Lenski argues for the 'limited nature' of the relationship between doctrinal orthodoxy and private devotion (which he describes as 'separate and independent

16. N. J. Demerath, *Social Class in American Protestantism,* Chicago, 1965, pp. 7-8.
17. J. W. Pickett, *Christian Mass Movements in India,* Lucknow, 1933, pp. 155 ff.

orientations'), and states that 'Protestant church attendance is increasing while at the same time both orthodoxy and devotionalism are declining'.[18]

Doubtless individuals may direct more energy toward one rather than another aspect of the religious life; doubtless, too, though not for long periods of time, changes in orthodoxy, private devotion, or church membership may outrun each other. But it does not seem particularly likely that church membership (on which we have so much evidence) is so little connected with other aspects of the religious life (on which we have virtually no evidence) that church membership is a useless indicator of changes or degrees in those aspects. Indeed, even Glock and Stark conclude that it is 'scarcely plausible that the various manifestations of religiosity are entirely independent of each other'.[19]

On the contrary, such evidence as is available on dimensions of religiosity other than church membership suggests that they are quite highly and positively correlated with membership, even if this may be less apparent in a period, such as the present, when religion might seem to become decreasingly formal and increasingly privatized. Hans Mol, who claims that 'church attendance' is not an 'adequate and representative' measure of religiosity, nevertheless shows in his book *Religion in Australia* that 'regular churchgoers' (who are those most likely to be on a church-membership roll) are, according to denomination, between twice and four times as likely to pray daily as are 'irregular churchgoers'.

Similarly the *Television and Religion* survey showed that 'regular churchgoers' were, according to denomination, between two and two-and-a-half times more likely to 'pray regularly' than non-regular churchgoers, and between one-and-a-half and six times more likely than they to 'read the Bible regularly'. Finally, Lenski's own figures seem to indicate that all Protestants who score 'high' on church attendance also score 'high' on devotionalism; while perhaps 80 per cent of all religious affiliates who score 'high' on attendance score 'high' on devotionalism too.[20]

On balance, therefore, we conclude that the religious statistics presented here are 'reliable' in the sense that they are in general accurately and honestly compiled; that they show few signs of tendentious manipulation; that they appear to measure something sensitively; that that something is church membership; and that church membership is a good indicator of religious activity. For these reasons, it seems both possible and useful to employ the data to analyse and elucidate the pattern of church membership in the British Isles.

18. Glock and Stark, op. cit., p. 22; Gerhard Lenski, *The Religious Factor, A Sociological Study of Religion's Impact on Politics, Economics, and Family Life,* New York, 1963, pp. 26, 58, 60.
19. Glock and Stark, loc. cit.
20. Hans Mol, *Religion in Australia, A Sociological Investigation,* Melbourne, 1971. pp. 22-4; *Television and Religion,* pp. 20, 27-30; Lenski, op. cit., p. 370.

II
Patterns of Church Growth

INDICES OF GROWTH

Church-membership series provide the best available indices of church growth. But these series are available for a fraction of the time since Christianity was introduced to Britain about the year A.D. 300, and indeed since it was reintroduced about the year A.D. 600. Despite the lack of data, what can be said of the period between 600 and 1800 is that church-membership increased very considerably, since the total population of Britain in the seventh century was probably little more than 1·5 million, while the major Protestant churches had about 1·1 million members in Britain in 1800. Over these centuries as a whole church membership probably increased approximately at the same rate as population, but there were no doubt periods during these years (as there have certainly been since 1800) when membership grew either much faster or much slower than population.

During the eighteenth century, the membership of the established churches seems to have fallen behind population growth. Historians argue that the Church of Scotland's communicant membership increased by no more, and perhaps less than the increase in total population, and evidence for the Church of England suggests that it may actually have declined in these years. Statistics of church building given by the 1851 Religious Census indicate that the stock of Church of England churches increased by 0·57, 1·00, and 2·81 per cent respectively in the years 1801-11, 1811-21, and 1821-31, figures which scarcely suggest pressure on church accommodation either in the first years of the nineteenth or the last years of the eighteenth century. Moreover, the number of resident incumbents and curates in England increased only 2·83 and 6·73 per cent respectively in 1811-21 and 1821-31, and these rates are rather low compared with those for the later years of the nineteenth century.[1]

1. See Alexander Hugh Bruce, *An Historical Account of the Rise and Development of Presbyterianism in Scotland*, Cambridge, 1911; and Tables D1 and E of the Appendix.

Table 2.1
Total Communicants in Selected Oxfordshire Parishes, 1738 – 1811

1738	911
1759	896
1771	868
1802	682
1811	755

NOTES
1. The parishes selected have been chosen solely on the grounds of the availability of relevant data at the maximum number of time-points and no parishes have been excluded which do afford such data. The parishes are thirty in number and comprise: Alvescot, Ardley, Britwell Salome, Charlton, Cowley, Deddington, Ducklington, Goring, Lower Heyford, Hook Norton, Horspath, Kencot, Mixbury, Northleigh,Oxford: St. Clement's, St. Giles, St. Mary Magdalene, and St. Thomas; Piddington, Great Rollright, Salford, Shilton, Shiplake, Shipton-on-Cherwell, Stoke Talmage, Stonesfield, Swerford, Waterstock, Watlington, Wroxton.
2. The following substitutions have been made because of the lack of data at a particular visitation: 1768 for 1771 – Oxford: St. Clement's and St. Thomas; Salford, Shiplake, Shipton-on-Cherwell, and Watlington; 1774 for 1771 – Horspath; 1808 for 1811 – Ducklington, Goring, Lower Heyford, Northleigh, Oxford: St. Mary Magdalene, and Shipton-on-Cherwell; 1814 for 1811 – Cowley.
3. The totals indicate average communicants at the 'Great Festivals' (Easter, Ascension, Whitsun, and Christmas) and would be lower than totals for Easter alone.

Source
Oxford Diocesan Visitations (Bodleian Library MSS.).

Table 2.1 summarises some corroborative evidence from the Oxford diocesan visitations for 1738-1811. These figures confirm the evidence of other visitations and parish records on the low number of communicants, since the totals in Table 2.1 represent less than 5 per cent of the total population of the parishes sampled. Further, the figures also show that the number of communicants in these parishes fell by a quarter between 1738 and 1802 and rose in 1811 to no more than 83 per cent of the 1738 total.

Non-resident incumbents were perhaps unusually common in eighteenth – and early-nineteenth – century Oxfordshire because many fellows of Oxford colleges then held benefices in the countryside round the city; but clerical neglect will account for only part of the fall in the number of communicants in eighteenth century Oxfordshire. Table 2.2 contains data for parishes in the archdiocese of York, where the number of Easter Day communicants fell by nearly 20 per cent but the population by only 10 per cent, between 1743 and 1764. Moreover, the very low level of the average number of communicants at the 'Great Festivals' in 1865 – when those receiving the sacrament amounted to perhaps no more than 3 per cent of the total population – indicates that the decline which marked the years 1743-64 must have continued well into the nineteenth century, during

Table 2.2
Communicants in Selected Parishes in the Archdiocese of York, 1743 – 1884

Easter Day Communicants		*Great Festivals Communicants*	
1743	3728	1865	1496
1764	3040	1877	2739
		1884	3181

NOTES

1. The parishes selected have been chosen at random from returns containing data for each year. The parishes are thirty-three in number and comprise: Atwick-in-Holderness, Birkin, Brafferton, Bridlington, Cherry Burton, Crathorne, Carnaby, Dunnington (York), Escrick, Featherstone, Feliskirk-with-Boltby, Fridaythorpe, Handsworth, Hotham, Hornsea, Inglesby Arncliffe, Kirkby Wharfe, Lofthouse, Lythe, Marr, Myton-on-Swale, Middlesborough, Normanton, Owston, Patrington, Sutton-in-Forest, Stokesley, Skidby, Skirpenbeck, Scarborough, Thorp Arch, Tunstall (Hull), and Whorlton.

2. Estimates were used in the following cases: Hornsea (1865, 1877), Lythe (1884), Myton-on-Swale (1764, 1884), Middlesborough (1877, 1884), Normanton (1764), Patrington (1884), Stokesley (1877), Skidby (1764, 1865), Scarborough (1877, 1884), Thorp Arch (1884).

3. The totals indicate communicants on Easter Day for the years 1743 and 1764, and the average number of communicants at the 'Great Festivals' (Easter, Ascension, Whitsun, and Christmas) for the years 1865-84. This average would be lower than the totals for Easter alone.

Source
Visitation Returns for the Archdiocese of York (Borthwick Institute MSS.).

which period the fall in the number of Church of England communicants must be quite largely attributable to the influence of Nonconformity.

If total church-membership in Britain rose during the eighteenth century, the increment must be largely or wholly attributable to churches other than the established churches, that is to say to the Nonconformists and the Catholics. Obviously, a certain number of the members of the pre-Reformation church remained loyal to Catholicism during the sixteenth and seventeenth centuries; but the Catholic population of Britain probably fell by about 40 per cent between 1720 and 1780, rising thereafter, chiefly through Irish immigration, to a total which we estimate at 129 000 in 1800. Similarly, though the independent congregations of the seventeenth century claimed many members, the 300 000 or so communicants who followed the ministers ejected under the Act of Uniformity in 1662 fell to less than 50 000 in number in 1750. Thereafter Nonconformity grew very rapidly. Between 1770 and 1810, the Wesleyans increased fivefold and the General Baptist New Connexion fourfold in membership, while the number of registered Congregational and Baptist places for worship also quadrupled. We estimate there to have been about 312 000 Nonconformists in Britain by 1810.[2]

2. See Tables 2.2, and A3-5 and D3 of the Appendix

These changes can be associated with certain well-known historical developments. From the Toleration Act of 1689 onwards, governments progressively withdrew the legal sanctions on public religious observance; and this policy, designed to preserve the principles of religious freedom implicit in the revolution of 1688, hastened the formation not merely of a non-Anglican but a non-religious public, especially in those parts of Britain where the religious tradition was already weak. Hence it was that the active membership of the Church of Scotland remained static, while that of the Church of England fell; and new voluntarist religious movements developed which recruited both disaffected members of the established churches and supporters of the old, and now declining, dissenting churches of the Civil War period. And the new voluntarist movements also benefited by the processes of industrialization and urbanization which began to accelerate about 1780.

Those processes have remained leading features of the post-1800 period, for which it is possible to construct the decennial totals of church membership given in Table 2.3 and illustrated in Figure 2.1. Certain problems are raised by material such as that presented in this table. Almost all the totals contain estimated values, which, indeed, predominate for the period 1800-90; and whether observed or estimated, since the type of data available varies, from series to series, from participation to roll and semi-demographic data, the estimated values also vary in character. In other words each type of data and estimated value bears a different quantitative relationship to 'true' church membership, which of course varies in significance from church to church. Nevertheless, not merely do the individual Protestant church-membership series summed in Table 2.2 correlate positively and significantly, but the Protestant *totals* included in that table also correlate positively and significantly, despite the large element of estimation involved in constructing the earlier values.

Taking each series as a whole, the Episcopalian, Scottish Presbyterian, and Nonconformist series correlate at 0·94-0·97; and taking year-to-year differences, the series correlate at 0·75-0·81: coefficients well above the level (0·59, N=18) at which there is only a probability of one in a hundred of the result arising by chance. It therefore seems reasonable to use the series in Table 2.3 as broad indicators of changes over time in the membership of the British churches.

The Catholic series shows sustained high growth between 1800 and 1840; very rapid growth between 1840 and the 1860s, and still high, but rather slower growth between the 1860s and 1970. The Protestant series shows high growth between 1800 and 1840; lower growth between 1840 and 1910; and a decrease between 1910 and 1970. These phases, too, can be associated with contemporary historical developments. Up to 1840 industrialization and urbanization continued at a rapid rate, giving increased facilities for voluntary religious movements, and stimulating Irish imigration to Britain. Then, though from about 1835 the Church

Table 2.3 Decennial British Church Membership Totals, 1800 – 1970 (thousands)

	Episcopalians	*Scottish Presbyterians*	*Nonconformists*	*Major Protestants*	*Catholics*
1800	577	313	211	1101	129
1810	599	346	312	1257	158
1820	622	398	437	1457	198
1830	658	450	600	1708	250
1840	821	503	835	2159	305
1850	953	603	1021	2577	846
1860	1078	723	1136	2937	1179
1870	1206	822	1290	3318	1213
1880	1332	949	1465	3746	1459
1890	1614	1053	1635	4302	1691
1900	2089	1164	1803	5056	2016
1910	2418	1232	2020	5670	2216
1920	2410	1281	1963	5654	2502
1930	2529	1299	2001	5829	2781
1940	2255	1311	1874	5440	3023
1950	2077	1304	1696	5077	3499
1960	2398	1332	1604	5334	4346
1970	1804	1179	1328	4311	4829

NOTES AND SOURCES

1. This table contains observed and estimated data on the membership, at decennial intervals, of the British churches for which adequate material was available. The figures are unweighted and, though they appear to indicate trends within each church or group of churches, are therefore of limited value as indices of comparative strength. During the present century, the ratio between the comparable active membership indicated by each unit of membership in the series given here for Episcopalians, Scottish Presbyterians, Nonconformists, and Catholics, seems to have been approximately 1·0:0·7:1·2:0·5. These weightings would give the following indices, taking Episcopalians in 1800 as 100:

	Episcopalians	*Scottish Presbyterians*	*Nonconformists*	*Major Protestants*	*Catholics*
1800	100·0	38·0	43·8	181·8	11·3
1850	165·2	73·1	212·3	450·6	73·3
1900	362·0	141·2	375·0	878·3	174·7
1950	360·0	158·2	352·7	870·9	376·6

But these indices are to be treated as very rough approximations, given present knowledge of church statistics.

2. The values for 1900-70 are derived from Tables A1-5 of the Appendix. Missing values for these years have been calculated by linear extrapolation. Values missing for earlier years have been calculated on the most probable simple assumptions. These assumptions vary according to the values being estimated.

3. The Episcopalian series includes data or estimated values for Easter Day communicants of the provinces of Canterbury and York of the Church of England as constituted in 1920, communicants of the Church in Wales as constituted in 1920 (or its constituent dioceses before that date), and communicants of the Episcopal Church in Scotland. The series is very largely shaped by movements in the number of Church of England Easter Day communicants, which

form about 90 per cent of the total; and is therefore very largely a participant-data series. The nineteenth-century values were obtained as follows:

(a) All values for 1890 and values for the Episcopal Church in Scotland for 1800-80 were derived or extrapolated from Table A1 of the Appendix.

(b) The values for England and Wales for 1800-80 were obtained as follows:

(i) According to data given in Tables A1 and D1 of the Appendix, there were 78·52 communicants or Easter communicants per resident incumbent or curate in the Church of England in England and Wales in 1885. In 1850 there were 12 994 resident incumbents or curates and, if this ratio then existed, 1 020 000 communicants. Extrapolating from data given by the Oxford visitations for a sample of thirty parishes in Oxford and Oxfordshire in 1834 and 1854, we calculate that in 1850 communicants at the 'Great Festivals' equalled 4·83 per cent of the total population of these parishes. If the same ratio obtained throughout England and Wales, there would have been 858 000 Episcopalian communicants in 1850. These estimates seem respectively too high and too low, since there were apparently fewer communicants per resident incumbent or curate in 1850 than in 1885, while the number of 'Great Festivals' communicants is an average always lower than Easter communicants. We have therefore averaged these figures and used the mean total of 939 000, a figure which assumes that the active communicant (that is, adult) membership of the Church of England in 1850 amounted to two-fifths of the worshippers in Church of England churches on the morning of 30 March 1851 (see Table F1).

(ii) The values for 1800-40 and 1860-80 were based on totals of resident incumbents or curates derived or extrapolated from Table D1 (the total for 1800 being estimated on the assumption that the number of resident clergy grew at an equal rate between 1800 and 1810 and between 1810 and 1820). The totals thus obtained were multiplied by 78·52; and, since the products would otherwise be inconsistent with the mean value adopted for 1850, they were multiplied in turn by 939/1020 or 0·9206.

4. The Scottish Presbyterian series includes data or estimated values for the Church of Scotland, the Free Church of Scotland, the United Presbyterian Church of Scotland, the United Free Church of Scotland, the Reformed Presbyterian Church of Scotland, and the Original Secession Church of Scotland. The series consists of roll data only, which (especially in the case of the Church of Scotland) appears by comparison with Nonconformist roll data to overstate active membership quite considerably. The nineteenth-century values were obtained as follows:

(a) The Church of Scotland total for 1800 was estimated on the assumption that this total equalled 14 per cent of the total population of Scotland (see note 2 to Table A2). The Church of Scotland totals for 1810-30 were estimated on the assumption that the number of Church of Scotland communicants grew at an equal rate between 1810 and 1834 and between 1834 and 1840. The Church of Scotland totals for 1840-90 were derived or extrapolated from Table A2.

(b) The Free Church of Scotland totals were derived or extrapolated from Table A2.

(c) The United Presbyterian Church of Scotland totals for 1800-50 were estimated on the assumption that communicants of this church and its constituents equalled 4·94 per cent of the total population of Scotland throughout 1800-60. The totals for 1860-90 were derived or extrapolated from Table A2.

(d) The United Free Church of Scotland totals were derived from Table A2.

(e) The Reformed Presbyterian and Original Secession Church totals for 1860 onwards and 1870 onwards respectively were derived or extrapolated from Table A2. The Reformed Presbyterian Church was assumed to have 3000 communicants in 1800-10, 4000 in 1820-30, and 5000 in 1840-50. The Original Secession Church was assumed to have 2000 communicants in 1800-40, and 3000 in 1850-60.

5. The Nonconformist series includes roll data or estimated values for Baptist, Congregationalist, and Methodist membership, and the communicants of the Presbyterian Church of England and the Presbyterian Church of Wales (Calvinistic Methodists). Baptist membership includes both General and Particular Baptists; Congregationalist membership includes the member-

ship of the Union of Welsh Independents; Methodist membership includes the membership of the Methodist Church and its constituents; Presbyterian Church of England membership includes membership of that church and its constituents. The nineteenth-century values were obtained as follows:

(a) (i) The English Baptist totals for 1800 and 1840-80 were derived or extrapolated from Table A4. The English Baptist totals for 1810-30 were estimated on the assumption that Particular Baptists increased at the same rate as the General Baptist New Connection.

(ii) Welsh Baptist totals were derived or extrapolated from Table A4.

(iii) Scottish Baptist totals for 1870-90 were derived from Table A4; while those for 1800-60 were estimated on the assumption that the number of Scottish Baptists grew at an equal rate between 1800 and 1864 and between 1864 and 1870.

(b) All English and Welsh Congregationalist totals, and Scottish Congregationalist totals for 1880-90, were derived from Table A4. Scottish Congregationalist totals for 1800-70 were estimated on the assumption that the number of Scottish Congregationalists grew at an equal rate throughout 1800-80.

(c) Except for the years 1810 and 1820, each Methodist total was taken from Table A7. To allow for the absence of published Bible Christian and Primitive Methodist data for those years, the Bible Christians were assumed to have 500 members in 1810 and 2500 in 1820; and the Primitive Methodists were assumed to have 900 members in 1810.

(d) Presbyterian Church of England totals for 1850-90 were derived or extrapolated from Table A2. Totals for 1800-40 were estimated on the assumption that the Presbyterian Church of England's constituent churches grew at an equal rate in 1800-40 and in 1840-60.

(e) Presbyterian Church of Wales totals for 1800-90 were derived or extrapolated from Table A4. Totals for 1800-30 were estimated on the assumption that the Presbyterian Church of Wales grew at an equal rate in 1800-38 and in 1838-48.

6. The Catholic series refers to estimated Catholic population and consists of semi-demographic data or equivalent estimated values. The nineteenth-century values were obtained as follows:

(a) The total for 1890 was extrapolated from Table A5.

(b) Totals for England and Wales for 1850-80 were estimated on the assumption that the Catholic population at those dates stood in the same ratio to total population as Catholic marriages did to total marriages. The same assumption was employed to obtain values for 1800-40, but it was necessary to estimate Catholic marriages for these years from observed data for the earliest available year, i.e. 1844, when Catholic marriages in England and Wales equalled 1·7 per cent of all marriages. It was estimated that Catholic marriages equalled 1·1 per cent of all marriages in 1800; 1·2 per cent in 1810, 1·3 per cent in 1820; 1·4 per cent in 1830; and 1·5 per cent in 1840.

(c) Totals for Scotland for 1860-80 were estimated on the assumption that the Catholic population at these dates stood in the same ratio to total population as Catholic marriages did to total marriages. Totals for 1800-50 were estimated on the assumption that the same ratio existed between the Catholic population of Scotland and that of England and Wales throughout the period 1800-60.

of England was partly reorganized and began to expand much faster than at any time in the previous fifty years, it apparently grew in part at the expense of Nonconformity. Meanwhile Irish immigration, and Catholic population, grew extremely rapidly between 1840 and the 1860s, and have continued to grow at a high rate since 1870, with a further acceleration after the Second World War. It would seem reasonable to explain the Catholic population curve very largely in terms of the relative economic position of Britain and Ireland, and, more particu-

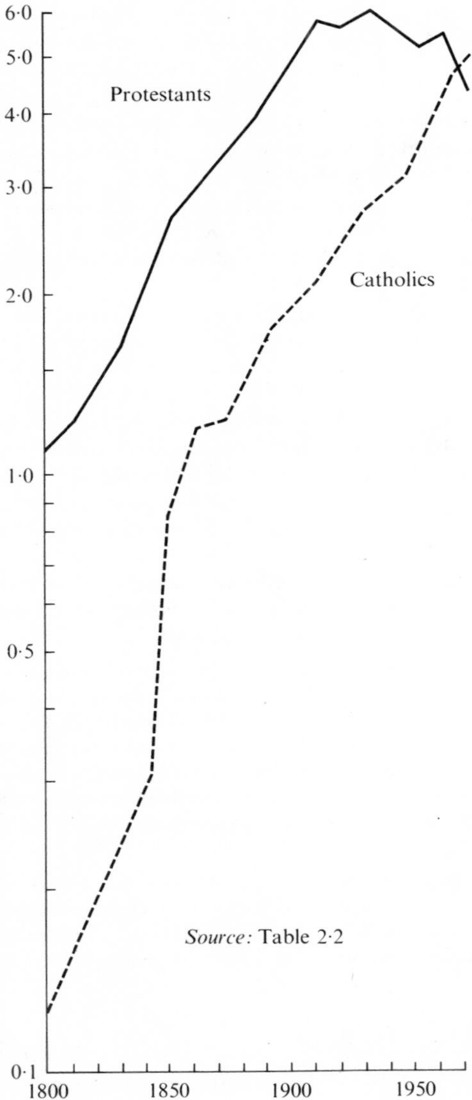

Fig. 2.1: Membership of the Major Protestant Churches and Estimated Catholic Population in Great Britain at Decennial Intervals, 1800-1970 (millions: semi-log).

Note: On a semi-logarithmic graph the slope of any curve indicates the rate of growth of the series plotted.

larly, of specific changes in the British demand for Irish migrant labour. Protestant membership since 1840 has not gained from immigration, and appears to have been influenced by a more complex set of factors. After 1840, British society was characterized by more stable urban and industrial institutions, and by greater freedom of travel, thought, and voluntary association; and, just as relaxation of

Fig. 2.2: Membership of the Major Protestant Churches and Estimated Catholic Population in Great Britain at Annual Intervals, 1900-1968 (millions).

state and legal pressures proved relatively unfavourable to public religious observance after 1689, so improved social and economic conditions proved relatively unfavourable to such observance after 1840.

After 1910 Catholic and Protestant experience became even more diverse: for in 1910 the membership of the major Protestant churches was more than twice as great as estimated Catholic population, while, by 1970, estimated Catholic population was rather greater than the membership of the major Protestant churches. These developments are illustrated by the annual data presented in Table 2.4 and Figure 2.2. Yet this striking divergence is almost entirely due to the differential effects of Irish immigration; and, as Figure 2.3 shows, comparison of the British Protestant-membership curve (in which England and Wales predominate) with the curve for Catholic conversions in England and Wales, indicates the highly *similar* experience of Protestantism and Catholicism in getting and keeping members from the indigenous British population during the present century.

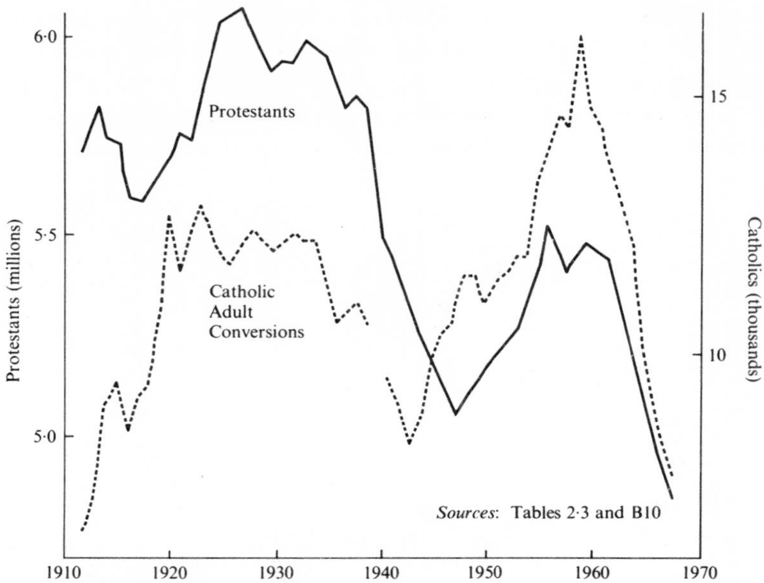

Fig. 2.3: **Membership of the Major Protestant Churches in Great Britain and Catholic Adult Conversions in England and Wales at Annual Intervals, 1912-70.**

Both Protestant and Catholic church membership reached peaks of some significance before 1914. This was followed by a sharp drop during the First World War, but from a low point in 1916-17 Catholic conversions and Protestant membership rose to new peaks in 1924 and 1927 respectively. The early 'thirties saw slight increases, the later 'thirties a minor fall. The Second World War brought a new low point, reached by Catholic conversion in 1943, and by Protestant membership no later and possibly earlier than 1947. Membership and conversions grew rapidly thereafter, reaching a peak in 1956 and 1959 respectively, but falling heavily after 1960. This pattern must cast considerable doubt on the commonly held doctrine that crises such as wars stimulate religious activity. For the evidence assembled here suggests that the two world wars had a most adverse effect on church growth; while both post-war revivals of church membership have been the precursors merely of new setbacks for organized religion during the political and economic crises of the late 'twenties and the 'thirties, and the 'sixties and the early 'seventies.

Table 2.4: Annual British Church Membership Totals, 1900 – 1970 (thousands)

	Episcopalians	*Scottish Presbyterians*	*Nonconformists*	*Major Protestants*	*Catholics*
1900	2089	1164	1803	5056	2016
1901	2136	1172	1824	5132	2061
1902	2212	1181	1860	5253	2106
1903	2238	1189	1893	5320	2117
1904	2293	1199	1939	5431	2129
1905	2113	1208	2024	5345	2141
1906	2177	1215	2057	5449	2153
1907	2213	1219	2048	5480	2165
1908	2303	1224	2039	5566	2180
1909	2356	1230	2031	5617	2190
1910	2418	1232	2020	5670	2216
1911	2507	1231	2014	5752	2242
1912	2405	1230	2004	5639	2291
1913	2524	1232	2006	5762	2339
1914	2437	1242	2003	5682	2389
1915	2416	1248	1997	5661	2438
1916	2301	1252	1980	5533	2434
1917	2297	1256	1975	5528	2456
1918	2330	1259	1974	5563	2466
1919	2369	1268	1967	5604	2493
1920	2410	1281	1963	5654	2502
1921	2453	1290	1962	5705	2517
1922	2410	1299	1969	5678	2514
1923	2540	1303	1988	5831	2567
1924	2570	1308	2002	5880	2599
1925	2650	1312	2008	5970	2633
1926	2642	1310	2018	5970	2646
1927	2662	1308	2019	5989	2660
1928	2606	1310	2015	5931	2711
1929	2575	1309	2005	5889	2762
1930	2529	1299	2001	5829	2781
1931	2556	1310	2000	5866	2813
1932	2549	1317	1991	5857	2843
1933	2608	1319	1982	5909	2855
1934	2601	1321	1973	5895	2891
1935	2580	1319	1961	5860	2933
1936	2520	1320	1944	5784	2950
1937	2504	1312	1921	5737	2968
1938	2531	1319	1907	5757	2976
1939	2515	1317	1896	5728	2990
1940	2255	1311	1874	5440	3023

	Episcopalians	*Scottish Presbyterians*	*Nonconformists*	*Major Protestants*	*Catholics*
1941	2209	1301	1849	5359	3033
1942	2165	1294	1824	5283	2996
1943	2120	1294	1807	5221	2970
1944	2076	1296	1793	5165	3022
1945	2031	1292	1773	5096	3057
1946	1987	1297	1746	5030	3094
1947	1944	1289	1731	4964	3136
1948	1989	1296	1713	4998	3235
1949	2033	1301	1707	5041	3370
1950	2077	1304	1696	5077	3499
1951	2105	1306	1684	5095	3557
1952	2134	1311	1675	5120	3591
1953	2161	1316	1669	5146	3643
1954	2241	1325	1664	5230	3713
1955	2322	1340	1661	5323	3800
1956	2401	1352	1654	5407	3927
1957	2354	1348	1641	5343	4064
1958	2309	1347	1627	5283	4123
1959	2360	1338	1615	5313	4210
1960	2398	1332	1604	5334	4346
1961	2395	1321	1589	5305	4406
1962	2392	1312	1572	5276	4459
1963	2288	1299	1543	5130	4539
1964	2184	1289	1525	4998	4647
1965	2152	1277	1496	4925	4782
1966	2117	1262	1468	4847	4828
1967	2059	1250	1440	4749	4830
1968	2001	1229	1402	4632	4907
1969	1903	1204	1361	4468	4964
1970	1804	1179	1328	4311	4829

NOTES AND SOURCES

1. For the composition of each series see the notes to Table 2.1
2. These figures were derived from Tables A1-5 of the Appendix. Estimated values have been used at points where there was a lack of data.

VARIATIONS IN GROWTH

Figures 2.4-7 illustrate some important membership series for individual churches. Given the composition of the membership series for 'Major Protestant Churches' presented in Table 2.4 and illustrated in Figure 2.3, it is obvious that the Church of England Easter Day communicant series (which constitutes 38 per cent of the values that compose the series) accounts for much of the pattern displayed by the aggregate series. Yet, as Figure 2.4 shows, the pattern of Easter Day communicants in England since 1900 is closely akin to the pattern of 'active' communicants – that is, persons who communicate at least once a year – in the Church of Scotland. The peaks and troughs closely coincide; and the major difference between the two series is that, whereas the trend of the Church of England series rises till about 1930 and then falls, the trend of the Church of Scotland series continues to rise until the 'active' communicant series ceases in 1959. The 'active' communicant series is not included in the series in Tables 2.3 and 2.4; but this upward trend is also indicated in the Church of Scotland communicant-roll series (illustrated in Figure 2.5) which does form part of those series. Indeed, between 1900 and 1956, the two Church of Scotland series show an almost identical increase of about 17 percentage points.

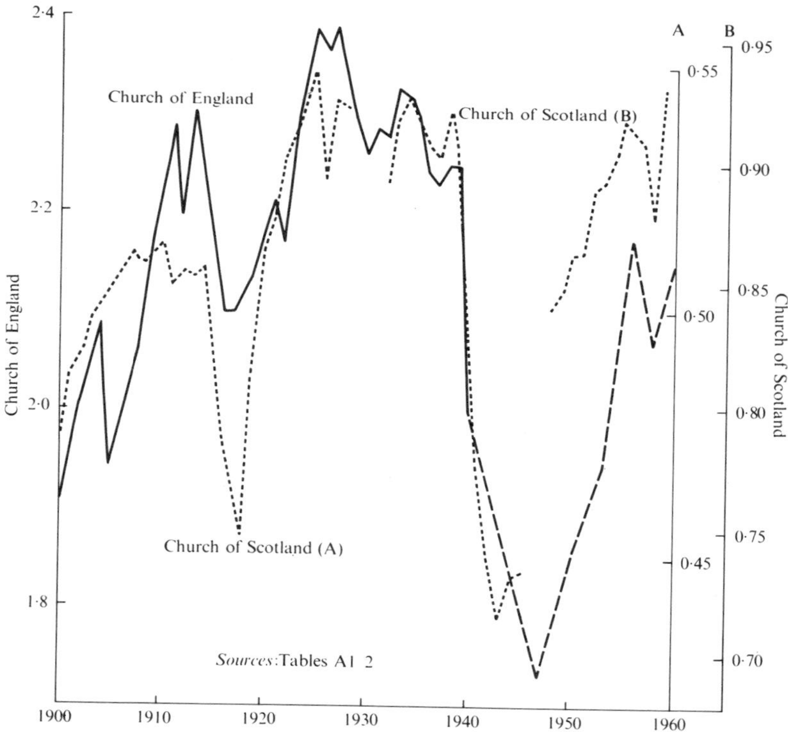

Fig. 2.4: Church of England Easter Day Communicants and Church of Scotland 'Active' Communicants at Annual Intervals, 1900-1960 (millions).
Note: After 1940, values for Church of England Communicants are given for the years 1947, 1950, 1953, 1956, and 1958 only.

In short, despite differences in medium-term trends, the two major participant-data series show much the same short-term configuration, a configuration also observable in the Catholic adult-conversions series. This pattern is largely con-

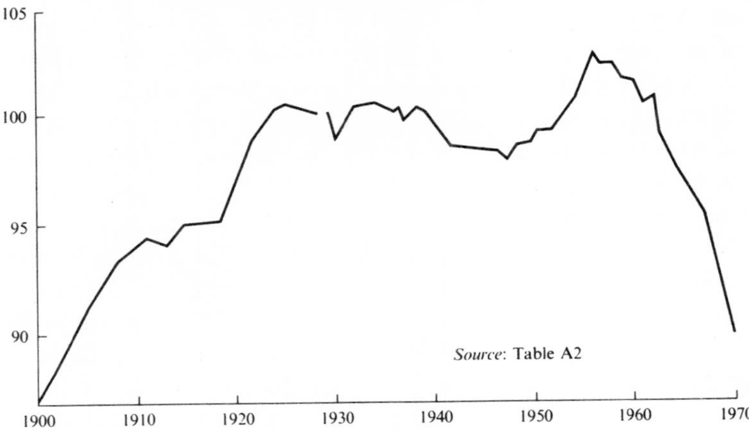

Fig. 2.5: Church of Scotland Communicant Roll at Annual Intervals, 1900-1970 (Index). Note: Membership on the roll is expressed as two indices in which 1928 (=100) is the base for the years 1900-28, and 1929 (=100) is the base for the years 1929-70.

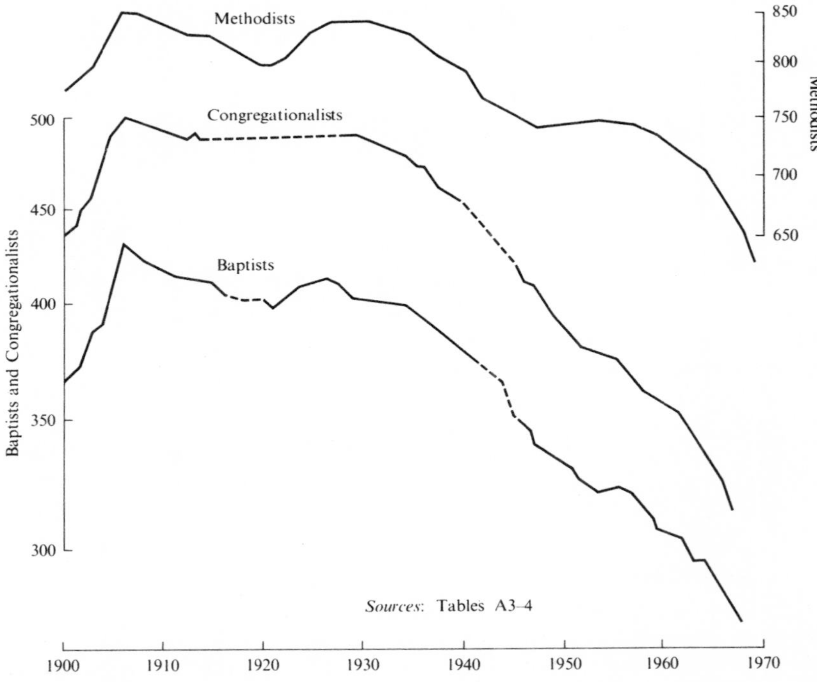

Fig. 2.6: Membership of the Baptist, Congregationalist, and Methodist Churches in Great Britain at Annual Intervals, 1900-1970 (hundred thousands: semi-log).
Note: The figure indicates the total membership of the constituents of the Methodist Church for the years 1900-1932.

firmed by the Church of England electoral-roll data, but a somewhat dissimilar pattern is seen in the three major Nonconformist series illustrated in Figure 2.6. Here the trend between 1900 and 1970 is distinctly downward; and, of course, since the curves are derived from roll data, year-to-year fluctuations are less clearly shown than in participant-data series. Yet the falls of the First and Second World War periods, the late 'thirties, and the 'sixties can clearly be seen; and the chief short-term differences between these series and the Church of England and Church of Scotland series seem to be the peak in Nonconformist membership in 1905-6 (not shown in the established churches' series) and the established chürches' peak in the middle or late 1950s (not shown in the Nonconformist series).

But the second of these variations may be less significant than this comparison suggests, for the roll data of the Nonconformist churches may obscure an increase in *participation* at a particular historical moment when people were more willing to attend church, or otherwise actively participate in church life, but not willing to be enrolled in the churches' records. Thus during 1953-6, while Church of England Easter Day communicants rose nearly 12 per cent, the number of names on the Church of England electoral roll fell almost 1 per cent; and during 1952-7, while Methodist membership as a proportion of the population aged fifteen and over fell 2 per cent, the Methodist share of marriages rose 4 per cent.[3]

Several smaller churches show growth patterns that do not immediately appear to correspond either to the established churches' or the Nonconformists' experiences. The Seventh Day Adventists (as can be seen from Figure 2.7) have grown both steadily and rapidly over the whole of the present century; and a pattern of steady rapid growth has also characterized the Pentecostalist churches, which have, like the Adventists, gained considerably from the West Indian immigration of the 1960s. The Society of Friends has, on the contrary, exhibited steady but low growth, while certain small religious groups have decreased sharply: since the beginning of the century, like the Churches of Christ and the New Church; since 1940, like Christian Science and the Salvation Army; or since the late 1950s, like the Open Brethren.

Perhaps the most successful of the smaller British churches are the Mormons (the Church of Jesus Christ of Latter Day Saints) and the Jehovah's Witnesses, membership series for both of which churches are shown in Figure 2.7. The Witnesses' cosmological teachings gained wider acceptance in the years immediately before the Second World War, and during the late 'forties and the 'fifties they again recruited many members. The Mormons also grew quite quickly about 1950, and again in the late 'fifties, but achieved remarkable growth during 1960-4, when they increased from 17 000 to 62 000 members by a large scale recruitment programme which probably appealed in quite large part to dissatisfied members of

3. See Tables A1, A3, H1, and H2.

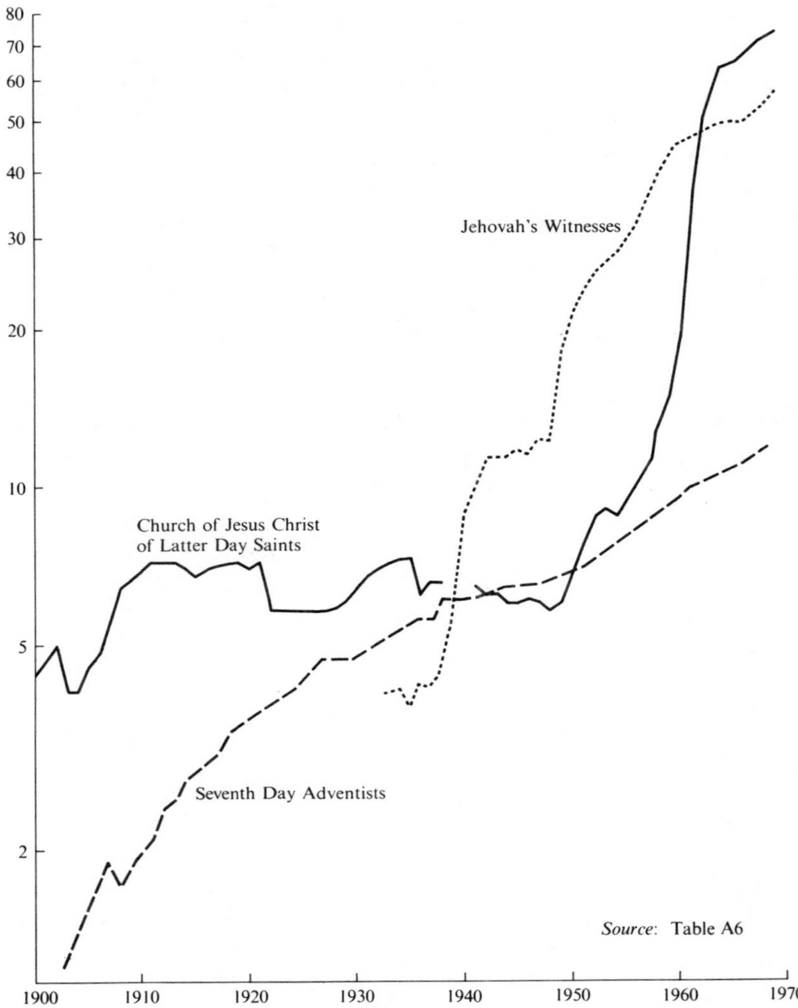

Fig. 2.7: Membership of the Church of Jesus Christ of Latter Day Saints, Jehovah's Witnesses and Seventh Day Adventists at Annual Intervals, 1900-1970 (thousands: semi-log).

larger religious bodies, who terminated church membership in considerable numbers during those years.

Yet, for all the special characteristics of these churches' growth patterns, there are some similarities in the fluctuations of these and other Protestant churches' membership. Indeed, the growth patterns of the Churches of Christ and the New Church, over most of the century, and Christian Science and the Salvation Army over the last few decades, exhibit a substantial identity with that of the major

Nonconformists. Despite drastic differences of trend there are even points of contact between the Mormons' and the Witnesses' growth curves and those of the larger Protestant churches. Thus, like those churches, the Mormons and the Witnesses found difficulty increasing their membership between 1943 and 1947/8; recruited more effectively from 1947 to 1960; and have again been less successful in the middle and late 'sixties.

It seems probable therefore that, while each church is itself a factor in determining its own growth by its specific recruitment policies, standards of discipline, and so on, the environment in which it operates is a still more influential factor. One good test of the degree to which any environment maximizes churches' opportunities to get and keep members is the degree to which the population uses facilities offered by churches to members and non-members alike. Tables H1-5 of the Appendix contain data on religious and non-religious marriages, from which it can been seen that the number of religious marriages solemnized in Britain fell from 95·7 per cent of all marriages in 1855 to 66·8 per cent in 1967. Moreover, even in 1967 the populations of the different countries of the British Isles responded in quite different ways to the churches' provision of facilities for religious marriages. In that year, 99·6 per cent of marriages solemnized in the Republic of Ireland were religious marriages; and so were 95·7 per cent of marriages in Northern Ireland; 74·8 per cent of marriages in Scotland; but only 65·9 per cent of marriages in England and Wales.

These differentials are reflected in the churches' growth. Between 1900 and 1968, the major Protestant churches increased 6 per cent in Scotland, and decreased 12 per cent in England and 18 per cent in Wales (variations between England and Wales being very largely explicable in terms of migration); while the Nonconformist churches increased 2 per cent in Scotland and decreased 21 per cent in England, 27 per cent in Wales. It is difficult to assess comparable changes in Ireland, since the Church of Ireland publishes no analogous data. However, the membership rolls of those Irish Protestant churches for which material is available increased about 29 per cent between 1900 and 1968, despite substantial migration out of Ireland.[4]

But there may also be local *short-term* variations. The Welsh Revival was associated with membership growth unmatched in England; for while, in England, the Baptists, Congregationalists, and Methodists increased 9·51, 10·40, and 9·29 per cent respectively, in Wales they increased 31·55, 17·93 and 20·52 per cent. Again, in the Second World War, net migration into Wales allowed many churches to sustain their membership rather more successfully in Wales than in England, since between 1940 and 1944 Baptists, Congregationalists, and Methodists de-

4. The membership rolls are those of the Presbyterian Church in Ireland, the Methodists, the Baptists, and the Congregationalists. It has been assumed that the Reformed Presbyterian Church had 3300, and the Congregationalists 1000 members in Ireland in 1968.

creased 5·57, 7·77, and 4·84 per cent respectively in England, while Baptists increased 0·88 per cent, and Congregationalists and Methodists decreased only 0·51 and 2·19 per cent, in Wales.[5]

Finally, the Anglo-Irish War and the Irish Civil War produced, during the years after 1918, a reduction in Irish Protestant church membership not matched in Britain. While Church of England Easter Day communicants, and Church of Scotland 'active' communicants *rose* 4·32 and 13·65 per cent respectively, Presbyterian Church in Ireland Easter communicants *fell* 0·6 per cent, between 1918 and 1921. Moreover, while the ratio between Catholics and Protestants remained virtually unchanged in Northern Ireland between 1911 and 1926, Catholics increased from 89·58 to 92·57 of the population of the Republic of Ireland, as the Protestant population declined by 32·54 per cent.[6]

But these divergences must not obscure the common configuration of church membership in the various countries of the British Isles. If the Nonconformist and major Protestant series given in Table 2.4 are divided into their English, Welsh, and Scottish components, the year-to-year differences of the Nonconformist and Protestant regional series thus generated correlate among themselves at 0·5-0·7 and 0·5-0·6 respectively, that is, well above the 1 per cent level of significance, which is in this case 0·3. Furthermore, the pattern of changes in Church of England Easter Day communicants and Church of Scotland 'active' communicants largely reappears in the movements of the number of 'active' communicants of the Presbyterian Church in Ireland, the total of these communicants reaching peaks before 1914, in the 'twenties and in the 'thirties, growing rapidly in the 'fifties, and falling in both world wars and in the 'sixties. It seems reasonable to conclude, therefore, that the differential effect of particular national environment is felt in the *trend* rather than the detailed *configuration* of changes in church membership.

THE GROWTH CYCLE

Fluctuations in time series such as those for church membership consist of endogenous changes, that is, changes arising from factors generated within the system measured, and exogenous changes, or changes arising from factors generated outside but impinging upon the system. In an economic system, for example, trade fluctuations might be attributed either to endogenous variations in consumption, savings, and investment, or to exogenous events such as conditions of weather resulting in good or bad harvests. Exogenous changes can cause fluctuations which are quite random when considered in the context of the system

5. See Tables A3 and A4. The Congregationalist figures for 1940-4 were estimated by extrapolation.
6. See Tables A1, A2, G1, and G2.

alone: but endogenous changes must be affected by the system and will therefore bear a significant relationship to it. If such endogenous changes are cyclical in nature, they presuppose a point or path of equilibrium about which the system tends to oscillate, just as a pendulum, constrained by gravity, swings either side of the vertical in such a way that the amplitude of each movement determines that of the counter-movement.

Church growth appears to display a largely cyclical pattern, the high and low points of which constitute uniform divergences from an equilibrium value related, over long periods of time, to the rate of growth of population; and these high and low points seem to indicate the operation of constraints which keep growth within certain limits. This observation is quite commonplace among church leaders, who have often concluded, as a Congregationalist put it in 1884, that 'The Kingdom of God comes by pulses, by wave movements'. Church leaders have most often associated these 'pulses' with 'revivals'; and, though they are not at all confined to periods notable for the special excitement generally included in the concept of a 'revival', they have usually been studied in connection with 'revivals'. C. G. Finney (who claimed that 'Almost all the religion in the world has been produced by revivals') noted that a 'revival' 'presupposes that a church is sunk down in a back-slidden state, and . . . consists of the return of the church from her backslidings, and in the conversion of sinners.' Finney reported that 'revivals' were said to 'come about once in five years', though he was anxious to argue that they could or should occur more frequently. William B. Sprague's *Lectures on Revivals of Religion*, first published in America in 1832, described 'the economy of revivals' as the system to which 'the church is much indebted . . . *for the increase . . . of her numbers*'. Sprague distinguished between 'seasons of revival' and 'ordinary circumstances'; he defined a 'revival' as 'the improved religious state of a congregation, or some other community'; and he traced a progression, in 'the economy of revivals' from 'a state of comparative depression', to the revival itself, and to the 'corresponding declension' or 'reaction' that follows.[7]

Sprague's perception of church growth as a cycle consisting of depression, revival, and declension approximates to the reality of membership change, as can be seen from evidence such as that presented in Table 2.5 and Figure 2.8. The time-trend of Wesleyan and Methodist growth falls from about 4·5 per cent per annum in 1770, to about 1.5 per cent per annum in 1870, and to about -1.5 per cent per annum in 1970. The growth rates of individual years fluctuate widely about this trend, yet more than 80 per cent of these years show growth rates that oscillate within a band defined by two limits – one, a line of maximum normal growth, so to speak, falling from 8 per cent per annum in 1770 to 4 per cent per

7. J. Brierley, 'The Philosophy of Revivals' *Congregational Magazine,* 1884, pp. 73-4; Charles Grandison Finney, *Lectures on Revivals of Religion,* Cambridge, Mass., 1960, pp. 9,15,20; William B. Sprague, *Lectures on Revivals of Religion,* London, 1959, pp. 7-8, 133-4, 233, 269.

Table 2.5

Wesleyan and Methodist Growth Rates (per cent)

		1811	5.52	1856	1.14	1901	0.55	1946	-0.78
		1812	6.53	1857	2.37	1902	1.81	1947	-0.50
1768	6.62	1813	4.43	1858	2.59	1903	1.05	1948	-0.29
1769	2.54	1814	7.33	1859	5.68	1904	1.29	1949	0.35
1770	4.78	1815	4.50	1860	5.98	1905	2.26	1950	0.18
1771	4.22	1816	5.48	1861	3.05	1906	2.80	1951	-0.43
1772	1.10	1817	1.05	1862	1.71	1907	-0.41	1952	0.27
1773	2.05	1818	0.74	1863	1.37	1908	-0.89	1953	0.05
1774	4.16	1819	0.41	1864	-0.01	1909	-0.23	1954	0.09
1775	4.49	1820	-2.39	1865	0.35	1910	-0.47	1955	-0.05
1776	3.64	1821	4.63	1866	0.11	1911	-0.62	1956	-0.25
1777	3.71	1822	5.66	1867	1.78	1912	-0.55	1957	-0.37
1778	5.11	1823	3.79	1868	1.58	1913	-0.09	1958	-0.39
1779	5.16	1824	3.44	1869	0.92	1914	-0.26	1959	-0.42
1780	3.22	1825	0.75	1870	0.85	1915	-0.49	1960	-0.69
1781	1.50	1826	1.05	1871	-0.40	1916	-1.06	1961	-0.69
1782	2.42	1827	2.68	1872	-0.07	1917	-0.80	1962	-0.59
1783	1.86	1828	3.35	1873	0.50	1918	-0.17	1963	-1.18
1784	7.01	1829	0.95	1874	0.88	1919	-0.78	1964	-1.33
1785	4.38	1830	0.43	1875	1.82	1920	-0.60	1965	-1.56
1786	7.17	1831	0.21	1876	4.15	1921	0.50	1966	-1.68
1787	6.20	1832	2.87	1877	2.51	1922	0.78	1967	-1.78
1788	6.67	1833	9.23	1878	-0.37	1923	1.51	1968	-2.34
1789	3.75	1834	4.29	1879	-0.86	1924	1.79	1969	-2.52
1790	2.60	1835	-0.33	1880	-0.25	1925	1.24	1970	-2.79
1791	0.97	1836	0.74	1881	1.14	1926	1.02		
1792	3.61	1837	-0.15	1882	3.36	1927	0.48		
1793	1.05	1838	1.40	1883	3.39	1928	0.36		
1794	13.52	1839	3.46	1884	0.81	1929	-0.10		
1795	8.30	1840	5.25	1885	0.68	1930	0.04		
1796	5.62	1841	1.74	1886	-0.19	1931	0.20		
1797	4.51	1842	-0.63	1887	-0.02	1932	0.03		
1798	2.83	1843	1.32	1888	0.85	1933	-0.41		
1799	7.61	1844	1.99	1889	1.24	1934	-0.75		
1800	-0.99	1845	0.94	1890	0.63	1935	-0.41		
1801	-2.00	1846	0.20	1891	0.14	1936	-0.86		
1802	3.82	1847	-0.61	1892	0.17	1937	-1.16		
1803	3.47	1848	-0.15	1893	0.66	1938	-0.50		
1804	9.87	1849	2.78	1894	1.32	1939	-0.31		
1805	4.94	1850	2.87	1895	1.01	1940	-1.28		
1806	8.72	1851	-15.65	1896	-0.53	1941	-1.70		
1807	6.96	1852	-6.93	1897	-0.82	1942	-1.51		
1808	6.82	1853	-3.66	1898	0.75	1943	-0.89		
1809	4.34	1854	-2.51	1899	1.14	1944	-0.53		
1810	4.48	1855	-1.25	1900	1.17	1945	-0.45		

NOTES AND SOURCES

1. The series indicates percentage change in the full membership of the Wesleyan Methodist Church (1768-1932), the Methodist Church and its constituent churches (1933), and the Methodist Church (1934-70). All figures refer to Great Britain.

2. Source: Table A7 of the Appendix.

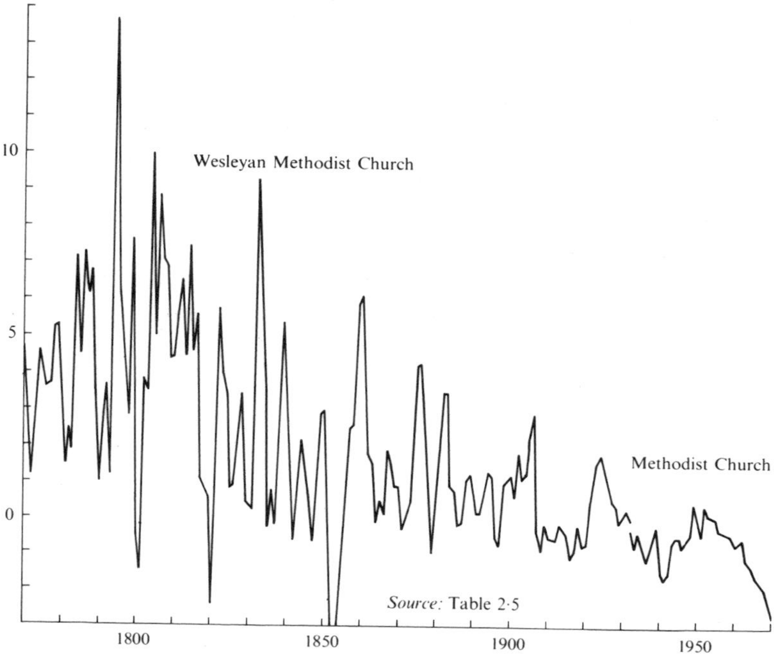

Fig. 2.8: Growth Rates of the Wesleyan Methodist Church and the Methodist Church at Annual Intervals, 1770-1970 (per cent).

annum in 1870 and 0 per cent per annum in 1970; and the other a line of minimum normal growth, falling from 1.5 per cent per annum in 1770 to -0.5 per cent per annum in 1870 and -2.5 per cent per annum in 1970.

Though peaks and troughs of these fluctuations occur at varying intervals, they are usually separated by five- or six-year periods. To specify the turning-points in these fluctuations is, as W. W. Rostow says of the turning-points of his British trade cycle series, 'a matter of judgement', both because of the imperfections of the data and because of the 'unique historical circumstances' of each period.[8]

In our series at least, these circumstances involve quite different combinations of endogenous and exogenous factors. Sometimes exogenous factors may so act as to permit the formation of growth cycles more or less regular in occurrence and in amplitude. The period 1886-1900, for example, provides three troughs (1886, 1891, and 1897) and three peaks (1889, 1894, and 1900), and the magnitude of each movement to and fro between peak and trough – 1·43, 1·10, 1·18, 2·14, and 1·99 percentage points respectively – varies little from cycle to cycle. Sometimes,

8. W. W. Rostow, *British Economy of the Nineteenth Century,* Oxford, 1948, pp. 32-3.

however, exogenous factors seem to be very powerful: for instance, in 1793-4, when political excitement attendant on war with France largely produced the uniquely high growth rate of nearly 14 per cent in one year; or in 1878-9 when the severity of the agricultural depression appears to have had considerable adverse effect on growth.

Despite interference from exogenous factors the cylical movement of growth does reassert itself from year to year, and not merely do peaks and troughs recur more or less regularly but the magnitude of each seems to determine the magnitude of the other. This may be seen in the Wesleyan Methodist curve even in years where growth exceeds the hypothetical normal limits, since most of these years follow directly upon each other. Thus 1791 and 1793 were years of excessively low growth; 1794-5 and 1799 of abnormally high growth; and 1800-1 of very low growth again. The Napoleonic wars saw no less than six years of very high growth, 1804, 1806-8, 1812, and 1814 (a sequence falling into three minor cycles, 1804-6, 1806-12, and 1812-14), followed by two years of excessively low growth in 1819-20; but the period 1804-20 does show the influence of unusually powerful exogenous factors. The year 1833 brought abnormally high growth again, and this was followed by two years of low growth (1835 and 1837); while high growth in 1840 was followed by low growth in 1842. The great Wesleyan schism resulted in something near to collapse in 1851-5, followed by a major period of very high growth in 1859-60 – though here too exogenous factors might be said to predominate. Finally 1876-83 produced the last complete cycle of abnormal growth.

These violent fluctuations seem inseparable from long-term high growth, as the evidence from Wesleyan history indicates. Ignoring the schism years of 1851-5, and dividing the total Wesleyan series into two periods, 1767-1850 and 1856-1932, it will be seen that twenty-two years of abnormal growth (high or low) occur in the first period, and only eight such years in the second. Moreover, while the first period is characterized by many peaks and troughs – of varying magnitudes – the latter is characterized by quite few. Yet the Wesleyan Methodist Church grew at an average rate of 3·36 per cent per annum in the first period, and at an average rate of only 0·85 per cent per annum in the second. During 1767-1850, then, Wesleyan growth rates fluctuated widely and frequently; and the hypothetical normal limits of growth, though widely spaced (being separated by 6·5 percentage points in 1770 and 4·5 in 1850) were frequently breached. During 1856-1932, however, Wesleyan growth rates fluctuated less widely and less frequently within hypothetical limits of growth separated by 4·5 percentage points in 1856 and 3 in 1932.

In Chapter I we argued that recruitment to church membership involves at least three distinct transfers of individuals: from the population as a whole (which is little disposed toward membership) to the external constituency of persons significantly disposed toward membership; from the external constituency to the internal constituency of non-member adherents who formally or publicly affirm their disposition toward membership; and from the internal constituency to membership itself. These transfers, as we shall show in Chapter III, occur at different rates, such that, in general, individuals transfer from the internal constituency to membership faster than from the external to the internal constituency, and they transfer from the external to the internal constituency faster than from the population as a whole to the external constituency.

These differentials arise, in a society where there is relatively little pressure toward church membership, because churches exert less influence over transfers sociologically more remote from them; and the result of these differentials is that, if the transfer of individuals from the internal constituency to membership is accelerated, that is, if growth rises, the internal constituency is depleted. But the internal constituency is not itself homogeneous, either at any one time or over time. For adherents' objective characteristics and circumstances will vary (for example, in eligibility by age, or degree of preparation for membership), making them more or less recruitable; and their responsiveness to recruitment will also vary, both between individuals, and between different periods in the same individual's life. Thus the internal constituency may diminish in a simple quantitative sense when growth rises – in other words, the *number* of potential recruits may fall – but it may also diminish qualitatively, in the sense that, even though unrecruited but objectively recruitable adherents remain in the internal constituency, those adherents become less responsive to recruitment.

But adherents do not always passively allow church members, or lay and clerical church leaders, or both, to be the sole active factors in the recruitment process. Sprague writes that, 'There is one grand principle of our nature, which the Holy Spirit makes great use of in a revival . . . I mean the principle of sympathy', that is, the communication of feelings, attitudes, expectations, and ideas between individuals. The stimulus toward a higher rate of recruitment may well first be received and transmitted by the full-time professional church leaders – indeed there are many instances, such as the reform and expansion of the Church of England in the 1830s, or the new missionary policy of the Mormons in the 1950s, where those leaders constitute a virtually predominant influence. But there is no reason why this must always be so when the 'sympathy' of individuals allows so much to be communicated and recommunicated between them; and many increases in church growth may originate from stimuli first perceived and transmitted by lay members, or even non-member adherents.[9]

However the stimulus to higher growth is received and transmitted, such growth nevertheless involves a paradox noted in Chapter I and illustrated in Chapter IV. Higher growth cannot be achieved simply by recruiting church

9. Sprague, op.cit., pp. 106, 133-4.

members' children, since the stock of such children is limited; and therefore children of non-members must also be recruited if churches are to grow more rapidly. But non-members' children are significantly less likely than members' children to retain membership; and therefore *increased recruitment must involve increased losses,* losses which occur well within the time-span of the average growth cycle: thus, in Finney's words, a '*constant tendency* . . . to declension and backsliding' characterizes 'converts of revivals'. This factor stongly interacts with the different rates of transfer between different categories of relationship to the church to determine the character of the growth cycle.[10]

Five phases can be identified in the growth cycle: and we wish (partly following Sprague) to term these phases periods of *depression, activation, revival, deactivation,* and *declension.* In the *depression* period, the pool of adherence which is the internal constituency is full but recruitment is low, and, because growth is therefore largely autogenous, losses are low. Church leaders are relatively inactive, and they may benefit from this period of quiet when there is little demand on their energies to get or to keep new members. Neither leaders, members, nor adherents expect high growth. This situation changes when the *activation* period commences. As Finney puts it,

> Most of the time the labours of ministers are, it would seem, directed to other objects [than revivals]. They seem to preach and labour with no particular design to effect the *immediate* conversion of sinners. . . . But when the attention of a minister is directed to the state of . . . his congregation, and his heart is full of the necessity of revival, and when he puts forth the proper efforts for this end, then you may be prepared to expect a revival.

The timing of the revival may be attributed to some political event, some crisis such as an epidemic, an economic upturn or, at the local level, some vicissitude in the lives of an individual or individuals within the congregation – such as the arrival of a new minister, the building of a church, or the tragic death of a member – which will cause adherents, members, leaders, or all three, to respond to the imbalance between the current recruitment rate and the size of the pool of adherence. Expectations of high growth will rise rapidly, because such growth is seen to be possible and – in the circumstances of the day – is *felt to be necessary.* Thus, for example, when the Methodist Quarterly Meeting in Hull met in 1826, it noted the losses of the previous year, and put in hand prayer meetings and other special activities, through which 'more than usual interest was excited', especially among previously less enthusiastic members, the 'half-awakened', attendants and lapsed members.[11]

The *revival* period soon follows. Leaders, members, and adherents are all highly activated; recruitment rate rises rapidly; and expectations of high growth may rise

10. Finney, op.cit., p.307.

11. Ibid., p. 33; R. Treffry, *Remarks on Revivals of Religion with Brief Notices of the Recent Prosperity of the Work of God in Hull,* London, 1827, pp. 7-9.

even faster. This period is typified by effort and excitement; and, in the special circumstances of what are commonly called 'revivals' high growth may be accompanied by new forms of religious behaviour, very frequent meetings for religious worship, and displays of great emotion both by individuals and by groups. Nevertheless, throughout this period the pool of adherence is decreasing as more and more adherents become members, and high recruitment rates are already beginning to produce higher losses.

The *deactivation* period is caused by four factors. Recruitment rate begins to fall because there are either few more potential recruits or because those few potential recruits that remain become, possibly through the operation of some exogenous factor, less responsive to recruitment. The loss rate is now high and this, combined with any exogenous check to recruitment causes an objective deceleration of net growth. *Expectations* of high growth therefore begin to fall, thus producing an endogenous check to recruitment by lowering efforts at, and responsiveness to, recruitment. And, finally, especially since losses are high, *and continue to rise even when recruitment falls,* leaders and members lose confidence in high growth and doubt both its efficacy and its validity.

Loss rate may continue to rise during the *declension* period which follows yet, since allogenous growth is decreasingly important during this period, both recruitment and loss rates fall together. The pool of adherence is beginning to refill; but expectations of high growth are rapidly falling; there is little pressure on the new adherents to become members; and, in this way, declension turns into *depression.* Once this happens, of course, the cycle is complete and conditions are right for a fresh activation of the church and its constituency. How the new cycle develops will be determined by the size of internal constituency and the rate at which it is growing; and these factors will, in turn, be influenced by changes in the whole population, so that demography comes to play a decisive part in shaping church growth.

III
Churches and their Constituencies

THE DEMOGRAPHY OF CHURCH MEMBERSHIP

'Church membership', as defined here, is a more or less voluntary association with a religious body, almost always expressed in some type of church attendance. Though the memberships of different churches can be distinguished by different cultural and socio-economic characteristics, they are sufficiently alike to be subject to influences affecting the total population; and, in particular, though each church generally recruits from part of the total population only, the demography of the part approximates to that of the whole. 'The expansion of religious communities', as Maurice Halbwachs observes, results 'most often from trends and movements affecting the entire population.'[1]

Figures 3.1 and 3.2 illustrate the churches' demographic dependence on the larger community. Over the long term, a church relies on recruitment of young persons disposed to membership through the influence of their families. During forty-six years of this century the Church of England baptized 21·9 million infants and confirmed 9·1 million persons aged twelve and over, but baptized only 0·5 million persons of 'riper years'. In other words, during these years baptisms of persons of 'riper years' constituted 2·39 per cent of all Anglican baptisms; and even if *all* these baptized persons of 'riper years' proceeded to confirmation, they constituted less than 6 per cent of the confirmed communicants of the Church of England. And, as Figure 3.1 shows, the number of infant baptisms in any given year (that is, the stock from which 95 per cent of the confirmees of about fifteen years later will be drawn) is determined almost entirely by the number of births in that year.[2]

So, too, churches' losses from deaths depend on fluctuations of deaths in the total population, as can be seen from Figure 3.2. In most denominations the chief

1. Maurice Halbwachs, *Population and Society, Introduction to Social Morphology,* Glencoe, Illinois, 1960, p. 54.
2. Statistical Unit of the Central Board of Finance of the Church of England, *Facts and Figures about the Church of England,* 3, London, 1965, p. 54. The years are 1902-40, 1947, 1950, 1953, 1956, 1958, 1960, and 1962.

Fig. 3.1: Births in England and Wales and Church of England Baptisms, 1900-1962 (thousands).
Note: Annual returns have been used for the period 1900-40. After 1940 only returns for the years 1947, 1950, 1953, 1956, 1958, 1960, and 1962 have been indicated in this figure.

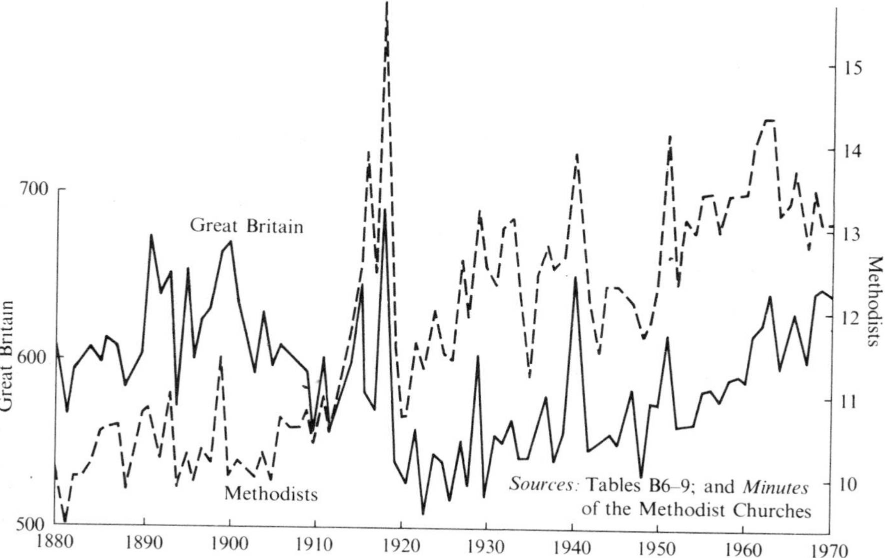

Fig. 3.2: Deaths in Great Britain and in the Methodist Church and its Constituent Churches at Annual Intervals, 1880-1970 (thousands).

source of membership loss is voluntary termination but loss from deaths has been, during this century, of a closely comparable magnitude. During 1933-69 inclusive, the Methodist Church removed 1 720 952 persons from its membership rolls. Of this total 617 298 were persons transferring their membership from one circuit to another; and of these 503 072 did complete their membership transfer, giving a true net loss of 1 217 610. Out of this net loss, 42·89 per cent (522 183) was due to voluntary membership termination, and 39·1 per cent (476 133) to death.[3]

The relationship between church membership and total population can be considered in two ways. On one hand, in so far as church growth is allogenous (that is, in so far as it arises from recruitment of children of non-members), it must be delimited by natural changes in the population available for recruitment. And on the other hand, in so far as church growth is autogenous (that is, in so far as it arises from recruitment of members' children), it must be delimited by natural changes in the size of members' families – which, in any event, will vary approximately as the total population of families varies.

The longer a church's history, the less likely is it to grow faster than the total population. Using the data presented in Tables 2.3 and 2.4 we estimate that, between 1800 and 1960, the mean annual growth rate of the Episcopalian, Scottish Presbyterian, and Nonconformist churches was 0·89, 0·91, and 1·28 per cent per annum respectively; and that the mean annual growth rate of the major Protestant churches as a whole was 1 per cent per annum. Since the total British population grew at a mean annual rate of 0·99 per cent per annum between these dates, only the Nonconformist churches appear to have grown faster than population during this period. Moreover, most of the Nonconformists' expansion occurred during the late eighteenth and early nineteenth centuries, and the mean annual growth rate of Nonconformity between 1820 and 1960 was only 0·93 per cent per annum. Long-term factors will, then, cause church growth to approximate to, or fall short of, population growth.

This tendency may be offset by entry into a population of migrants specially responsive to recruitment by a particular church. During 1910-70, the Presbyterian Church of England became increasingly dependent for its growth, as Figure 3.3 shows, on migration to England of members of Scottish Presbyterian churches. After 1931 this dependence greatly increased, since the number of persons resident in England and Wales but born in Scotland rose from 366 000 in that year to 654 000 in 1961; and, after 1946, Scottish migrants became the chief source of membership growth, accounting for 42 per cent of all persons newly entered on the Presbyterian Church of England's communicant rolls. Moreover, during peacetime, Scottish migrants provided the Presbyterian Church of England with a flow of recruits much steadier than that afforded by the English population: English recruitment and Scottish transfers falling 20·05 and 10·33 per cent

3. See Table B9 of the Appendix.

Fig. 3.3: New Members of the Presbyterian Church of England Recruited in England and Transferred from Scotland as a Percentage of Communicant Membership at Annual Intervals, 1911-1968 (per cent: semi-log).

respectively between 1920 and 1938, and 25·00 and 5·03 per cent respectively between 1946 and 1967.[4]

While Scottish migration has merely checked the decrease of the Presbyterian Church of England, Irish migration has enabled the Catholic church to increase very rapidly throughout Britain. There were about 250 000 Irishmen in Britain in 1820, and about 375 000 in 1840. Large-scale migration, stimulated partly by the Irish famine, partly by British demand for labour, raised the number of Irishmen in Britain to 800 000 by 1860. Thereafter the total fell to 550 000 in 1920,

4. Tables A2 and B4; 1931 and 1961 *Censuses*. The rates of recruitment and transfer were calculated by expressing the number of those 'admitted first time' and of those received 'by certificate' from a non-English church as a proportion of communicant membership in each year.

but rose (especially after 1945) to 1 000 000 by 1960. Though many Irishmen were short-stay migrants, many others settled, married, and raised families in Britain, so that the total *Irish* (as opposed to Irish-born) population of Britain grew faster than these figures suggest.

The size of the Irish – or indeed the Anglo-Irish – population of Britain is quite unknown, as is the proportion of British Catholics who are Irish or Anglo-Irish. But the significance of Irish migration for the British Catholic community may be indicated by a comparison of estimates of the Catholic population of Britain in the eighteenth and twentieth centuries. In 1781, on the eve of the industrial revolution, when comparatively few British Catholics were Irish, the Catholic population of Britain probably numbered about 120 000. If this population had, like the membership of British Protestant churches, more or less kept pace with the growth of the total population, by 1960 the estimated Catholic population of Britain would have been about 680 000; but, according to the parish priests, it was then in fact about 4·3 million, while other estimates put it as high as 6·4 million. Some of the 3·5-5·75 million Catholics thus unaccounted for must be British adult converts: for there were about 740 000 adult conversions to Catholicism in Britain between 1900 and 1960, perhaps a half or three-quarters of which represented a lasting increment to the Catholic population. Moreover, some of these 3·5-5·75 million Catholics will be European migrants, such as the 100 000 Poles who came to Britain during the 1940s. But plainly, at least according to the estimated size of the Catholic population in Britain, half and perhaps three-quarters of the total must be Irish migrants and their descendants.[5]

Churches may also exhibit a growth rate significantly different from that of the population as a whole if either the proportions of the sexes and the various age groups in its membership, or its membership's fertility and longevity, vary from that of the total population. The fertility of Irish migrants in the 1960s has been estimated at about 40 per cent higher than that of the English and Welsh population as a whole; while Catholic fertility in England and Wales has been estimated to be 66 per cent higher than non-Catholic fertility in 1914, and 31 per cent higher in 1962. These differentials must be attributed partly to the high proportion of young people in a migrant population, partly to the stimulus toward large families, and the inhibitions on artificial contraception, inherent in Catholic teachings and culture. And, regardless of particular cultural influences, a similar differential in fertility would be found in any church that entered upon a *progressive* relationship with the population at large. For such a church will derive by far the greater part of its high net gains from allogenous growth; and in the modern world such growth will arise, to a quite disproportionate extent, from recruitment

5. Table A5; John Archer Jackson, *The Irish in Britain*, London, 1963, *passim;* and A. E. C. W. Spencer, 'The Demography and Sociography of the Roman Catholic Community of England and Wales' in L. Bright and S. Clements (eds.) *The Committed Church*, London, 1966.

of young people in the most fertile age groups. Thus not merely will an expanding church obtain many new members but these members will in turn provide further young members from their own families.[6]

The contrary is of course true of a church that enters a *recessive* relationship with the population at large. Such a church will derive a decreasing part of its diminishing growth from children of non-members and will, therefore, be characterized by an increasing reliance on recruitment of members' children. Wastage among these recruits cannot be offset by recruits from outside the community, nor can younger persons be brought in to redress the demographic imbalance of the community as the remaining members get older — with the result that the church's fertility must fall. Table 3.1 shows this process at work. The death-rate of the total population aged fifteen and over has steadily declined and then become more or less stable; but the death-rate of the three denominations selected here has first fallen and then risen, so that the mortality of their membership is now higher than it was a century ago. The permanently unfavourable relationship of denominational death-rates to the death-rate of the total population is attributable very largely to these denominations' disproportionate recruitment of socio-economic and regional groups characterized by high mortality. But the *deterioration* of the denominations' death-rates since the First World War (illustrated also by Figure 3.2) can be explained only by the increasing predominance of older age groups within the denominations.

In order to expand, therefore, a church must increase its stock of young potential recruits by first increasing its stock of young adult members or adherents. Figure 3.4 illustrates this process in operation in the dependence of infant baptisms on church marriages in British Catholicism. It is of course possible to have marriages without baptisms: during the late 'twenties and the 'thirties, and again in the late 'sixties Catholic — like Protestant — couples restricted their families in the face of political and economic uncertainties and difficulties. But since, over the century as a whole, more than 90 per cent of births have been legitimate births, at least nine-tenths of each increase in baptisms is the product of an immediately anterior increase in marriages.

The number of baptisms in any given year will tend to determine the number of new members about fifteen years later. Wastage, recruitment of members or adherents of other churches, and of members of the non-churchgoing population, and fluctuations in the responsiveness of the various categories of potential recruits, will all serve to obscure the underlying delayed influence of baptisms on membership. Yet that influence will provide much of the trend of recruitment, as Figure 3.5 shows. Over the years 1890-1935, the number of new members

6. Juliet Cheetham, 'Immigration', in A. H. Halsey (ed.), *Trends in British Society since 1900*, London, 1972, p. 472; Spencer, op.cit., pp. 74-5.

Table 3.1
Selected Death-Rates (per cent)

	England and Wales	*Methodists*	*Presbyterian Church of England*	*Presbyterian Church of Wales*
1880	1.48	1.55	1.39	
1885	1.51	1.41	1.50	
1890	1.56	1.42	1.45	
1895	1.43	1.32	1.47	1.84
1900	1.44	1.48	1.35	1.67
1905	1.24	1.24	1.26	1.55
1910	1.17	1.29	1.28	1.55
1915	1.33	1.38	1.54	1.71
1920	1.12	1.51	1.47	1.53
1925	1.18	1.38	1.46	1.61
1930	1.15	1.48	1.38	1.61
1935	1.21	1.36	1.42	1.71
1940	1.45	1.75	1.67	1.72
1945	1.19	1.63	1.77	1.68
1950	1.27	1.70	1.88	1.91
1955	1.30	1.80	1.62	1.93
1960	1.29	1.85	1.54	1.94
1965	1.30	1.92	1.65	2.09

NOTES AND SOURCES

1. The England and Wales death-rate refers to the number of deaths per cent in the age-group fifteen and over. The number of deaths in each year was derived from the *Returns* and *Reviews* of the Registrar-General for England and Wales.

2. The Methodist death-rate refers to the number of deaths per cent among members of the Methodist Church and its constituents. The figures for 1880-1935 include Scotland, where there were few Methodists. Souces: Tables A3 and B6-9 of the Appendix; and the *Minutes of Conference* of the Bible Christians and the Methodist New Connexion.

3. The Presbyterian Church of England and Presbyterian Church of Wales death-rates refer to the number of deaths per cent among the communicants of those churches. The two churches were virtually confined to England and Wales respectively during the period covered by this Table. Sources: Tables A1, A4, B4-5 of the Appendix.

admitted to the Presbyterian Church of England was closely determined by the number of baptisms in that church during the years 1876-1920. Indeed there are only two major breaches in this relationship: one, during 1901-5 when membership rose very sharply through the Nonconformist (and Liberal) revival; and the other, during 1914-15 when the coming of war sharply reduced recruitment. These exceptions, are, however, variations upon the demographic trend. Such variations may, from time to time and from church to church, become so pronounced as to override the trend altogether; but once the exogenous causes of these variations are removed, the endogenous factors that sustain membership within certain normal limits of growth will be seen still to operate.

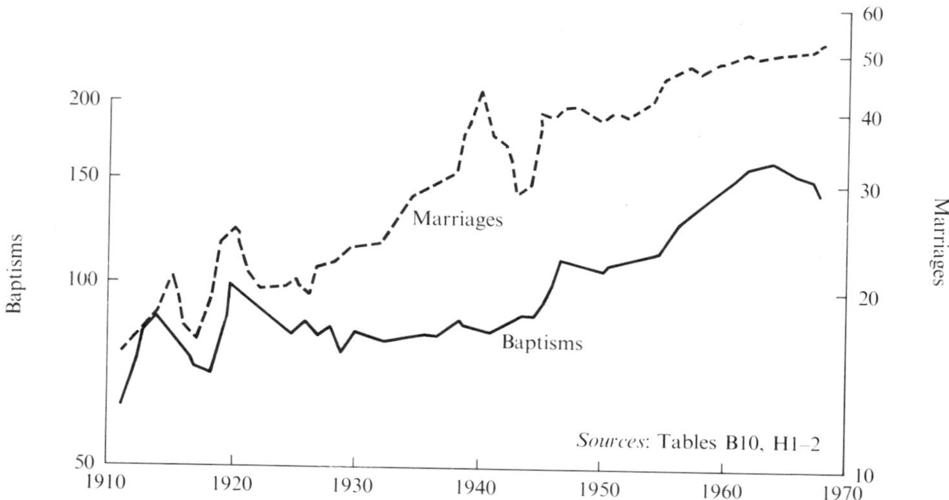

Fig. 3.4: Catholic Marriages and Baptisms in Great Britain at Annual Intervals, 1911-1968 (thousands: semi-log).

Fig. 3.5: Admissions and Baptisms in the Presbyterian Church of England at Annual Intervals, 1891-1935 (thousands: semi-log).
Note: Baptisms have been lagged fifteen years.

CONSTITUENCIES

General demographic changes tend to determine changes in church growth because the fertility and mortality of the total population also characterizes the membership of the churches. Yet, in a pluralistic society which contains many churches, and indeed many non-church members, each individual church might seem able, at least in theory, to recruit sufficient new members for a long enough period to secure, even over very many years, a growth rate much higher than that of the population as a whole. In 1900, for example, when the major British Protestant churches had a membership of about 5 000 000, and when perhaps another million and a half persons aged fifteen and over were members of other churches, the total population of Britain aged fifteen or over was about 25 000 000; and to have recruited the entire adult population over the length of the nineteenth century, the churches would have needed to treble or quadruple their growth rates.

Churches do not obtain these growth rates because they can recruit so few isolated individuals outside their particular 'constituency', that is, outside a more or less cohesive section of the population which is significantly disposed toward church membership. A church recruits from its constituency; and since that constituency responds to demographic forces at work in the population as a whole, each church is influenced by those forces almost as much as if its membership were coterminous with the total population.

The notion of a special relationship between church and constituency is fundamental to the sociology of religion. Weber discovered the origins of the different religions of the world among different classes: Confucianism among literary intellectuals, Buddhism among mendicant monks, Islam among world-conquering warriors, Christianity among itinerant artisans, and so on; and he emphasized the 'characteristic contrasts in what religion must provide for the various social strata', each of which has its special 'religious need', and hence its 'distinctive class religion'.[7]

Richard Niebuhr applied the concept of the nexus between a religion and a social group to the analysis of individual churches, arguing that these collectivities are 'caste-organisations', since 'the division of churches closely follows the division of men into the castes of national, racial and economic groups'. And this analysis, has, in turn, been applied to the study of church growth by Donald McGavran, who divides society into what he calls *homogeneous units*, characterized by certain common cultural or socio-economic features. 'Men like to become Christians', observes McGavran, 'without crossing racial, linguistic or class barriers' such as those that delimit homogeneous units.[8]

7. Max Weber, *From Max Weber, Essays in Sociology* (trans. and ed. H. H. Gerth and C. Wright Mills), New York, 1946, pp. 268-9; *The Sociology of Religion* (trans. E. Fischoff), London, 1965, pp. 101-7.

8. H. R. Niebuhr, *The Social Sources of Denominationalism*, Cleveland and New York, 1965, pp. 6, 21; Donald A. McGavran, *Understanding Church Growth*, Grand Rapids, Michigan, 1970, pp. 85, 198, 208.

These writers' 'strata', 'groups', 'castes', or 'homogeneous units' correspond to what may be called *external* constituencies as distinct from the *internal* constituency which, contained within the external constituency, consists of those persons who, without yet taking up full membership, have translated their disposition towards a particular religious allegiance into some formal or public act of adherence to a given religious organisation. Some external constituencies may, in a sense, be delimited by a church itself when, for example, a religious organization confines itself (like certain Lutheran bodies in England) to ethnically specific migrant groups. But more often, in the pluralistic post-Reformation era, a population, free to choose its religious allegiance, coheres slowly and informally into very loose groups susceptible to recruitment by one or other of the religious bodies operative within the population. In this sense at least, the external constituency comes into being, demonstrates its demand for religious facilities, and so induces a supply of those facilities by the appropriate church.

Though many individuals may belong to more than one external constituency, and though each such constituency may display a number of different characteristics, we may perhaps identify a few important types of constituency which, though they overlap in practice, are theoretically separable and can be defined in terms relevant to the religious preferences of their constituents. Individuals and groups might then be categorized not by an exhaustive definition of their relationship to a particular religious organization, but by specification of those qualities that would be expected to dispose them toward membership of one church rather than another.

Some groups acquire from a particular religion an identity in a plural society. For this type of constituency a certain religion, a certain church, becomes 'our religion', 'our church', and – to a greater or lesser degree – membership of another religion or church, or no religion or church, becomes a species of deviance ranging from eccentricity to betrayal. The most obvious example of this tendency is afforded by the Irish who, in Britain as in America, have closely identified themselves with Catholicism; while the century of the separate existence of the Presbyterian Church of England illustrates many Scottish migrants' desire to retain, so far as possible, a specifically Scottish religious identity in a non-Scottish community. Moreover, in Wales, the divisions between English- and Welsh-speaking communities has produced not only the antithesis of the episcopalian Church in Wales and the Presbyterian Church of Wales, but also linguistic distinctions *within* churches, such as the Welsh-speaking Union of Welsh Independents and the English-speaking North and South Wales Unions in Congregationalism, and the Welsh-speaking 'Wales' Districts and the English-speaking Cardiff and Swansea District in Methodism.[9]

9. McGavran, op.cit., p. 141; Will Herberg, *Protestant-Catholic-Jew, An Essay in American Religious Sociology*, New York, 1960, pp. 142 ff.

These instances are ethnic. But there are other cultural or regional groups that, without a distinct ethnic character, nevertheless repose at least part of their collective identity in a specific religious commitment. The Bible Christians who originated in Devon and who, in 1901, represented less than 4 per cent of British Methodists but 29 per cent of the Methodists of Devon and Cornwall, gained great advantages in those counties from their special regional appeal as the only predominantly West Country Methodist church run by West Countrymen, and generally holding its annual conference in the West Country. Both the Free Church of Scotland and the Episcopal Church in Scotland exemplify the tendency to regional or cultural particularity on a larger scale: for, though the former is overwhelmingly, and the latter predominantly, Scottish, by their religious affiliations both mark themselves off from the Lowland majority loyal to the Church of Scotland. Finally, the English Recusants seem, over most if not all their history, to have expressed, by their Catholicism, a complex dissociation from a cultural majority in many ways hostile to them, yet certainly no more English.

A further type of constituency consists of persons of a common socio-economic status and, possibly, of similar occupations. The existence of such constituencies underlines Niebuhr's 'theory of class-denominationalism'.[10] At present, the best evidence on such socio-economic constituencies in Britain is that relating to Nonconformity. During the first four decades of the nineteenth century, artisans, colliers, and miners were very heavily over-represented, merchants, manufacturers and tradesmen somewhat over-represented, labourers rather (and farmers heavily) under-represented, and the aristocracy virtually unrepresented, in the ranks of Nonconformity. Thus the chief socio-economic elements in the external constituencies of the Nonconformist churches were the business classes and skilled manual workers, including miners. Moreover, the business elements in Nonconformity at this period largely consisted of small businessmen, while skilled workers who were Nonconformists were either self-employed artisans or employees in small workshops.[11]

The growth of large-scale enterprises after 1840 probably inhibited the increase of small businessmen, while continued development of the factory system both greatly reduced the class of skilled manual workers which formed about 60 per cent of the male membership of the Nonconformist churches in 1840, and created a new class of manual workers which Nonconformists could not recruit in any large numbers. That Nonconformity did not appeal to manual workers in large factories can be seen from the relative weakness of Nonconformity in south-east Lancashire, the historic centre of large-scale factory production, and its relative strength in other manufacturing areas, such as Leicester, the Trent valley, and the

10. Niebuhr, op.cit., p. 78.

11. Alan D. Gilbert, *Religion and Society in Industrial England,* London, 1976, pp. 59-67.

West Riding, and also in mining areas such as Northumberland and Durham, Cornwall, and South Wales. Moreover the distribution of Nonconformist activists in trade unionism points to the same conclusion. For, while the mining unions had many Nonconformist leaders, cotton, metal, and general workers' unions (that is, the unions of factory workers *par excellence*), had few.

Socio-economic changes after 1840 thus diminished the traditional constituencies of the Nonconformist churches but – perhaps because of the relatively small increase in white-collar labour *during this period* – provided them with no new sources of membership sufficient to compensate for this loss. And as these churches' external constituencies dwindled, the number of their adherents fell, and they could only recruit at a much lower rate. The major Methodist denominations, for example, grew at a mean rate of 3·94 per cent per annum during 1800-40; 0·93 per cent per annum during 1840-80; and 0·51 per cent per annum during 1880-1920.

Finally, there are constituencies consisting of persons related to each other by their association with a particular position within the structure of social and political power – whether that position is one in which they objectively participate, or one to which they owe a subjective loyalty. These associations will be shaped by the presence or absence of 'relative deprivation', that is, of deprivation (or a sense of deprivation) arising from the perception (or imagined perception) of obtainable goods either no longer possessed or now possessed only by others. Whether or not 'felt deprivation', as Charles Glock argues, is 'a necessary precondition for the rise of any organised social movement', those who feel relatively deprived by the social and political position with which they associate themselves may tend to join that type of religious organization generally known as a 'sect', for such organizations' members are very often drawn, to use Bryan Wilson's words, from 'groups who are . . . socially disenfranchised, or whose aspirations are unconfirmed or unlegitimated in the general social order'. Those who, because of their social position, feel little or no relative deprivation will tend to join the type of religious organization known as a 'church', which, as Troeltsch puts it, 'utilises the State and the ruling classes'.[12]

The relationship between the Church of England and the Conservative Party has been well attested historically and may be said to continue today, if in somewhat diminished form. For both the most active Anglicans (those who may be said to be 'members' of the Church of England, in the rather restricted sense used here) and those who attend Church of England services less frequently (and may be classified as 'adherents' who, in the right conditions, could become 'members') are more likely to be Conservatives than are individuals from other sections of the

12. W. G. Runciman, *Relative Deprivation and Social Justice, A Study of Attitudes to Social Inequality in Twentieth-Century England,* London, 1972, p. 11; Charles Y. Glock, 'The Role of Deprivation in the Origin and Evolution of Religious Groups', in Robert Lee and Martin E. Marty (eds.), *Religion and Social Conflict,* New York, 1964, p. 29; Bryan R. Wilson, *Religion in Secular Society, A Sociological Comment,* London, 1966, pp. 183-4; Ernst Troeltsch, *The Social Teaching of the Christian Churches,* New York, 1931, p. 33.

population. The Gallup Poll *Television and Religion* sample of 1963-4 gave the Labour Party a 4 per cent lead over the Conservatives; but those who claimed an affiliation to the Church of England, and those who regularly attended Church of England Services, gave the Conservatives respectively a 1- and a 30-per cent lead over Labour.[13]

Butler and Stokes obtained more detailed results from a sample survey taken in the summer of 1963. While these authors emphasize the higher proportion of Conservatives among *middle-class* Anglicans, and the lower proportion of Conservatives among *working-class* Anglicans, they conclude that 'Among middle and working class Anglicans alike, involvement in religious observance and commitment to the Conservative Party go together'. Forty-one per cent of those who claimed an affiliation with the Church of England, and 36 per cent of the total sample, identified themselves as Conservatives. Forty-five per cent of those who supported *either* the Labour *or* the Conservative party identified themselves as Conservatives, but 48 per cent of Anglican Labour-or-Conserative supporters identified themselves as Conservatives. Moreover, while only 38-42 per cent of nominal Anglicans (those who attended church once a year, less, or never) who were *either* Labour *or* Conservative supporters identified themselves as Conservatives, 53-63 per cent of such Anglicans who attended church monthly or at least several times a year identified themselves as Conservatives. These figures suggest that almost all the internal constituency, and perhaps much of the external constituency, of the Church of England does associate itself with Conservatism: an association which can reasonably be said to denote an absence of relative deprivation.[14]

Little is known of the political character of 'sects', though many Christian Scientists, and probably Adventists and Brethren also, are Conservative. But some evidence suggests that they are politically rather inactive: indeed Jehovah's Witnesses and Exclusive Brethren do not vote. Such a position might express indifference toward the given political and social order, but is more likely to indicate a defiance or rejection of a system held to offer no worthwhile goals to those who, according to traditional sectarian ideology, are 'separate' from the world. An attitude of defiance is certainly expressed by the norms of these organizations. For adoption of doctrines widely and notoriously unacceptable, refusal to take legal oaths, resistance to military service, opposition to blood transfusions and other medical treatments, all imply a condemnation of the world in which the sect finds itself. And what is true of the style and life of the members of sects would appear to be true also, if in lesser degree, of the adherents of sects.[15]

13. Social Services (Gallup Poll) Ltd., *Television and Religion,* London, 1964, pp. 16-17.
14. David Butler and Donald Stokes, *Political Change in Britain, Forces Shaping Electoral Choice,* London, 1969, pp. 124 ff, 469.
15. Cf. Bryan R. Wilson, *Sects and Society, A Sociological Study of Three Religious Groups in Britain,* London, 1961, pp. 287-8.

All external constituencies arise from the operation of cultural and historical forces largely beyond the churches' power. Nevertheless they are by no means totally passive. Their very existence affects the religious attitudes of the population, and this effect becomes the stronger as people get closer to membership. Thus, while churches may have little influence upon the transfer of individuals from the population as a whole to the external constituency, they obviously have much greater influence on transfers between the external and internal constituencies and between the internal constituency and membership. The churches' share in these latter processes may be said to depend upon *proximity, congruity,* and *utility.*

Since church membership involves in almost every case attendance of church or participation in a collective rite, a church must achieve a physical *proximity* to those it seeks to get and keep as members by provision of buildings, religious professionals, or both. Evidence collected by a Parliamentary Commission on church building, which reported in 1853, indicated that – given good roads and weather – people would travel a mile to church, but probably no farther; and it may be doubted whether churches have ever recruited more than a very small fraction of their membership from persons living as much as 2 miles distant from the nearest church building.[16]

The significance of proximity in the development of pre-Reformation Christianity can hardly be over-estimated, for the English Church never achieved a uniform distribution of its buildings and personnel. In 1811, Church of England parishes east of the Tamar and south of a line from the Severn to the Wash extended on average over about 4 square miles, as did parishes in Lincolnshire and the Trent valley. In the West Midlands and in Cornwall, however, parishes were on average between 4 and 5·5 square miles in extent; in Wales and in Yorkshire, about 10 square miles; and in Cheshire, Lancashire, the Lakes, Northumberland, and Durham, 18.5 square miles. As radii of 1 and 2 miles about a church would enclose circles of about 3 and 12·5 square miles in area, while parishes were virtually never compact enough even to approximate to the circular, probably at least a quarter part of every parish without a chapel of ease lay more than a mile from a church building; while one third part of every northerly parish so circumstanced lay more than 2 miles from a church building. For this reason, Christianization was by no means complete by the Reformation; and, in many parts of Britain – especially remote or isolated areas such as Cornwall, the Fens, the Pennines, and the Highlands – pre-Christian religion and traditions have persisted into modern times.[17]

16. 'Report of the Commission appointed to Inquire into the Practicability and Mode of Subdividing Parishes, respecting the immediate Want, as reported by them, for Six Hundred New Churches . . . , *Pp.* 1852-3, LXXVIII, pp. 23-60.

17. 'Population Abstract, 1811', *Pp.* 1812, XI. On pre-Christian religion and traditions see, inter alia, K. M. Briggs, *Fairies in Tradition and Literature,* London, 1967; T. C. Smout, *A History of the Scottish People, 1560-1830,* London, 1972; Keith Thomas, *Religion and the Decline of Magic,* London, 1971.

The desire to increase proximity stimulated both the eighteenth-century Methodist system of itinerancy, whereby preachers made circuits or rounds throughout the country to conduct services in remote areas, and the large-scale church-building and clergy-training programme which the Church of England initiated in the 1830s. Both schemes were highly successful, and have stimulated the churches' modern interest in rationalization of resources and extension of religious facilities. Yet the 'leakage' of members who move from one area to another unserved or less well served by churches of their own religious affiliation provides further evidence of the importance of proximity. Between 1883 and 1907, the Bible Christians admitted 83 000 new members, but lost 37 000 members chiefly through migration to urban areas where this denomination had built no churches; and between 1957 and 1970 the Church of Scotland admitted 415 000 new members, but lost 59 000 members chiefly through migration to England where the Church of Scotland builds very few churches.[18]

Probably the most striking evidence of leakage comes from the records of the Wesleyan and the Methodist Church. During 1881-1932, when the Wesleyans increased their accommodation by about a quarter, the number of members who 'leaked' in transit from one Wesleyan circuit to another fell from 37·74 to 20·95 per cent of the total number of members moving between circuits. When the Wesleyan, Primitive, and United Methodist Churches united to form the Methodist Church, leakage rose sharply (reaching 28·27 per cent in 1933) apparently because of a high rate of leakage in the Primitive and United Methodist Churches, which had relatively few churches compared with the Wesleyans, but which had difficulty persuading their migrant members to attend Wesleyan chapels. Thereafter, the consolidation of the three churches' network of church buildings, and the steadily increasing willingness of each church's migrant membership to attend churches previously regarded as belonging to another denomination, enabled the Methodist Church to reduce leakage to 3·82 per cent of all inter-circuit transfers by 1960.[19]

Proximity is, however, not always enough either to encourage the formation of a constituency or to make adherents and members, as the case of Catholicism shows. The Catholics have nearly 4000 churches and 8000 priests, and the Methodists 2600 ministers and proably about 10 000 churches and chapels, in England and Wales. While Catholicism has grown very fast in England and Wales since 1945, and is perhaps still growing, Methodist membership decreased nearly 15 per cent between 1945 and 1970. Yet the Methodists are only a little less able

18. For itinerancy and for the reconstruction of the Church of England, see R. Davies and G. Rupp, *A History of the Methodist Church in Great Britain,* Vol. 1, London, 1965, and R. Soloway, *Prelates and People: Ecclesiastical Social Thought in England, 1783-1852,* London, 1969. For recent church interest in rationalization of resources see E. R. Wickham, *Church and People in an Industrial City,* London, 1958; L. Paul, *The Deployment and Payment of the Clergy,* London, 1964; and the various editions of *Facts and Figures about the Church of England,* published by the Church Information Office.

19. See Tables B8 and B9.

than the Catholics to recruit adults from outside the circle of their immediate adherents.

In England and Wales, in 1961, 1965, and 1966, the only years for which all the relevant evidence is available, the Catholics conducted 395 000 baptisms and recruited (from among the non-churchgoing population, or from the membership of other churches) 34 000 converts, aged fourteen and over, a number equivalent to 8·5 per cent of baptisms. In the same years, however, the Methodists baptized 138 000 infants, and recruited from other churches 7300 members aged fourteen and over, a total equivalent to 5·25 per cent of baptisms. Since some of the 57 000 new Methodist members of these years must have been recruited from the non-churchgoing population, this percentage should probably be raised to a point not far short of the Catholic figure. In other words, despite all the advantages, and all the apparent dynamism of Catholicism, the Catholic Church is, proportionately speaking, hardly if at all more successful in recruiting outside its own ranks than is the Methodist Church, a weakness attributable chiefly to the general perception of Catholicism in England and Wales as something 'foreign'.

What the Catholic Church lacks in this situation is *congruity,* that is, a similarity to the indigenous population of England and Wales, such as would enable individuals from that population to become Catholics without regarding this act as a withdrawal from the structures, commitments, and routines of their lives. The Catholics' incongruity resides above all in their cultural dissimilarity as a largely Irish, migrant community in a non-Irish country. Yet cultural congruity is perhaps less well attested in the social-historical and sociological literature than the congruity which arises from common socio-economic traits among the ministers, members and adherents of churches such as those analysed in Niebuhr's *Social Sources of Denominationalism.*

While cultural congruity (or incongruity) is likely to persist over very many generations, socio-economic congruity might be disturbed in little more than a generation if the socio-economic status of a church either rose or fell in relation to that of its external constituency. McGavran, in his work on church growth, uses the term *lift* for the phenomenon whereby, as Niebuhr puts it, 'The churches of the poor all become middle class churches sooner or later'. This phenomenon may consist in the process through which, in Wesley's words, 'true Christianity' causes 'diligence and frugality, which, in the natural course of things, must beget riches'; but it is more likely to arise from inter-generational status change effected by the improved education of lower social groups that take up church membership.[20]

Out of 8632 Nonconformists whose occupations were recorded in the Non-Parochial Registers during the first four decades of the nineteenth century,

20. McGavran, op.cit., pp. 261 ff; Niebuhr, op.cit., p. 54; John Wesley, *Sermons on Several Occasions,* London, 1876, Vol. III, p. 325.

1375, or 16 per cent, can be regarded as persons with higher-status occupations (including farmers and shopkeepers), and 7257, or 84 per cent, as persons with lower-status occupations (including artisans, colliers, and miners). Since the Second World War, however, Gallup Poll surveys have divided Nonconformists' occupations approximately 45 and 55 per cent between two categories, middle and upper-middle class (lower professionals, salaried clerical workers, teachers, shopkeepers and shop managers, non-manual supervisory grades, and small farmers), and lower-middle and working class (skilled and semi-skilled manual workers, shop assistants, and wage-earning clerical workers). Between about 1840 and 1950, therefore, the status profile of Nonconformist membership has radically changed, substantial inequality between the size of the higher- and lower-status groups being very largely eliminated.[21]

This change must be attributed to the development of urbanization and factory production and the expansion of government which followed this development. For Nonconformist membership in the mid-twentieth century was chiefly drawn from the supervisory and salaried clerical workers of large productive units; from the shop-keeping and shop-managing groups called into being by the modern urban need for an extensive class of retailing workers; and from the teachers and civil servants employed in training and regulating this mass society. Mid-twentieth century Nonconformity therefore differs radically from mid-nineteenth century Nonconformity; and the transition has been, for the Nonconformist churches, peculiarly unhappy. Their predominantly lower-class membership first rendered them incongruous with these new occupational groups – the 'educated' and 'respectable' whose recruitment and retention remained so difficult a problem for church leaders; while whatever success they had in recruiting the 'educated' and 'respectable' rendered them incongruous with the lower occupational groups on which they had relied for their early strength. In short, through 'lift' Nonconformity suffered a loss of congruity with its original (but in any event dwindling) external constituency unmatched by any very efficacious congruity with the growing middle-class occupation groups.[22]

Neither proximity nor congruity will *suffice* to secure church growth. Church membership involves costs of time, money, and effort; and, once church membership becomes more or less voluntary, these costs must be balanced by commensurable benefits. A church must possess a utility for those whom it seeks to get and keep as members; and its utility will be linked to its *primary* or *religious* functions that is to say, those functions that relate to use of means wholly or partly supernatural; its *secondary* or *cultic* functions, which relate to the ritual activation of

21. Gilbert, op.cit., pp. 62-7, Social Surveys (Gallup Poll) Ltd.

On the social problems of nineteenth-century Nonconformity, see Gilbert, op.cit., pp. 145-74; and R. Currie, *Methodism Divided,* London, 1968, pp. 120-40.

such means; and its *tertiary* or *organizational* functions, which relate to the life of the church as an organization able to carry out such rites.

The appeal of a church's strictly religious functions will depend upon prevalent opinions on the existence, character, and activity of the supernatural, so that, for example, a member of a strongly religious society will need only a weak belief in God, while a member of a secularized society will need a very strong belief in God, if he is to attribute a high utility to a church's religious functions. A church's secondary or cultic functions will attract persons to, or sustain them in, membership in so far as its rites satisfy a cultural demand not otherwise met by society: through preaching such as characterized traditional Nonconformity, for instance, or through an elaborate liturgy such as that practised by the Catholic Church and certain sections of the Church of England. When part or all of a community lacks educational and recreational facilities, individuals will be more responsive to religious rites, whatever those individuals' ideas about the supernatural. But as public education becomes more freely available, and as the development of the media affords other possibilities of recreation and entertainment, individuals may well become less interested in religious rites, irrespective of their views on the supernatural.

A church's tertiary or organizational functions will depend for their appeal upon general and individual perceptions of that church as a social collectivity. An individual will be attracted toward membership of a church if, for example, he finds in that church a community to which he wishes to belong, or an identity which he wishes to assign to himself. Moreover, people will be encouraged to seek membership of a church thought to enjoy social prestige or social power – through its members' votes, for instance, or through its influence over other social institutions such as political parties. But in so far as a church is not thought to enjoy social prestige or social power, it will not attract members, quite regardless of the attitudes toward the supernatural or religious rites held by those whom it seeks to recruit.

The period from about 1850 to the beginning of the First World War marked a significant change in estimates of the utility of church membership. Scientific theories, especially geological and biological theories which cast doubt on the biblical account of creation, impaired the credibility of the supernatural; while technological changes that raised living standards, lowered mortality, and gave people both an increased sense of security and greater control over their own lives, reduced the number of ends to the achievement of which the supernatural might be thought appropriate or useful. The churches' primary functions therefore lost some of their apparent utility. At the same time, the increase in public education (especially after 1870), and the growth both of a popular press and of characteristic urban recreations such as association football and the music hall, weakened the appeal of the churches' secondary functions as a source of instruction and entertainment.

Finally, though the anomic conditions of the new urban areas had, during the industrialization period, offered the churches a remarkable opportunity to provide the population of these areas with community structures otherwise unavailable, by 1850 that opportunity had virtually disappeared as the urban population consolidated its own largely secular community structures, based on the pub, the club, the trade union, and neighbourhood relationships. At the same time, the political conflicts of the early nineteenth century, between a pre-industrial upper class on one side, and industrial management and industrial labour on the other, a conflict in which the Church of England and Nonconformity played a major part, began to give way to a new political struggle between organized manual labour on the one hand and almost all sections of the middle and upper classes on the other. In this struggle Nonconformity was divided and denominational allegiances began to lose most of their political significance. Thus during the years 1850-1914, the churches lost both their appeal as communities and their relevance to political life; and a decline in the apparent utility of their tertiary functions could be the only consequence.

MEMBERSHIP DENSITY

Since a church does not recruit the whole population of a country, but only that external constituency disposed toward membership of it, any measure of density that directly relates church membership to total population (or to that part of the population formally eligible for membership – for example, by age) cannot provide an entirely precise indication of a church's success, or lack of success, in bringing into membership those who in practice constitute the stock of its potential recruits. But as accurate calculation of a church's external constituency seems to be impossible, the best available measure of density is the one that assumes the external constituency to be equal to population, an assumption which will, in a sense, understate 'true' density, but will give a reasonably good picture of density fluctuations over time. Such a measure is illustrated, by reference to the Wesleyan Methodist and the Methodist Churches, in Table 3.2 and Figure 3.6

Any given pattern of membership density must be the product of several factors, among which can be specified: the size and fluctuation of the total population of which the external constituency forms a part; the size and fluctuation of the external and internal constituencies, and the variation of their responsiveness to the attractions of the recruiting organization; trends in membership retention; the different combinations of children of church members, and children of non-church members (each with their characteristic levels of membership retention at any one time), recruited at different times; the organization's supply of facilities

Table 3.2:
Membership Density of the Wesleyan Methodist Church and the Methodist Church in Great Britain

	Population aged 15 and over (thousands)	*Membership Density (per cent)*		*Population aged 15 and over (thousands)*	*Membership Density (per cent)*
1800	6769	1.34			
1801	6823	1.31	1846	12 634	2.70
1802	6880	1.35	1847	12 803	2.65
1803	6959	1.38	1848	12 973	2.61
1804	7055	1.38	1849	13 143	2.65
1805	7161	1.42	1850	13 314	2.69
1806	7265	1.53	1851	13 482	2.24
1807	7366	1.61	1852	13 632	2.06
1808	7462	1.70	1853	13 782	1.97
1809	7560	1.75	1854	13 929	1.90
1810	7656	1.80	1855	14 060	1.86
1811	7756	1.88	1856	14 206	1.86
1812	7874	1.97	1857	14 354	1.88
1813	8000	2.03	1858	14 480	1.91
1814	8126	2.14	1859	14 628	2.00
1815	8261	2.20	1860	14 772	2.10
1816	8400	2.28	1861	14 921	2.14
1817	8534	2.27	1862	15 102	2.15
1818	8665	2.25	1863	15 264	2.16
1819	8790	2.23	1864	15 445	2.13
1820	8923	2.14	1865	15 607	2.12
1821	9071	2.21	1866	15 793	2.10
1822	9225	2.29	1867	15 959	2.11
1823	9375	2.34	1868	16 149	2.12
1824	9515	2.39	1869	16 319	2.12
1825	9647	2.37	1870	16 513	2.11
1826	9774	2.36	1871	16 695	2.08
1827	9902	2.40	1872	16 914	2.05
1828	10 042	2.44	1873	17 112	2.04
1829	10 179	2.43	1874	17 337	2.03
1830	10 313	2.41	1875	17 566	2.04
1831	10 452	2.38	1876	17 772	2.10
1832	10 577	2.42	1877	18 006	2.12
1833	10 696	2.62	1878	18 243	2.09
1834	10 835	2.69	1879	18 457	2.05
1835	10 981	2.65	1880	18 700	2.01
1836	11 127	2.63	1881	18 912	2.01
1837	11 256	2.60	1882	19 143	2.06
1838	11 390	2.61	1883	19 378	2.10
1839	11 551	2.66	1884	19 614	2.09
1840	11 706	2.76	1885	19 854	2.08
1841	11 846	2.78	1886	20 097	2.05
1842	11 994	2.72	1887	20 342	2.03
1843	12 146	2.73	1888	20 620	2.02
1844	12 297	2.75	1889	20 900	2.01
1845	12 465	2.73	1890	21 184	2.00

	Population aged 15 and over (thousands)	*Membership Density (per cent)*		*Population aged 15 and over (thousands)*	*Membership Density (per cent)*
1891	21 476	1.98	1931	34 011	1.47
1892	21 788	1.95	1932	34 208	1.46
1893	22 105	1.93	1933	34 347	2.43
1894	22 456	1.93	1934	34 498	2.40
1895	22 812	1.92	1935	34 693	2.38
1896	23 174	1.88	1936	34 897	2.35
1897	23 540	1.86	1937	35 098	2.30
1898	23 913	1.85	1938	35 297	2.28
1899	24 295	1.84	1939	35 541	2.25
1900	24 678	1.83	1940	35 759	2.22
1901	25 029	1.82	1941	35 781	2.18
1902	25 281	1.83	1942	35 941	2.13
1903	25 603	1.83	1943	36 269	2.10
1904	25 928	1.83	1944	36 469	2.07
1905	26 258	1.85	1945	36 634	2.05
1906	26 591	1.87	1946	36 706	2.03
1907	26 928	1.84	1947	36 981	2.01
1908	27 270	1.80	1948	37 392	1.98
1909	27 616	1.78	1949	37 660	1.97
1910	27 967	1.75	1950	37 897	1.97
1911	28 205	1.72	1951	37 980	1.95
1912	28 507	1.69	1952	38 082	1.95
1913	28 794	1.68	1953	38 152	1.95
1914	29 207	1.65	1954	38 213	1.95
1915	29 577	1.62	1955	38 319	1.94
1916	29 830	1.59	1956	38 452	1.93
1917	30 027	1.56	1957	38 592	1.92
1918	30 122	1.56	1958	38 710	1.90
1919	30 167	1.54	1959	38 884	1.89
1920	30 493	1.52	1960	39 124	1.86
1921	30 867	1.51	1961	39 486	1.83
1922	31 200	1.50	1962	39 848	1.81
1923	31 533	1.51	1963	40 131	1.77
1924	31 937	1.52	1964	40 372	1.74
1925	32 139	1.52	1965	40 596	1.70
1926	32 515	1.52	1966	40 773	1.66
1927	32 836	1.52	1967	40 954	1.63
1928	33 121	1.51	1968	41 562	1.57
1929	33 372	1.49	1969	41 164	1.54
1930	33 689	1.48	1970	41 251	1.50

NOTES AND SOURCES

1. Population aged fifteen and over was calculated as follows. The proportion of the population aged fifteen and over in each census year was calculated from the age-breakdowns given in the Census of Population. The proportion of the population aged fifteen and over in each intercensal year was derived by linear extrapolation of the decennial series thus obtained. These coefficients were then used to reduce the Registrar General's, annual estimates of the total population at mid-year to obtain estimates for the mid-year population at age fifteen and over. See the Census *Reports* and the Annual and Quarterly *Reports* and *Reviews* of the Registrar-General for England and Wales and for Scotland.

2. During 1915-20 and 1940-8 the population series refers only to the British civilian population.
3. See Table A7 of the Appendix for the membership of the Wesleyan Methodist Church and the Methodist Church.
4. The fall in density in 1851-7 is largely attributable to schism.
5. From 1933 onwards the density series refers to the Methodist Church.

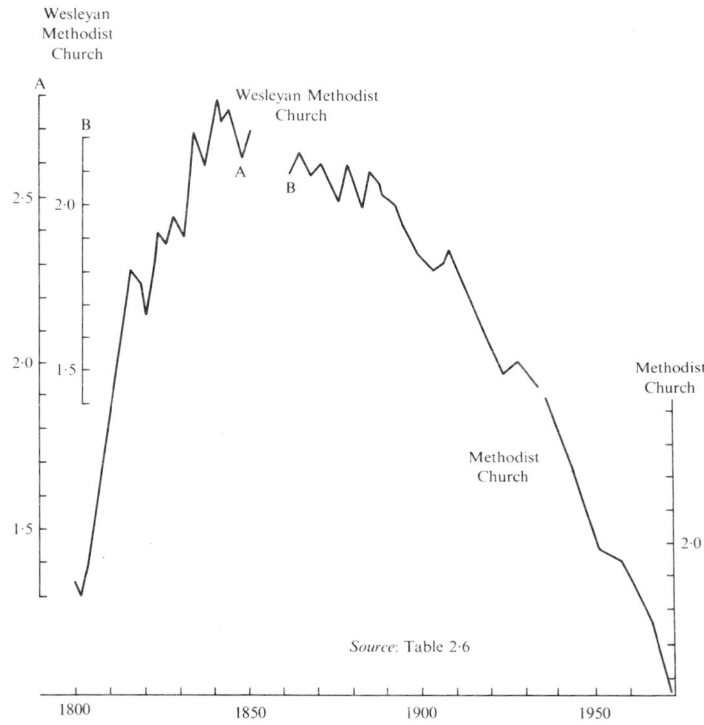

Fig. 3.6: Membership Density of the Wesleyan Methodist Church and the Methodist Church at Annual Intervals, 1800-1850, 1860-1932, and 1933-1968 (per cent).

for membership, including both buildings and full- and part-time leadership; and the varying appeal of membership itself. The density pattern is therefore highly complex, and it is not assumed here that each empirically observed pattern necessarily corresponds in all its particulars with the model of density already outlined in Chapter I.

Fundamental to that model is the assumption that population is either stable or increasing, so that any external constituency, once formed, will at least tend not to decrease over a fairly lengthy period after the recruiting organization's inception. The external constituency has its origins in some historical process: a societal cleavage, the development of a sense of relative deprivation, or perhaps merely the failure of existing religious organizations to recruit populations nominally within their purview. Such a process is likely to bring into being, at approximately the same time, both a new organization's potential recruits and the organization able to appeal to the hitherto unorganized or ill organized. This coincidence is the objective cause of the subjective sense of opportunity which buoys up so many founders of new religious organizations, among whom John 4:35, 'Lift up your eyes and look on the fields; for they are white already to harvest', acquires therefore something of the status of a cliché. In the first fifteen days of April 1739, when Wesley commenced 'field-preaching', that is, preaching to any audience which would listen to him, he claimed to have addressed gatherings of 3000, 1500, 1000, 'about 1000' (twice), 900-1200, and 5000-6000; and on 17 April 1739, his congregation being too many for the floor on which they stood, the boards gave way beneath them. Thus, while in 1738, the membership density of Wesleyan Methodism must be accounted zero, by 1838 (when there were, in addition, many non-Wesleyan Methodists), it constituted 2.61 per cent of the British population aged fifteen and over.

Such a rapid increase in density is, however, not simply the result of a large and responsive constituency, the easy recruitment of which results in the apparently unhindered advance of a religious organization during the *progressive* phase of its history. For the organization itself enjoys certain advantages which are lost to it in later years. Precisely because it begins from zero, the organization has no 'membership' at all (but merely a small cadre of activists and would-be leaders), and therefore no membership at variance with the constituency already formed for it; and even as the organization begins to acquire a membership, its members have for some time an exposure to intra-organizational influences quite insufficient to differentiate them from those potential members who remain yet unrecruited. Thus potential members see in membership relatively little change in their habits or their identity. Moreover, though the organization is almost invariably short of capital – whether to build buildings or to support full-time leaders – that capital can be applied wherever and whenever the needs of expansion dictate. For since there has as yet been no or virtually no investment of capital, there are no calls upon the available resources to maintain existing commitments, for example, to meet dilapidations, or to service loans already utilized. Finally, given the extent of the organization's opportunities, and the freedom and efficacy of its activites, it is able to adopt in its most unqualified form what has, in recent years, been known as a 'theology of mission', that is to say, an uninhibited ideology of expansion, which reinforces all its efforts.

During the progressive phase recruitment exhibits certain important characteristics not found in subsequent phases. The appeal of church membership is, by comparison with later years, both extensive and intensive, because potential recruits find in membership at once a resolution of very many of their problems and a goal towards which they feel themselves to be impelled by inexplicably powerful forces. The primary, or strictly religious, functions of the organization alone provide an adequate representation of this appeal; and the secondary or tertiary functions of the organization have little *overt* influence upon the consciousness of recruits. In this way, the organization's hold over its members is, within the context of its history as a whole, uniquely effective, and the membership retention of all types of membership is, *for each type*, uniquely high.

Those who are recruited into membership at the beginning of this phase of the organization's history are, by definition, those whose parents are non-members, and therefore those whose retention of membership is lower than that of those hypothetical children of church members whom the organization lacks at this stage in its development. Membership can therefore only be increased at the price of substantial losses; but these will be concealed by the very rapid rate of membership gains indicated, for example, in Figure 3.6, and in the growth of the Jehovah's Witnesses, illustrated in Table A6 and Figure 2.7. During this period, too, a religious organization will tend to recruit more men than women, unless – as has not been the case hitherto in Britain at least – cultural norms permit women to be as adventurous as men in adopting new social or organizational relationships. Some of these male recruits will later bring families with them, but enough others will not for there to be a preponderance of men in the organization's membership. A recent study of early Methodism in north Nottinghamshire between 1760 and 1851 notes, for example, that 74 per cent of identified Wesleyans, and 71 per cent of identified Primitive Methodists were men. Such a preponderance of men of course minimizes the organization's difficulties in recruiting male lay leadership, and probably maximizes unit contributions to the organization's funds; and these factors will tend to facilitate expansion of the organization's supply of the facilities for membership.[23]

In the case of Wesleyan Methodism the progressive phase of membership density lasted well into the nineteenth century; for Wesleyan density doubled between 1800 (1·34 per cent) and 1834 (2·69 per cent). Density still stood at 2·69 per cent in 1850, however, having reached its highest point (2·78 per cent) in 1841. After 1834, in other words, Wesleyan membership density ceased to increase rapidly; and since the rate of increase in density was already falling sharply by 1834, it is reasonable to situate the end of the progressive phase of Wesleyan growth somewhat before that year. The *marginal* phase which ensued probably lasted from the 1820s to the 1880s, a period perhaps shortened by the adverse effects of the great Wesleyan schism of the 1850s, when membership density fell to 1·86 per cent, a level not again reached till 1897. By 1860, density had risen to 2·1 per cent (that is to say, had once more surpassed the level of 1813); and density was still 2·1 per cent in 1883. From 1883 onwards density fell

23. Barry J. Biggs, 'Methodism in a Rural Society: North Nottinghamshire 1760-1851', Nottingham Ph. D. Thesis, 1975, *passim*.

without a break until 1901, when it reached 1·82 per cent; and this fall, unaccompanied by any internal crisis in Wesleyanism, must be taken as indicating the end of the marginal phase.

The largest single cause of a transition from the progressive to the marginal phase should be a decline in the rate at which people transfer from the population as a whole to the organization's external constituency, which thereafter would tend to grow no faster than the total population. Yet a fall in the responsiveness of the external constituency to pressures to join the internal constituency of those who have made some formal or public profession of a disposition toward membership, as well as a fall in the responsiveness of the internal constituency to pressures to take up membership of the organization, must also be accounted significant factors in this characteristic development in the organization's history. In the case of Wesleyan Methodism, the development, after 1815, of economic changes less rapid, and social conditions more adverse, than those experienced during the first years of industrialization and the prolonged period of war with France, apparently involved some diminution in the number of persons objectively inclined toward membership of a Methodist church. But these persons' responsiveness toward *Wesleyan* Methodism was probably also reduced by the emergence of new types of Methodism, represented above all by the Bible Christians and the Primitive Methodists, who held their first conferences in 1819 and 1820 respectively.

Other factors also hastened the coming of the marginal phase in Wesleyan Methodism. The progressive phase marks the creation from, and largely by, a small group of activists, of a substantial membership, which eventually begins to display on a larger or smaller scale specific political, socio-economic, and cultural characteristics. This specificity imparts to the organization an appeal more or less limited to the same type of people as those who are already members; and the constituency therefore acquires a certain rigidity or fixity, since there are now few if any hitherto unrecruited social groups which, because they lack any exact 'image' of the organization's membership, can readily identify themselves with existing members. When Wesley began recruiting followers, for example, he could, other things being equal, have appealed to many different social groups; but a hundred years later 'the Methodists' were closely associated in very many people's minds with the shopkeepers, small employers, artisans, and other manual wage-earners who in fact predominated in the membership of the Wesleyan Methodist Church. Similarly, when the Christian Scientists began organizing in England about 1900, they could, other things being equal, have drawn support from widely varying sections of the population; but a generation later they would have experienced considerable difficulty in recruiting outside the suburban middle and upper-middle classes whose members composed almost the entirety of their societies.

Moreover, by the end of the progressive phase, a religious organization has usually invested heavily in the supply of membership facilities in those areas where demand for such facilities was, in earlier years, found, or expected, to be high. By 1801 Wesley's followers occupied about 800 chapels and preaching places, services in which were conducted by 334 full-time and about a thousand part-time preachers; while the number of chapels and preaching places was increasing by about half-a-dozen, and the total of full-time preachers by about thirty, a year. The full-time preachers were in theory entirely mobile, though their mobility was decreasing by the 1830s; the chapels and preaching places were of course fixed; and the preachers' salaries and the chapel debts greatly reduced the amount of resources freely available for use wherever a new demand for Methodist membership might arise. Circumstances such as these compel a religious organization, however flexible, to exploit its existing capital investments rather than to seek entirely new ventures; and even when – as widely occurred throughout mid-nineteenth-century Nonconformity – lavish 'revival campaigns' were mounted as an ostensible supplementation to the ordinary course of denominational activities, such 'campaigns' tended to concentrate on areas and groups in which membership had already been heavily advertised.

In a sense, therefore, the transition from progressive to marginal phase is a transition from recruitment to retention. The organization now lays more emphasis on maintaining existing facilities, and on satisfying existing members, than on undertaking new enterprises in regions over which it has hitherto enjoyed no influence. In the case of Wesleyan Methodism, for example, those regions of Great Britain which contained 81 per cent of Wesleyan membership in 1801, still contained 76 per cent of Wesleyan membership in 1901. And the consolidation indicated by such data of course interacts with changes in the character of the organization's growth. During the progressive phase, the organization (which began by recruiting only non-members' children) comes to derive new membership more and more from its members' families – whose natural rate of increase, corresponding to demographic trends in the population as a whole, closely determines the organization's growth rate. Such a shift from allogenous to autogenous growth implies an increase in the level of membership retention, since, even if in the long run all members' commitment declines over time, members' children are always more retentive of membership than non-members' children. Hence, while efforts to keep new recruits are relatively unsuccessful in the progressive phase, they are much more successful during the marginal phase; and this very success tends to reshape the organization's attitudes and policies.

Among the attitudes that develop especially during the marginal phase, perhaps the most significant is an explicit consciousness of the church as a social entity. The overriding influence of the church's primary or religious functions is now modified by increased concern with secondary, or cultic, and tertiary, or organizational, functions; and the membership identifies itself as a continuing community in a standing relationship with an organization which confers both duties and rights upon those who belong to it. Loyalty to the organization becomes a merit for the social group that inheres within it; while the organization's conformity to certain cultural and even material standards – scholarly exposition of doctrine, well-run services, comfortable and convenient pews – is exacted by the individuals upon which it depends for its existence. Debates about the conduct of services, the orthodoxy of sermons, and the behaviour of ministers may now ensue. In Wesleyan Methodism such debates – about candlesticks on the altar, the use of an organ, a theological college, or the alleged *hauteur* of ministers of religion – led to a number of schisms during the marginal phase; yet even these controversies did not so diminish the disputants' sense of a shared identity that they could not bequeath to their descendants a consciousness of a common allegiance sufficient to enable their reunion, many years later, into one Methodist Church. In a somewhat similar fashion, the Church of Scotland was divided, between the early eighteenth and mid-nineteenth centuries, by wide-ranging debates about the appointment of ministers, which led to secessions in 1733 and 1761, and to the Disruption of 1843; but which were ultimately followed by the reunion of most Scottish Presbyterians in 1929.

Finally, it should perhaps be noted that, during the marginal phase, membership of a religious organization will – unless it is very small – approximate both to the age and sex distribution and to the family structure of the population as a whole. The earlier preponderance of men (and no doubt of young men at that) will give way to a more even balance of the sexes and to the growth of an older membership. This change may inhibit the expansion of the organization's leadership, unless women are conceded an extended role in the organization's work; and will almost certainly introduce elements of conservatism and repetition into the organization's policies and procedures. So, too, as the family unit becomes central to the organization, and the organization itself becomes more familial in outlook, the rigours of the organization's earlier demands, especially as regards devotions or ascetic practices, will be modified to accommodate the needs of members and adherents, some of whom are now very old, and others very young.

The marginal phase gave way to a *recessive* phase in Wesleyan Methodism about 1883, when membership density stood at 2·1 per cent. By 1932, when the Wesleyans merged into the Methodist Church, Wesleyan density had fallen to 1·46 per cent; and though the density of the new Methodist Church stood at 2·43 per cent in 1933, it had fallen to 1·57 per cent by 1968 (when the density of the 'Wesleyan' component of the Methodist Church was perhaps no more than one per cent). Thus, as Table 3.2 and Figure 3.6 indicate, with the brief exceptions of the revival of the early 1900s, and the very modest post-war expansion which occurred after 1920 and about 1950, Methodist membership density has now fallen for nearly a century. A similar experience has befallen other Protestant groups in Britain; for, as Tables 2.3 and 3.2 show, between 1880 and 1960, all Nonconformists fell from 7·83 to 4·1 per cent, and Episcopalians from 7·12 to 6·13 per cent, of the British population aged fifteen and over.

For the Methodists this development constituted an unprecedented reversal of earlier trends. Its onset must be attributed to the quantitative decline of the Methodists' constituency, and to a qualitative decline in that constituency's responsiveness. The Presbyterian Church of Wales data contained in Table 4.1 show that that church's 'attendants' decreased between 1895 and 1968 from nearly 89 000 to less than 6000; and the Methodists have evidently suffered losses of this order among their adherents. One major element in the decline of the Methodist constituency (as indeed of the constituencies of other Nonconformist churches) is no doubt the decay of high Victorian politics – with its battles between Nonconformists and Liberals, on the one hand, and Anglicans and Conservatives on the other. For those politics began to collapse, and new secular politics based on economic redistribution began to develop, following the defeat of the first Home Rule Bill, and the Liberal *débâcle* in the general election of 1886. But other factors must also be considered, notably the expansion of the non-sectarian, instrumentalist trade unionism which first caught public attention with the 'New Unionism' of 1889-90.

During this period (as, indeed, would be the case during the recessive phase of any religious organization's history) the contrived 'revival campaigns' of the marginal phase were virtually abandoned, since they now offered such small rewards. In any event, the decrease of the organization's constituency involves a decline in allogenous growth, and a further concentration on recruitment from existing members' families. As the recessive phase proceeds, the membership is, of course, ageing faster than the total population, partly because of the decline in new members, partly because of the wastage of new (that is, young) members as the level of membership retention declines still further among both members' and non-members' children; and such ageing must reinforce recessive tendencies within the organization simply by lowering its members' fecundity. At the same time the increase in female membership, first significant during the marginal phase, continues as male adherents become more reluctant to acquire membership, and more anxious to abandon it once acquired; and this tendency continues to render recruitment to lay and clerical leadership more precarious.

The effective withdrawal of the organization from the society in which it exists heightens internal emphasis upon the narrower society that it provides for its members. Tertiary functions assume an ever greater importance, if only in the subjective perceptions of the organization's members, who explain their preference for the organization (rather than the larger society) especially in terms of the kind of people, and the kind of social interaction, to be found within the organization. Local churches may concentrate much of their energies upon the creation and sustenance of ancillary organizations, 'circles', 'clubs', 'meetings', and 'fellowships', which serve to express a heightened interest in the 'social life' of the organization. Meanwhile, the organization's intelligentsia becomes increasingly involved in a debate about those 'principles' which seem to be cast in doubt by the indifference, and even contempt, of the larger society, whose respect for, and interest in, the organization can be aroused once more, so some will argue, only by the adoption of new, 'modern', or 'up-to-date' principles. Hence those disputes – such as the hellfire debate in Methodism, the 'Downgrade' controversy among the Baptists – which commence about the onset of the recessive phase, and continue thereafter, in varying forms, almost without a break.

The final resolution of the recessive phase is rather obscure. Obviously there comes a point in the organization's decline at which the external constituency has virtually ceased to exist, and recruitment (if any) can arise *only* from within the families of church members. If it be assumed that membership retention continues to fall, even among church-members' children, then the recessive phase must conclude in the extinction of the organization. However, the procedures, capital, and traditions of an organization may be said to create, among its last few members, an inertia which prevents them from abandoning it altogether while a few random recruits can be brought in from outside. In such a case extinction – or transformation – may be preceded by a *residual* phase, in which a very few members and their families preserve a minimal continuation of the organization's activities, in such a fashion as to keep pace with population without ever gaining on it, of course. Certain very small groups may provide an empirical approximation to this model; but it is not clear how far this can be argued without qualification.

IV
Membership Gains and Losses

FROM ADHERENCE TO MEMBERSHIP

A religious organization's internal constituency, the group of persons already linked to it by some formal act of affiliation, must be the chief source of that organization's growth. 'If it be asked', wrote Sprague, 'whence come the greater number of the subjects of our revivals, we answer, from our Sabbath schools, and Bible classes, and from families in which the parental influence is decidedly religious'.[1]

Sociologists have so far shown themselves little interested in the definition and analysis of groups formally and openly disposed toward church membership. Nor have the churches themselves made many efforts to count their potential recruits. The statistical inquiries begun by the Newman Demographic Survey and continued by the Catholic Education Council for England and Wales do, in effect, include some assessment of the number of those formal Catholics who will supply, from their numbers, the *active* Catholics of the future; and the Statistical Unit of the Central Board of Finance of the Church of England does publish annual totals of new Anglican confirmees. The Church Membership Committee of the Methodist Church has gone a little farther than this by attempting to specify and enumerate the 'Methodist community', but the data so far collected cannot compare with the enormous volume of statistical material relating to Methodist *membership*.

Thus considerable significance attaches to the Primitive Methodist series on 'adherents', and the Presbyterian Church of Wales (Calvinistic Methodist) series on 'the whole congregation' contained in Tables B5 and B10 of the Appendix. The former measures those non-member associates of the Primitive Methodist Church whose names were known to that body's ministers. The latter is a composite series consisting of full communicant members, probationer members, children of church members, and a residual category of persons who, in David Jenkins's words, were 'regular attenders at places of worship, and "hearers" of the Word, without being members'. We have extracted his residual category, which we wish to call 'attend-

1. William B. Sprague, *Lectures on Revivals of Religion*, London, 1959, pp. 144-5.

ants', in Table 4.1. This series, when added to church members' children, probably corresponds quite closely to the internal constituency of the Presbyterian Church of Wales; but the Primitive Methodist adherents series is perhaps more inclusive. As was noted in Chapter II, however, no internal constituency is uniformly responsive to recruitment, and neither the Primitive Methodist nor the Calvinistic Methodist series indicate the number of persons ready for recruitment at any one time.[2]

These series suggest that internal constituencies increase more slowly and decrease more quickly than membership. Between 1880 and 1908, Primitive Methodist membership increased 24·52, and Primitive Methodist adherence only 13·09, per cent; while between 1895 and 1905 Calvinistic Methodist membership increased 28·42 per cent, and Calvinistic Methodist attendants *decreased* 19·62 per cent. On the other hand, between 1908 and 1932, Primitive Methodist membership fell 3·52, and Primitive Methodist adherence 21·7, per cent; while between 1920 and 1968 Calvinistic Methodist membership fell 39·39, and Calvinistic Methodist attendants 90·94 per cent.

Changes in adherence appear to effect changes in membership. Primitive Methodist adherence fell from 520 000 to 518 000 during 1880-7, and during 1885-93 Primitive Methodist membership increased only from 181 128 to 181 444. But during 1887-1905 Primitive Methodist adherence rose from 518 000 to 604 000, and during 1893-1908 Primitive Methodist membership increased from 181 444 to 206 834. Thereafter, Primitive Methodist adherence declined from 604 000 in 1905 to 552 000 in 1922, and Primitive Methodist membership decreased from 206 834 in 1908 to 198 471 in 1922. The heterogeneity of a group such as that indicated in the Primitive Methodist adherence series precludes any close statistical relationship between these fluctuations: yet turning-points in the Primitive Methodist adherence series such as 1887 and 1905 do seem to locate turning-points in the growth of the true internal constituency of the Primitive Methodist Church.

Since new adherents do not speedily replace those adherents that churches make into members, any increase in the rate of recruitment to membership reduces the possibility of further increase, because potential recruits are recruited and not replaced; and any decrease in the rate of recruitment reduces the possibility of further decrease, because potential recruits are not recruited and are therefore available for future recruitment. Hence the cyclical pattern, discussed in Chapter II, in which after a period of depression and low growth, recruitment is activated (partly because there are so many potential recruits); revival and high growth ensue; recruitment is deactivated (partly because there are so few potential recruits); declension follows; and finally depression and low growth return.

2. David Jenkins, *The Agricultural Community in South West Wales at the Turn of the Twentieth Century*, Cardiff, 1971, p. 210.

Table 4.1:
The Internal Constituency of the Presbyterian Church of Wales

	Attendants	*Constituents*		*Attendants*	*Constituents*
			1931	42 742	102 397
			1932	40 576	99 387
			1933	38 800	96 000
			1934	38 000	93 200
1895	88 549	155 639	1935	36 200	90 100
1896	87 574	155 159	1936	33 500	85 300
1897	89 021	157 738	1937	31 400	80 900
1898	91 459	159 794	1938	29 100	77 900
1899	87 035	156 788	1939	25 400	73 400
1900	86 314	159 054	1940	23 700	70 900
1901	86 565	161 087	1941	21 900	68 300
1902	88 458	162 788	1942	20 800	66 500
1903	89 019	164 472	1943	20 200	65 200
1904	78 985	156 812	1944	18 900	63 100
1905	71 178	151 543	1945	19 100	62 500
1906	75 138	157 596	1946	18 300	60 900
1907	71 957	154 717	1947	18 800	60 700
1908	70 772	153 083	1948	19 100	60 200
1909	74 727	157 863	1949	18 800	59 100
1910	71 359	154 862	1950	18 000	57 600
1911	68 295	151 433	1951	17 400	56 300
1912	73 793	152 248	1952	17 300	55 400
1913	75 151	152 729	1953	17 600	54 900
1914	72 540	148 433	1954	18 000	54 500
1915	71 179	147 091	1955	18 200	54 000
1916	65 315	140 384	1956	18 900	53 900
1917	63 220	137 665	1957	18 100	52 400
1918	63 246	137 277	1958	13 700	47 200
1919	64 725	137 719	1959	10 000	42 700
1920	65 593	137 603	1960	9000	41 000
1921	58 159	130 423	1961	7800	39 100
1922	57 495	127 915	1962	7400	37 800
1923	57 402	126 577	1963	7000	36 700
1924	57 660	126 427	1964	6200	35 100
1925	56 738	124 343	1965	6300	34 500
1926	56 067	121 284	1966	6400	33 800
1927	52 783	117 643	1967	5900	32 500
1928	52 425	116 461	1968	5900	31 800
1929	47 835	110 586	1969	6300	31 400
1930	46 814	107 871	1970	5500	29 900

NOTES AND SOURCES

1. 'Attendants' are those members of the 'Whole Congregation' who are not 'Children in the Church', probationers, or full communicant members. From 1933 onwards, the values given are estimates rounded to the nearest hundred. These estimates are derived from estimated values for probationers (1933 onwards) and for 'Children in the Church' (1938 onwards), but from observed values for the 'Whole Congregation' and for full communicant members. The estimates for probationers were calculated on the assumption that the annual proportionate decrease from 1932 onwards was equal to the average annual proportionate decrease between 1895 and 1932. This assumption gave an estimated value of nil probationers for 1945 onwards. The estimates for 'Children in the Church' were obtained by linear extrapolation between the values for 1937 and 1968.

2. The series for 'Constituents' was derived by summing the values for 'Attendants' and 'Children in the Church' derived as indicated in note 1.

3. Sources: Tables A4 and B5 of the Appendix.

In the Welsh Revival, for example, high growth was activated by Liberal and Nonconformist political resistance to the Education Act of 1902 and, to a lesser extent, by the Free Church Council Simultaneous Mission of 1901, and by the evangelical campaign stimulated by the Keswick conventions. High growth continued from 1903 to 1905 and, in some cases, into 1906. During 1903-5 the Presbyterian Church of Wales's communicants increased by 23 946 or 14·49 per cent; but its attendants decreased by 17841 or 20·04 per cent. This dramatic increase in membership very largely caused its own deactivation simply because almost all attendants ready for membership were recruited. Between 1905 and 1913, therefore, communicant membership fell by 4474 or 2·37 per cent; but the pool of attendants, no longer drained by heavy recruitment, rose by 3973 or 5·58 per cent. A similar pattern appears in Welsh-speaking Wesleyan Methodism, which, during 1901-4, 1905, and 1906-8, recruited new members at a rate equivalent to respectively nearly 8, 25, and 5½ per cent of existing membership.

The initiative in the periods of high growth, which so strongly characterize the early years of a church's history, may come from ministers, lay leaders, or members. But, though the demand for increased recruitment can never result in high growth without being diffused among *all* these groups, there appears to be a shift over time from high growth arising either from lay (or lay and ministerial) initiative to high growth arising largely or entirely from ministerial initiative. Throughout the nineteenth century 'revivalism' was strongly associated with laymen, and was looked on with suspicion by full-time ministers. It is unlikely, therefore, that ministers were always among those who originated movements toward a higher rate of recruitment, whether those movements were accompanied by 'revivalism' or not. By about 1900, however, independent lay evangelization had largely decreased in many churches; recruitment was increasingly regarded as a strictly ministerial function; and the difficulties of maintaining growth stimulated much interest in all matters relating to membership gains and losses.[3]

One indicator of the new significance of the full-time ministry in initiating higher growth may be the changing sequence of gains and losses after 1900 in the Wesleyan and the Methodist Churches, the Presbyterian Church of Wales, and some other bodies such as the Presbyterian Church of England. Up to 1907, peaks in losses in the Wesleyan Methodist Church tend to *follow* peaks in gains, for reasons discussed below. Thus, for example, recruitment of new members reached peaks in 1883, 1894, and 1906, while peaks in those who 'ceased to be members'

3. Robert Currie, *Methodism Divided*, London, 1968, pp. 49, 54 ff; Alan D. Gilbert, 'The Growth and Decline of Nonconformity in England and Wales, with Special Reference to the Period before 1850: An Historical Interpretation of Statistics of Religious Practice', D. Phil. Thesis, Oxford, 1973, pp. 416 ff.

occurred in 1884, 1896, and 1907. But after 1907, greatest losses in both the Wesleyan and the Methodist churches tend to *precede* greatest gains, as indicated in Tables B8 and B9. Thus, for example, recruitment of new members reached peaks in 1924, 1938, and 1947, but peaks in those who 'ceased to be members' occurred in 1920, 1936, and 1945.

This change is probably partly attributable to the change in the ministerial role in recruitment. Up to 1900, full-time ministers responded to rather than initiated higher growth; and part of their response was to purge the membership roll. After 1900, however, ministers were more active in promoting higher growth; and – perhaps paradoxically – they purged the roll at a relatively early stage in the movement toward higher growth, simply because an increased ministerial concern with membership could issue in deletion of names from the membership roll more readily than in additions thereto. That removals from the roll do not continue to rise thereafter must be explained partly on the assumption that these deletions do fully purge the roll, and partly by reference to the characteristics of the different types of recruit discussed below.

AUTOGENOUS AND ALLOGENOUS GROWTH

Various studies have demonstrated that the family is by far the most important instrumentality through which individuals acquire personal, cultural, and social self-identification. Thus, for example, a number of investigations have served to show that voters support a political party with which they identify themselves, and that this identification is mediated to them through their parents' influence. Butler and Stokes observe that 'A child is very likely indeed to share his parent's party preference,' and add that, 'children of parents who were united in their party preference' are 'overwhelmingly likely to have absorbed the preference at the beginning of their political experience.' This preference remains largely unaffected throughout the individual's life: 75 per cent of Butler and Stokes's respondents whose parents were both Conservative, and 81 per cent of those whose parents were both Labour supporters, retaining their parents' political allegiance.[4]

A similar process affects recruitment to church membership. Sprague, as was noted above, attributed the 'greater number' of converts to the effects of a 'decidedly religious' parental influence. Starbuck, in his study of conversion, found that 39 per cent of female and 52 per cent of male respondents explicitly attributed their conversion to the *'influence of home'*. 'The influence and example of parents', Starbuck concluded '. . . . is often spoken of as the most powerful of all

4. David Butler and Donald Stokes, *Political Change in Britain, Forces Shaping Electoral Choice*, London, 1969, pp. 47-8.

. . . influences.' This effect must characterize most recruitment to church membership, whether or not accompanied by a conversion experience, for most new church members are, except in periods of unusually high growth, juveniles. As we noted in Chapter III, only a tiny fraction of Church of England baptisms and confirmations are attributable to recruitment of persons of 'riper years'; while, over the period 1895-1968, 57 per cent of the Presbyterian Church of Wales's new members were classified as 'children of the church'.[5]

Parental influence affects not merely the adoption but the retention of a political or a religious allegiance. Any such allegiance is more likely to be retained if it expresses parental allegiance than if it does not; and church growth can therefore be analysed into two types: *autogenous* growth, accruing from recruitment of church members' children, and *allogenous* growth, accruing from recruitment of non-members' children. Rapid expansion of church membership must almost always involve a large element of allogenous growth, for then the stock of members' children rarely constitutes an adequate supply of recruits. But allogenous growth is less likely to sustain membership over a longer period of time, because non-members' children are less likely to retain membership.

Figure 4.1 illustrates the effect of the two types of growth on membership retention in the Presbyterian Church of Wales. Over the period 1895-1960, recruitment of 'children of the church' rose from 54·03 to 72·09 per cent of membership gains, while the annual rate at which existing membership was lost (from all causes excluding death) fell from 2·4 to 1·62 per cent of the whole. A still more pronouncedly inverse relationship obtains in the short run. Autogenous growth fell from 55·64 to 23·03 per cent of gains between 1900 and 1905 and rose to 58·86 per cent by 1910. The loss rate (excluding deaths) rose, on the contrary, from 2·39 to 4·47 per cent between 1900 and 1905 and fell to 3·21 per cent by 1910. But allogenous growth is essential to a high recruitment rate. In 1906 the Presbyterian Church of Wales recruited 18 737 more new members than it had in 1900, and of these 91 per cent were non-member attendants; while in 1923 it recruited 668 more new members than it had in 1919, and of these 87 per cent were non-member attendants.

Reliance on allogenous growth must bring a heightened loss rate; and this is particularly noticeable during 1902-7, which may be regarded as the last period of growth similar to that experienced by most churches during the late eighteenth and nineteenth centuries. In 1902 the Presbyterian Church of Wales's losses (from all causes other than death) equalled 3·07 per cent of its full communicant membership, and this figure fell to 2·41 and 2·43 per cent respectively in 1903-4. Recruitment of non-member attendants rose from a level equal to 2·62 per cent

5. Sprague, loc. cit.; Edwin D. Starbuck, *The Psychology of Religion, An Empirical Study of the Growth of Religious Consciousness,* London, 1899, pp. 51-2, 294-5.

of membership in 1902 to 5·43 per cent in 1904 and 11·01 per cent in 1905, and fell to 2·14 and 1·93 per cent respectively in 1906-7. This change greatly increased losses, which equalled 4·47 of membership in 1905, and 3·98 and 3·78 respectively in 1906-7. The new members recruited in 1904-5 were less loyal than the members recruited in earlier years; and high growth in 1904-5 therefore produced high losses in 1906-7.

The Presbyterian Church of Wales's returns show that the new members of 1904-5, unlike the members recruited in earlier years, were overwhelmingly non-member

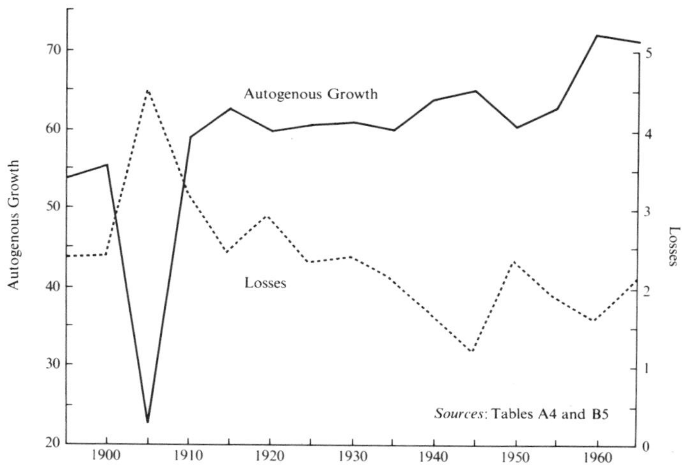

Fig. 4.1: Autogenous Growth and Membership Losses in the Presbyterian Church of Wales at Quinquennial Intervals, 1895-1965 (per cent: semi-log).
Note:'Autogenous growth' is here indicated by expressing 'children of the church' as a percentage of total new admissions; and 'losses' by expressing all membership terminations otherwise than by death as a percentage of communicant membership.

attendants rather than 'children of the church'. Such distinctions do not occur in other churches' returns; but where gains and losses can be compared, the statistics provided by such returns do behave as if, just as in the Presbyterian Church of Wales, high growth chiefly meant allogenous growth with low membership retention. Table B2 shows, for example, that admission 'by profession' in the Church of Scotland rose from 26 054 in 1900 to 28 218 in 1905 only to fall to 26 583 by 1908; but losses otherwise than by death or by certificated transfer also rose from 15 853 in 1900 to 17 911 in 1905, and remained as high as 17 181 in 1908. And, while admissions by profession rose from 21 734 in 1918 to 32 280 in 1920, only to fall to 28 400 by 1925, losses otherwise than by death or certificated transfer rose from 14 583 in 1918 to 15 964 in 1920 and to 18 869 in 1925.

Over the last hundred years many churches have suffered a prolonged decline in recruitment to membership. In 1883 the Wesleyan Methodist Church recruited new members equal to 14·89 per cent of its existing membership. But this recruitment rate fell to 4·93 per cent by 1933; and the Methodist Church, of which the Wesleyans formed the largest single component, saw its recruitment rate fall from 4·69 to 1·91 per cent between 1933 and 1970. This decline has been largely caused by a failure to sustain allogenous growth, as Figure 4.1 indicates. In the Presbyterian Church of Wales recruitment of 'children of the church' fell from a level equal to 3·29 to 1·16 per cent of membership between 1905 and 1968; but recruitment 'from without' fell from a level equal to 11·01 to 0·54 per cent of membership during the same period. And this latter drop is largely attributable to the drop in the number of non-member attendants, who equalled 37·63 per cent of members in 1905 but only 5·23 in 1968.

A decline in recruitment, and specifically a decline in allogenous growth, must cause losses to decline, because those who do become members will be more loyal to the organization. This is probably one cause of the characteristic tendency of most churches since 1914 not to show rising losses after rising gains. In pre-twentieth-century conditions, even given an initial ministerial purge of the membership roll, losses would continue to rise with gains because new members would very largely be drawn from outside existing members' families. But in recent decades most churches have made so few new members, and so few of these have been recruited from outside members' families, that a short term increase in growth usually produces no significant rise in losses. This would be true, for example, of the periods 1936-8 and 1945-7.

It would also be generally true, in the longer term, of the last hundred years, as Figure 4.2 indicates. In 1882, Wesleyan membership increased 3·36 per cent, and new members, and those who ceased to be members, were equal in number to 14·07 and 6·4 per cent of full members respectively. In 1970, Methodist membership fell 2·79 per cent, and new members, and those who ceased to be members, were equal to 1·91 and 2·2 per cent of full members respectively. In other words, during 1882-1970, Wesleyan/Methodist growth fell 6 percentage points, recruitment rate fell nine-tenths and loss rate fell two-thirds.

Since similar developments occur in all churches for which relevant data is available, turnover of membership appears to bear a direct relationship to membership growth both in the short and the long run. High growth means high turnover, so that when a church increases its gains it also increases its losses. During the progessive phase of membership density, these losses may be very high. The membership of the Primitive Methodist Church quadrupled during 1820-4; remained virtually unchanged in 1825; fell by unknown amounts during 1826-7; and only passed the 1825 total in 1829. In the same way, membership of the Church of Jesus Christ of Latter Day Saints increased six times between 1956 and 1964, grew only 3·25 per cent per annum during 1964-9, and decreased in 1970. Such abrupt changes in the rate of net growth indicate a high rate of membership losses, masked in earlier years by the high rate of membership gains.

But evidence from the last few decades serves to complicate the simple conclusion that a progressive phase involves high turnover which decreases thereafter as a church's relationship to total population becomes first marginal and then recessive. For several churches' statistics indicate a new relationship between recruitment to, and retention of, membership. As Figure 4.2 shows, since the late 1950s, gains and losses in the Methodist Church seem to have shifted from

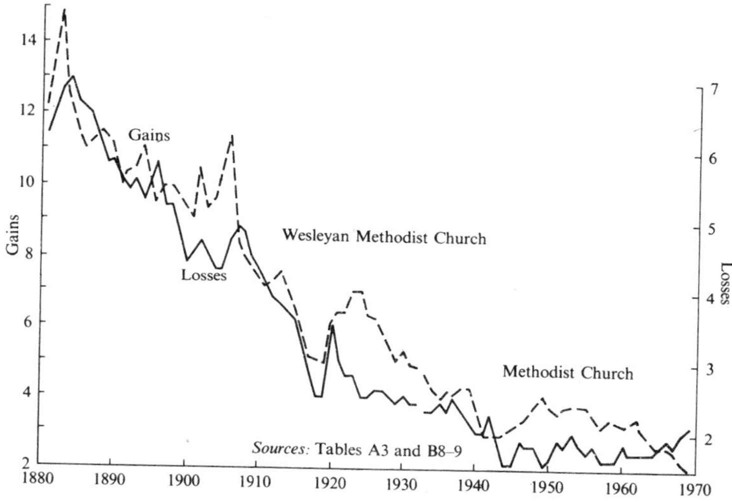

Fig. 4.2: Gains and Losses as a Percentage of Full Membership in the Wesleyan Methodist Church and the Methodist Church at Annual Intervals, 1881-1969 (per cent).
Note: 'Gains' indicates 'New Members' only; 'Losses' 'Ceased to be Members' only.

a direct to an inverse relationship, in which losses *increase* as gains *decrease* in relation to total membership. Between 1957 and 1970, while Methodist new members fell by half, from 23 898 to 11 806, those who ceased to be Methodist members increased by a fifth, from 11 232 to 13 547.

Other churches seem to have experienced the same development. Between 1955 and 1970, admissions 'by profession' to the Church of Scotland have fallen 58·1 per cent from 45 832 to 19 204, but losses otherwise than by death or certificated transfer have risen by 26·24 per cent from 17 999 to 22 722. The Church of England provides no comparable figures but, though confirmations fell 59·25 per cent, from 190 713 to 113 005, between 1960 and 1970, Easter Day communicants fell sharply during the same period, from 2·2 to 1·6 million, a fall of nearly 30 per cent, which must indicate a substantial rise in the annual losses of the Church of England.

This new situation may be attributable to a decline in the loyalty of churchmembers' children. Certainly it cannot wholly be attributed to a new decline in the loyalty of members recruited from non-churchgoing families, since most churches enjoy very little allogenous growth. One possible cause may be a lowering of the age of recruitment of new members, partly due to a desire to keep up numbers in a period when membership is rapidly falling, and partly perhaps to changes in attitudes towards the age of maturity. There is little evidence of such an alteration in the age of recruitment; but the proportion of Catholic 'adult conversions' of persons aged thirteen and under seems to be rising, as Table B10 indicates; while it is reported that a greater proportion of confirmees and new members in various Protestant churches are under fifteen years in age. Such a development might well increase losses since the younger people are when they acquire church membership the less likely they are to regard it as a binding act of their own volition.

DIRECT AND INDIRECT RECRUITMENT

Most churches recruit most successfully in the earliest years of their history, when, given a relatively large constituency and a relatively small membership, they are able to achieve their highest growth rates. The Primitive Methodist Church, for example, grew from no more than a few dozen members in 1800 to over 7800 members in 1820 and, as late as 1821-2, grew 53 per cent in one year. Wesleyanism experienced similar growth rates in the mid-eighteenth century, and so have many Christian churches in Asia and Africa in the nineteenth and twentieth centuries.

During this progressive phase of very high growth, churches recruit whole communities or whole families, rather than isolated individuals, and they recruit adults rather than children. The population so recruited must be religiously minded to the extent that it believes in the supernatural and expects the supernatural to act, when correctly treated, both favourably and efficaciously. Moreover, it may well be necessary for the recruited population to know at least something of the recruiting organization's particular ideas about the natural and the supernatural.

Both the Wesleyan and the Primitive Methodist Church enjoyed these advantages. For even when they recruited exceedingly ill-educated populations in out-townships of remote and neglected parishes, or in the more or less autonomous new industrial districts, they were appealing to people both religious in a general sense and Christianized, if only to a small degree. When Christian churches have attempted to recruit Asian and African populations, they have been dealing with highly religious if not highly Christianized nations; and the high growth rates achieved by these churches have largely depended either upon a prolonged preliminary education in Christian ideas – whether conducted by themselves or by some other agencies – or upon thorough-going assimilation of Christianity to the indigenous religion of the region under recruitment.

Populations ready for, and responsive to, recruitment have not been a feature of modern British history and, indeed, despite the Methodists' success, opportunities for churches to achieve prolonged very high growth were fast disappearing by the late eighteenth century. Two distinct though related factors tended to reduce the religiosity of the British people. First, the division and despoliation of the Church of England during the Reformation and the Civil War seriously hindered the established church's efforts to provide religious instruction for a population which was, in any event, increasing much faster than it had done before the Reformation. As many eighteenth-century episcopal visitations show, the communion was often received by no more than 1 or 2 per cent of the parish; church attendances were little higher; and the clergy abandoned a great part of their parishioners to irreligion.

Secondly, industrialization created an urban population quite remote even from such desultory religious ministrations as obtained in many country places. The parish church of Sheffield, for example, served 2000 people in 1615 and 10 000 in 1736. By 1851, when Sheffield had grown to be a town of 135 000 persons, it contained sixteen churches and chapels of the Church of England, and forty-three buildings belonging to other bodies, which provided in all 43 000 seats, or one for every three citizens. Such conditions prevented any church from counteracting the secularizing tendencies of industrial technique and an industrial, urban life-style. City dwellers did retain certain residual religious notions or 'superstitions', but these came to play a very small part in the lives of individuals who, moreover, were largely ignorant of the churches' concerns, ideas, and teachings. In these circumstances, the urban areas became 'missionary territory' in which the preliminary work of Christianization and even religious socialization had to start virtually from the beginning.[6]

Despite great outlay of capital and labour, churches cannot achieve high growth rates in these circumstances; and, in order to obtain net gains, must abandon attempts at *direct* recruitment of a population, already made responsive to recruitment by other agencies (such as other churches or earlier generations), and institute a system of *indirect* recruitment which involves, first a religious socialization quite distinct from membership, and then, and only then, recruitment to membership itself. Indirect recruitment must always be more lengthy – and therefore less rewarding – than direct recruitment, simply because it involves an extra stage of activity; yet indirect recruitment has come to characterize most churches in twentieth-century Britain. One measure of this trend is the churches'

6. E. R. Wickham, *Church and People in an Industrial City*, London, 1957, pp. 34, 41, 281; F. Boulard, *An Introduction to Religious Sociology, Pioneer Work in France*, (trans. M. J. Jackson), London, 1960, *passim*.

increasing reliance on re-recruiting lapsed members who have already received thorough religious socialization during their previous period of membership. Thus, for instance, 10 per cent of those whose names were entered on the communicant rolls of the Church of Scotland in 1896 were lapsed and restored members; but by 1970 this figure had risen to 21 per cent.

The chief means whereby the churches could indirectly recruit a population was by creating, or co-operating in, educational institutions that, though more or less distinct from the churches, were managed by churchmen and had among their various aims – as the authors of one such scheme put it – the inculcation of 'the leading and incontrovertible principles of Christianity'. These institutions were the Sunday schools, which began at the end of the eighteenth century, and which, by the end of the Napoleonic Wars, were clearly seen as agencies for the preparation of persons for church membership. The purpose of the Sunday schools, declared the President of the Methodist Conference in 1827, was 'that the children may be habituated to a regular and devout attendance upon the public worship of Almighty God'.[7]

But a population too secularized to be directly recruited to church membership would not readily accept a programme of religious socialization as part of a process of indirect recruitment. Hence Sunday schools had to provide their pupils with some service in return for which they would submit to such socialization. This service was the provision of 'useful learning', including self-evidently utilitarian skills such as reading and writing, and less tangible social skills such as manners, punctuality, and self-discipline. 'Useful learning', apparently unlike religious socialization, was a commodity for which a demand existed; but it was a demand quite unrelated to religious concerns, and once that demand fell off, or was otherwise satisfied, Sunday schools would be jeopardized.[8]

Moreover, while a religious population regards church membership as a natural concomitant of normal adult life, a secularized population tends to feel that normal adults 'outgrow' church membership, in a biological sense, just as the entire secularized culture has 'outgrown' religion in a historical sense. The association of 'useful learning' with religion is therefore unattractive to adult members of such a population, and these adults have in general failed to attend Sunday schools except where some overriding motive has obtained. One such motive was afforded by Welsh nationalism which found in the Nonconformist Sunday schools institutions well adapted to the maintenance of the Welsh language: but the Welsh Sunday schools were unique in their power to recruit and retain adults. Other schools had to be content with children, who are, in any event, more likely than adults to accept, or to be required to accept, learning whether useful or not.

7. W. R. Ward, *Religion and Society in England 1790-1850*, London, 1972, p. 14; Methodist *Minutes*, 1827, p. 285.
8. Ward, loc. cit.

And once Sunday schools became almost entirely involved with children, they *institutionalized* the notion that religion was for children only, and exacerbated precisely the difficulty that led to the creation of Sunday schools, namely, the churches' lack of appeal to new members.

The salience of the Sunday school in the indirect recruitment process can be seen from the relationship between Sunday-school membership and church membership, the former tending to be relatively larger where the recruitable population was most secularized and the recruiting church most anxious to make members. Thus Catholic Sunday schools remain quite unimportant both in Ireland and Great Britain because in both countries the Catholic constituency is both large and highly responsive to recruitment. In Scotland, Presbyterianism enjoys an authority unknown to any Protestant church in England, where the population is more thoroughly secularized; and the Sunday schools of both established and unestablished Presbyterian churches in Scotland have rarely had half as many pupils as their parent churches had communicant members.

In England, the established church has traditionally recruited from those middle- and upper-class elements that are, of all the population, most closely connected, through their general education, with the Christian tradition. Moreover for very many years, the Church of England has only infrequently and partially seen itself as a proselytizing organization. Thus Anglican Sunday schools, at their height, contained approximately only as many pupils as the Church of England had Easter Day communicants. The Nonconformists, however, saw their task, over several generations, as the recruitment of the least-educated and most-secularized sectors of the population. Most Nonconformist Sunday schools therefore enrolled, by the end of the nineteenth century, at least twice as many pupils as their parent churches enrolled members.

Sunday schools have always contained many persons too young for membership, and, of those scholars that are at or near a recruitable age, relatively few come from families sufficiently close to the recruiting church to be accounted part of its internal constituency. There is therefore a very considerable wastage between the Sunday school and church membership. In 1906, for instance, the Wesleyan Methodist Church had 1 000 000 Sunday-school scholars and 100 000 junior members, made 57 000 new members, and achieved a net increase of 14 000 full members. Nevertheless, where figures are available, the fluctuation of Sunday-school membership does correlate with that of church membership: in the Church of England, during 1891-1962 at 0·76; in the Church of Scotland, during 1929-59 at 0·69; and in the Methodist Church, during 1932-68, at 0·88.

The history of Sunday schools falls into three distinct phases. Large numbers of these institutions were formed from the mid-1780s onwards. The early Sunday schools emphasized 'useful learning'; were, in many cases, interdenominational; and won the support of local magistrates and businessmen by purporting to assist public order. There were about half a million Sunday-school scholars by 1818, and at least 5 000 000 by 1900. During this period, therefore, the Sunday schools grew at about 3 per cent per annum, that is, a good deal faster than both church membership and the internal constituency for church membership. Most of this growth was, however, concentrated in the years before 1880. Between 1841 and 1880, Primitive Methodist Sunday school membership and church membership grew at mean rates of 4·59 and 2·03 per cent per annum respectively.

But as the threat of public disorder declined, and as secular authorities became less reliant on religion as a means to secure law and order, the promoters of Sunday schools found greater difficulty in obtaining support and assistance for their projects. Furthermore, Sunday schools became less attractive to those whom they were meant to render responsive to recruitment. Interdenominational schools rapidly gave place to denominational schools whose allegiance to a particular religious organization made manifest their religious socialization, rather than their general educational, functions; and this change in the public image of Sunday schools could not increase their growth among a secular population. Finally, a series of measures, culminating in the Act of 1870, created a system of more or less *secular* education which greatly reduced the utilitarian appeal of the Sunday schools as institutions providing 'useful learning'. By 1880, therefore, the Sunday school was already a partial failure as a stage in the process of indirect recruitment. Thereafter declining Sunday-school membership necessarily reduced the growth rate of those churches that had large schools which had provided a significant proportion of juvenile church members.

About 1880 Sunday schools entered a second phase which lasted till about 1920. Between 1880 and 1920, Primitive Methodist Sunday-school membership, adherence, and church membership increased at mean rates of 0·83, 0·13, and 0·46 per cent per annum respectively. During this period, though Sunday-school membership was still growing faster than adherence or church membership, the demand for Sunday-school instruction was plainly declining. This may be attributable partly to a decline in the under-fourteen age-group as a proportion of the population; but it is probably also due to the extension and expansion of the system of free elementary day schools. For, since growth in church membership fell slightly less than growth in Sunday-school membership, the declining appeal of the *churches* appears not to have been a decisive factor in the declining appeal of the *schools*.

Since 1920, Sunday schools have entered a phase of very severe decline. Between 1920 and 1960, Church of England and Baptist Sunday-school membership has fallen respectively 48 and 49 per cent; and the Sunday-school membership of the Methodist Church and its constituents has fallen 62 per cent from 1·5 to 0·6 million. In the same period, however, the membership of these churches has fallen only 2, 22, and 9 per cent respectively. This fall cannot be attributed to a decline in the under-fourteen age-group, for that has remained virtually constant as a proportion of the total population, and has substantially increased in number. Nor can it be explained entirely in terms of the appeal of rival educational agencies, because at least since the First World War Sunday schools have become little more than Bible classes offering virtually no instruction in either reading or writing. Since the modern Sunday schools' failure to provide 'useful learning' has been quite common knowledge for so long a period, it is unlikely that the lack of such a facility has *continuing* influence on the decline in the number of Sunday-school scholars.

One possible factor is the decline in the status of the schools. As Gorer's *Exploring English Character* shows, the claim to send a child to Sunday school seems to have a status value since, as late as 1951, whereas 54 per cent of Gorer's respondents claimed so to do, giving the schools about 5 000 000 pupils in England and Wales, the schools themselves counted about 3 000 000 pupils: a total bound to fall as the status value of these claims diminishes. Finally, some of the recent decline of Sunday schools may be due to the decline of parental sanctions, and to changes in recreation. One major function of the Sunday school has been the provision (especially, as Gorer shows, for large families) of cheap or free child-minding, but in recent years parents have perhaps been less able or less willing to send their children out of the house to receive institutional supervision on Sundays, when, in any event, new forms of shared leisure such as television and motoring, may make parents more willing to accept their children's company.[10]

The decline in Sunday schools must be a large factor in the decline of church membership, even were the schools now more efficient in their religious socialization than in earlier years. Other elements in the indirect recruitment process certainly do not seem to offset these difficulties. Religious education remains a semi-compulsory element of public education, but there is little evidence of its contribution to church membership; and it is not easy to see how a form of instruction that is generally held to have what Wilson calls 'low status as a subject' can have a great influence on behaviour.[11]

Furthermore, religious broadcasting, as Tables I1 and I2 show, does not appeal to the general population as any efficient form of religious socialization must if indirect recruitment is to provide the churches with an adequate supply of members. Broadcast religious services that had audiences of 8, 10, 11 per cent of the adult population in 1940 were listened to by 3 or less per cent of adults by 1955. Even the audience for the relatively popular 'People's Service', still 11 per cent of the total population in 1964, had fallen to less than 5 per cent by 1970. Part of this decline is due to the appeal of television, but the B.B.C.'s religious

10. Geoffrey Gorer, *Exploring English Character*, London, 1955, pp. 245-8, 454-5.
11. Bryan R. Wilson, *Religion in a Secular Society, A Sociological Comment*, London, 1966, p. 58.

television programmes also have lost much of their audience. Between 1963 and 1970, the audiences for the television Morning Service, the discussion programme 'Meeting Point', and the music programme 'Songs of Praise' have fallen 60, 40, and 30 per cent respectively. Independent Television's religious programmes, whose content and presentation were quite markedly altered in the late 1960s, were viewed by 21·7 and 22·4 per cent of homes receiving Independent Television in 1958 and 1970 respectively; yet the programmes broadcast immediately after the 'religious slot' were viewed by 42·7 and 40·3 per cent of these homes in 1961 and 1971 respectively.

MEMBERSHIP TERMINATION

A church's power to recruit arises from its proximity to, congruity with, and utility for those whom it recruits. These characteristics vary widely, but all may be associated with the church's existence as a community, and its relationships both to the community or communities that make up its constituency and to the larger society. A church itself is a community the utility of whose tertiary or organizational functions profoundly influences attitudes toward it. Its congruity with the community or communities that it recruits is a vital determinant of its growth. And its proximity may be regarded as the physical distance between it and a recruitable community.

Sociological theory has emphasized the notion of religion as the expression of a community. In terms of this theory, 'rites are means by which the social group reaffirms itself', as Durkheim put it. For individuals born into a church-centred community, church membership would be closely connected with the affirmation of a particular group, while membership termination would be as closely connected with the dissolution of that group, whether such dissolution occurs in the objective reality of the group or in the individual's subjective perception of and relation to the group.[12]

Most conversion crises occur in the 13-20 age-group, and what is true of conversions is true also of other types of entry to church membership. Thus, over 80 per cent of Church of England confirmees in 1958 and 1960 were aged between twelve and twenty. On the other hand, according to opinion polls, 60 or 70 per cent of those who have ceased attending church claim to have done so in the 10-20 age-group; so that the teens appear to be the period in which most individuals who join churches join, and in which most individuals who stop going to church stop.[13]

12. Emile Durkheim, *The Elementary Forms of the Religious Life*, London, 1968, p. 387.
13. Michael Argyle, *Religious Behaviour*, London, 1958, pp. 60-1; Statistical Unit of the Central Board of Finance of the Church of England, *Facts and Figures about the Church of England*, 3, London, 1965, p. 55; Social Surveys (Gallup Poll) Ltd., *Television and Religion*, London, 1964, p. 128.

The critical nature of this phase of life scarcely needs stating. This is a period when, in the early teens, individuals 'come of age', in the sense of leaving childhood and taking on a life and personality distinct from, yet still linked to, the life of the parents, and when, in the late teens or early twenties (according to the biological circumstances and cultural norms of the period) they reach adulthood, in the sense of acquiring a life and personality quite separate from that of the parents. The *mores* and norms of the community, as adopted and mediated by the parents, must exert a powerful influence on the individual teen-aged attendant's or member's relationship to the church. If the parents are themselves members of a church, church membership will in most cases be seen as a concomitant of adulthood which, on the individual's 'coming of age' he will desire (and be encouraged) to obtain for himself: and such pressures must account for much of any church's new membership. Most parents are, however, not now members of churches, but rather belong to a community in which church-going is either not the norm, or the norm for children only. In either case, the individual – if he goes to church – will on 'coming of age' desire (and perhaps be encouraged) to cease attending church: hence much of any church's loss of *attendance,* though probably only a small part of any church's loss of *membership,* since such individuals are relatively unlikely to have acquired membership.

There will be a few who, on 'coming of age', will reject their community's norms and *mores* but they are much more likely to do so when they approach or reach adulthood. At that point in their lives, individuals may continue to accept parental attitudes, may form other personal opinions about church membership, or – more likely – may be swayed by the norms and *mores* of communities other than those to which their parents belong. Throughout the last hundred years the probability has increased that the norms and *mores* of the communities with which young people might wish to identify themselves will be hostile to church membership. Hence, a very few individuals will cease church attendance, on 'coming of age', in deference to parental and community attitudes, but, on reaching or approaching adulthood, will recommence church attendance and perhaps take up church membership; but many more individuals will take up church membership on 'coming of age' in deference to external pressures of this sort only to terminate membership in their late teens or early twenties.

Some individuals, having taken up membership of one church may of course relinquish that membership in order to join another church. In Britain, few persons do so, however. The Church of England received on average 14 775 communicants a year from other churches during 1954-6, and 8250 in 1962. Of the former total, 3480 had been members of the Catholic Church, and 11 295 members of other churches. The latter total was composed of 2620 Catholics and 5630 members of other churches. Total Anglican receptions from other churches in 1962 were equivalent to 0·38 per cent of Easter Day communicants; and the numbers of Catholics and non-Catholics received into the Church of England in that year were equivalent to 0·13 and 0·21 per cent of Catholic mass attendance and the membership of the major non-episcopalian Protestant churches respectively. Adult conversions to the Catholic Church in England and Wales largely represent persons transferring church membership, but when conversions reached a peak of 16 250 in 1959 they equalled only about 0·4 per cent of the major Protestant churches' membership, and 0·5 per cent of estimated Catholic population, in England and Wales.

Wesleyan and Methodist gains from, and losses to, other churches reached peaks of 0·48 (2231) and 0·69 (3192) per cent respectively of Wesleyan membership in 1921; and 0·42 (2676) and 0·48 (2838) per cent of Methodist membership in 1969 and 1968 respectively. But in 1921, 1968, and 1969 the number of those who ceased to be members, and were not recorded as joining another church, were equal in number to 2·99, 2·05, and 2·1 per cent of Wesleyan or Methodist membership. Losses to another church are, presumably, a minimum figure, since those who leave one church and join another are quite likely to do so without the cognizance of the leaders of the church they are leaving. But this source of error would have to be very large indeed for the number of persons who left either the Wesleyan or the Methodist churches for another church to approach the number of persons who left those churches to join the non-churchgoing population.

That people do tend to move from church membership into the non-member population during their late teens and early twenties is shown by various pieces of evidence indicating a decline in church attendance from the age of sixteen onwards. In such cases, membership termination may be linked to some change in life circumstances associated with, or symbolic of, personal maturity and rejection of parental habits and ideas. Such changes would include starting further education (especially if this involves living away from home), marriage, the birth of children, or a first job or a change of job (especially if this too involves migration from the parents' district). The relationship between migration and membership termination is of particular significance. Between 1933 and 1970, 15·59 per cent of Methodist losses from all causes other than death and emigration were attributable to 'leakage' of persons whose membership was being transferred from one circuit to another; while such leakage accounted for 27·02 per cent of Wesleyan Methodist losses from all causes other than death and emigration between 1906 and 1932. These figures represent a minimum of persons actually terminating membership on migration.

Leakage may well be partly due, as was argued in Chapter III, to an inadequate spread of religious facilities, since, if church members move from an area close to a church of their persuasion to an area farther from such a church, their membership may lapse. But that leakage is not solely due to an inadequate supply of the facilities of membership can be seen from the general tendency of leakage to conform to the pattern of other membership-termination series. This is particularly noticeable in the Wesleyan Methodist Church where, over the period 1881-1932, leakage and cessation of membership correlate at 0·97 or, taking year-to-year changes, 0·66, that is, well above the 1 per cent level of probability (0·35).

Evidence published by the Presbyterian Church of England also suggests that members 'leak' on migration from one area to another as a convenient and appropriate means of terminating a membership they wish to relinquish, rather than because they move to an area ill supplied with churches of their persuasion. Leakage in the Presbyterian Church of England fell steadily between 1911 and 1940 from 1·49 to 0·81 per cent of membership. But after the Second World War leakage remained stable and then rose between 1956 and 1968 from 0·77 to 2·37 per cent of membership. The geographical spread of Presbyterian Church of England churches did not materially diminish during these years; but membership of the church, which had fallen at a mean rate of 0·42 per cent per annum during 1911-40, fell at 0·93 per cent per annum during 1956-68, and in 1972 the church merged with the Congregational Union of England and Wales to form the United Reformed Church.[14]

Unilateral membership termination by members who 'leak' on moving to another area, or who remain in the same area while allowing membership to lapse, expresses very clearly the objective or subjective dissolution of the church-centred community that consists of the church members and the constituency for membership. Only if membership termination becomes a *bilateral* process in which the church itself is able to expel the member by a significant formal procedure, recognized by the member, does the withdrawal of the member lose some of its meaning – at least for the member – as a dissolution of the church-centred community.

For an *expelled,* as opposed to a *lapsed,* member may be deemed to have undergone and, in a sense, accepted a judgement acknowledged by that community; and hence the universal possibility of restoration to membership even of excommunicated persons who, by being excommunicated, certainly have not withdrawn from the whole community of which the church is a part. It is a measure of the *denominationalism* of the churches in a pluralist society that, in recent years, all forms of expulsion and excommunication have virtually fallen into disuse, since this development can only be attributed to the churches' inability to appeal to a constituency sufficiently enclosed and controlled for expulsion to be a meaningful process of membership termination.

The history of expulsion is illustrated by data published by the Presbyterian

14. It is assumed that transfers from the Presbyterian Church of England to Scottish Presbyterian churches are not significant; that transfers from Presbyterian Church of England churches are therefore transfers to English Presbyterian churches only; and that, to calculate leakage, these losses by transfer should be set against gains by transfer from English Presbyterian churches only.

Church of Wales for the years 1895-1957. Figure 4·3 indicates trends both in rate of expulsion of members and in the *number* of non-member attendants of the Presbyterian Church of Wales. Between 1906 and 1920 the expulsion rate remained virtually stable (falling from 14·91 to 14·4 per cent of the total number

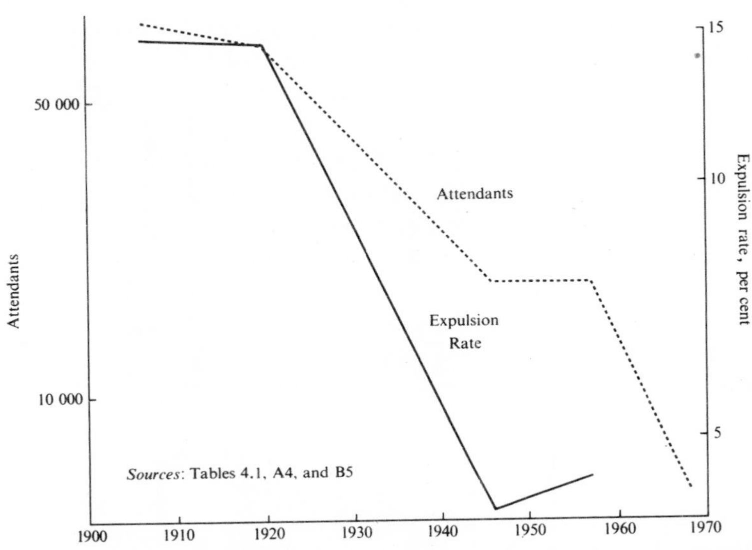

Fig. 4.3: Attendants and Expulsion Rate in the Presbyterian Church of Wales in 1906, 1920, 1946, 1957, and 1968 (semi-log).
Note: For a definition of 'Attendants' see Table 4.1. 'Expulsion rate' refers to members expelled, expressed as a percentage of all members ceasing membership otherwise than by death or by leakage in transfer.

of persons ceasing membership otherwise than by leakage or death), while the number of attendants fell from 75 138 to 65 593, a drop of only 12·7 per cent. Between 1920 and 1946 both expulsion rate and the number of attendants fell sharply: the former from 14·4 to 4·05 per cent of losses so defined; the latter from 65 593 to 18 264, a drop of 72·2 per cent. From 1946 to 1957 expulsion rate rose slightly, from 4·05 to 4·46 per cent of losses so defined, and the number of attendants fell from 18 264 to 18 136, a drop of only 0·7 per cent. In 1958, a year in which attendants' decreased by nearly 25 per cent, the Presbyterian Church of Wales ceased publishing the number of expulsions; and it seems probable that expulsions have now fallen to a very low level.

This data does suggest a very close, positive association between expulsion rate and developments within the internal constituency. The number of replacement or potential replacement members does seem to determine the number of members expelled; and over the period 1895-1957 there is a 0·65 correlation between the year-to-year differences of numbers of expulsions and members 'received from without', a figure well above the 1 per cent level of probability (here 0·32). In other words, the evidence may be held to show that the practice of formal expulsion does rest upon the continuance of a church-centred, even church-controlled, community.

Such communities are rapidly ceasing to exist. The decline in church membership and church attendance, and the growth of the population, causes a steady increase in the non-churchgoing elements of the population, both absolutely and relative to the number of churchgoers. Thus the possibilities for individual church members to move, through some commonplace life circumstance, such as further education, marriage, or a change of job, from a church-centred to a churchless community are always increasing; and these movements, by causing yet more membership terminations, provide further increases in the non-churchgoing population, and yet further possibilities for church membership to decrease.

V

External Influences on Church Growth

THE PRIMACY OF EXOGENOUS FACTORS

It was suggested in Chapter I that the formation of the *internal* constituency, and still more the recruitment of new members, were cases of supply-induced demand: that is to say, the provision of religious facilities for both adherents and members stimulated demand for those facilities. In this sense, factors endogenous to the organization give rise to growth. Moreover, as has been argued in Chapters II and IV, fluctuations in the transfer of adherents to membership are influenced by variations in the recruiting activities of those laymen and clergy or ministers who, in the different churches, are responsible for bringing persons into membership; and here too endogenous factors are obviously highly significant.

Wesleyan Methodism affords one of the most striking examples of a conscious attempt to induce a demand for church membership by the supply of religious facilities. Wesley organized his assistants into an annual conference which debated and formulated policy and appointed the tasks for the 'travelling preachers' during the coming year, above all by specifying the area in which they were to recruit and service members. Each area consisted of a 'circuit' or group of chapels and preaching places so arranged that all new and poor societies of members were linked to older-established and richer societies able to assist them. The travelling preachers visited the chapels and preaching places in turn according to the different societies' needs. Moreover, the travelling preachers selected and trained both 'local preachers' who lived in the area and preached throughout the circuit, and 'stewards' and trustees to administer the chapels that were built.

Wesley spoke of his system as a 'connexion', and termed the deployment of travelling preachers 'itinerancy'; and the realization of these two notions, the centralization and interconnection of all the parts of the organization, and the movement of full-time professionals about the organization, proved extraordinarily successful. Furthermore, Greaves's study of Yorkshire Methodism can be said to show that the success of Wesleyanism in co-ordinating and recruiting from its internal constituency depended at least partly upon the efficient operation of the system, as well as upon a pre-formed demand for the religious facilities offered by Wesleyanism, since the new church spread mainly where the roads were good enough to allow the travelling preachers to reach a responsive local population.[1]

The pattern of Mormon membership in Britain provides further evidence of the effects of a church's policy on its growth. The Church of Jesus Christ of Latter Day Saints increased rapidly in Britain in the first half of the nineteenth century, reaching a total of 32 894 members in 1851. Thereafter membership steadily fell till 1892 when it reached 2604, and rose again slowly to 9691 by 1956. But since 1956 the British membership of the church has greatly increased: in 1969 there were 72 899 Mormons in Britain. During the nineteenth century, British Mormons were encouraged to emigrate to Utah, and between 1840 and 1913 at least 52 000 did so; but the Mormons laid less emphasis on migration in the late nineteenth century, and, after the First World War, American immigration restrictions inhibited movements of British Mormons across the Atlantic, and British membership therefore gradually increased. From 1956 onwards, however, as a result of decisions taken in Salt Lake City, a large missionary campaign commenced in Britain, where membership grew very rapidly indeed.

Yet Mormon growth in Britain during recent years has been sufficiently varied to suggest that, even in this case, policy was by no means sufficient to produce expansion. While the church increased its membership by 69·52 and 53·86 per cent in 1961 and 1962 respectively, its growth decreased sharply thereafter and never exceeded 5 per cent per annum throughout 1964-9. This fall in growth may be partly attributed to the logistic problems of continuing to increase membership by more than 50 per cent per annum, partly to the fall in membership-retention inseparable from very high allogenous growth; but very probably the Mormons failed to maintain their very rapid expansion after 1962 above all because of the same obstacles, insuperable by any policy, that so severely reduced the numbers of other churches during these years.

Similar conclusions can be drawn from the early Wesleyan case. Though the Wesleyan system maximized expansion, it could not prevent fluctuations in growth which seem to arise from exogenous factors. The connexional and itinerant method was worked no less efficiently in 1772 than in 1771, yet in the earlier of these years the Wesleyan Methodist Church grew 4·22 per cent, and in the later only 1·1 per cent. Moreover, the evidence of Yorkshire Methodism does after all show the significance of the entirely exogenous factor of road communications; and the *over-all* geographical spread of Methodism suggests that, among exogenous factors, roads were not decisive. Communications were no worse in Middlesex and

1. B. Greaves, 'An Analysis of the Spread of Methodism in Yorkshire in the Eighteenth and Early Nineteenth Centuries (1740-1831), with Special Reference to the Environment of this Movement', M. A. Thesis, Leeds, 1961; 'Methodism in Yorkshire 1740-1851', Ph.D. Thesis, Liverpool, 1968.

London than in Yorkshire, for example; yet by 1801 the Wesleyans had recruited 2·5 per cent of the population of Yorkshire and only 0·3 per cent of the population of Middlesex and London.

Church policy does therefore seem to be only one, and perhaps not the most significant, factor in church growth. Indeed it seems probable that, whatever efforts are expended by a church, increased recruitment cannot be obtained in unfavourable exogenous conditions. Between 1943 and 1947, the Methodist and certain other churches organized schemes of 'team evangelism' under the title of Christian Commando Campaigns. The Campaigns were described as 'attacks on entrenched indifference to organised religion' by churches 'prepared' to engage in 'evangelistic enterprise'. In short, this recruitment campaign laid great stress on the churches' own activities. But, while the Methodist Church suffered a net loss of 23 854 members during the four years up to the 'official end' of the campaign (1944-7), it enjoyed a net gain of 1812 members in the following four years (1947-50); a gain by no means confined to those areas in which Commando Campaigns had occurred.[2]

There are two further indications of the primacy of exogenous factors. Whatever the significance of endogenous factors in causing membership growth to assume a cyclical pattern, almost all available evidence suggests that this pattern tends to be common to all churches, a phenomenon difficult to explain except on the hypothesis that the activation phase of each cycle is often synchronized in different churches by exogenous factors operating upon every church. Moreover, since 1900 exogenous events have had a very obvious effect upon the increase and decrease of church membership: above all, both world wars have coincided with severe falls in membership which were at least partly made up at the end of the war period, an association in which it is difficult not to see a casual connection.

However a church fares, it relies for its growth not only upon an internal constituency but upon an external constituency over the formation of which it exercises little or no control. The external constituency is almost entirely the product of exogenous factors; and the incipient demand for religious facilities indicated by the external constituency's existence tends to induce the supply of those facilities, rather than vice versa. This can be seen most clearly from the geographical spread of religious organizations, since very many churches move, or, rather, are drawn, into areas where a demand for church membership is, for whatever reason, neglected by other churches. Thus Congregationalists and Baptists recruited where the Church of England was weak in southern England, and the Methodists recruited where all three churches were weak in northern England,

2. Frank Baker, *A Charge to Keep*, London, 1947, p. 149; Colin A. Roberts (ed.), *These Christian Commando Campaigns*, London, 1945, pp. 7, 47.

while each new Methodist church tended to make its members in districts as yet unrecruited by existing Methodist groups. Even if in every case a church's movement into an area was an act of conscious policy, that policy must itself arise from perception of a prior, exogenously generated demand for membership created by the formation of an external constituency.[3]

SECULARIZATION

One very powerful external influence upon church growth is the 'secularization' of modern culture and society. Some scholars have doubted both the usefulness of the term and the existence of the development to which it refers, arguing that the word itself is imprecise and, in any event, tendentious; and that evidence about trends and magnitudes in 'real' religion does not demonstrate the existence, at least in that kind of religion, of the symptoms which would be expected to arise from the operation of 'secularization'.[4]

But secularization, in the sense of a diminished resort to supernatural means, can be seen in the British Isles; and this process is manifested in a diminution of both the quantity, and what Wilson calls the 'social significance', of 'religious thinking, practice and institutions'. That very many opinion-poll respondents claim to 'believe in God' is scarcely evidence to the contrary since the very concept of God has undergone, even in the thought of church leaders and theologians, certain well-attested changes which hardly contribute to the perception of God as a concrete, effective supernatural entity. Thus, when in 1963 a bishop of the Church of England wrote that 'to say that "God is personal" is to say that . . . in personal relationships we touch the final meaning of existence as nowhere else', he would seem to have adopted a notion of God secularized by comparison with the statement made by a Church of England Commission in 1938 that God is 'a living God, on whose act of will creation itself depends, and who has a purpose for mankind, to accomplish which He is Himself active in history'.[5]

3. F. Tillyard, 'The Distribution of the Free Churches in England', *The Sociological Review*, 1935, pp. 1-18; R. Currie, 'A Micro-Theory of Methodist Growth', *Proceedings of the Wesley Historical Society*, 1967, pp. 65 ff; A. D. Gilbert, *Religion and Society in Industrial England: Church, Chapel, and Social Change, 1740-1914*, London, 1976, pp. 115-21.

4. e.g. David A. Martin, 'Towards Eliminating the Concept of Secularization', in Julius Gould (ed.), *Penguin Survey of the Social Sciences*, 1965, pp. 169 ff; P. G. Forster, 'Secularization in the English Context: Some Conceptual and Empirical Problems', *Sociological Review*, 1972.

5. Bryan R. Wilson, *Religion in Secular Society, A Sociological Comment*, London, 1966, p. xiv; John A. T. Robinson, *Honest to God*, London 1963, pp. 48-9; *Doctrine in the Church of England, The Report of the Commission on Christian Doctrine Appointed by the Archbishops of Canterbury and York in 1922*, London, 1938, p. 42.

Moreover, the widespread claim, again among opinion-poll respondents, to engage in private prayer or other secret devotions is not strong evidence against secularization, both because the claim not to do so is now more widespread, and because over time the incidence of these devotions, as recorded by such data, is decreasing. And of course all other forms of religious activity are decreasing also. As can be seen from Table 2.3, the membership of the major British Protestant churches fell from 5 to 4½ million between 1900 and 1970, while the total British population rose from 37 to 53 million; and though the Catholic population rose through immigration, the number of British recruits to Catholicism also fell. The audiences for religious broadcasts too, have declined, as Tables I1 and I2 show, especially in the case of those broadcasts whose religious content is most overt. Given such evidence, it would seem difficult to argue that 'secularization' is not at work in Britain.

Two available quantitative measures of secularization, other than church-membership series themselves, are the membership of secularist organizations (see Table C2) and the Registrars'-General data on civil marriages (contained in Tables H1-5). People contract civil marriages for various reasons. Such marriages are expeditious, cheap, and more readily available to divorced persons who, in 1966, constituted 15 per cent of all those marrying. But among such reasons must be counted the fact that a civil marriage is not a religious ceremony; and, since the civil-marriage rate (that is, marriages not conducted according to a religious rite as a proportion of all marriages) in England and Wales rose from 2·6 to 34·1 per cent between 1844 and 1967, the number of persons who contract civil marriages because they object to religious ceremonies must have increased substantially. In any event, such objections are clearly entertained by members of the Rationalist Press Association, whose growth — following a very rapid expansion up to 1914 — has been similar to the growth in civil marriages: the former increasing 48·7, and the latter 41·49 per cent, between 1914 and 1967. It therefore seems reasonable to treat the civil-marriage rate as an indicator of secularization.

The relationship between secularization so measured and church growth probably falls into three periods: up to 1914, from 1914 to 1940, and since 1940. During 1840-1914, secularization appears chiefly to have checked or retarded church growth, for though civil marriages in England and Wales increased from 2·6 to 24·1 per cent of all marriages, the membership of the major Protestant churches grew from 18·42 to 19·61 per cent of the British population aged fifteen and over. In other words, while civil marriages increased rapidly, Protestant church membership also expanded. Secularization may have delimited the number of church members and potential church members, therefore, but it did not greatly affect membership retention.

After 1914, however, this relationship altered. Between 1914 and 1939 civil-marriage rate rose from 24·1 to probably about 29 per cent in England and Wales, and from 12·56 to 16·58 per cent in Scotland; but between 1914 and 1940 membership of the major Protestant churches fell from 19·61 to 15·37 per cent of the British population aged fifteen and over. In other words, a rise of about a fifth in the civil-marriage rate accompanied a fall of about a fifth in Protestant density; and it seems probable that during this period, secularization, as measured by the civil-marriage rate, had begun to affect the behaviour of both church members and potential members. There is some evidence, indeed, that short-term fluctuations in the civil-marriage rate and church membership were now linked, probably for the first time. Thus, church membership, having fallen substantially during 1914-19, increased again to 1924 and, during these years of increased membership, the civil-marriage rate fell slightly in England and Wales and quite sharply in Scotland.

After 1940, the loyalty even of church members' children began to fall significantly and this development can perhaps be associated with a more rapid secularization of British culture. Furthermore, from 1940 onwards fluctuations in church membership seem to become quite closely connected with fluctuations in support for explicitly secularist organizations. Figure 5.1 shows that, over the twenty-five year period 1940-65, there was a very high negative correlation between membership of the major Protestant churches and membership of the Rationalist Press Association, the former decreasing when the latter increased, and vice versa. The disparity between the size of the Association's membership and that of the churches is far too great for the Association's expansion to be at all a significant cause of the churches' declension. But during this period the short-term increase of rationalists, and the short-term decrease of church members, do for the first time seem to arise from the operation of the same, or very closely connected, causes; and those causes would appear to consist, above all, in short-term changes in the level of secularization.

ECONOMIC FACTORS

Secularization affects all other exogenous determinants of church growth because the long-term result of cultural changes tending to reduce the appeal of church membership is to minimize the effect of all factors promoting growth and to maximize the effect of all factors inhibiting growth. Yet there are many other factors that would, quite apart from secularization, reduce church growth in the British Isles since 1700.

Because churches recruit from a more or less coherent constituency of potential members, rather than from the population as a whole, churches greatly rely upon the influences and sanctions of a community to induce people to get and keep church membership. Just as trade unions recruit large groups of workers rather than single employees, so churches recruit families rather than single individuals; and these families must regard church membership as an appropriate and desirable characteristic of their community. In the long run church growth would be

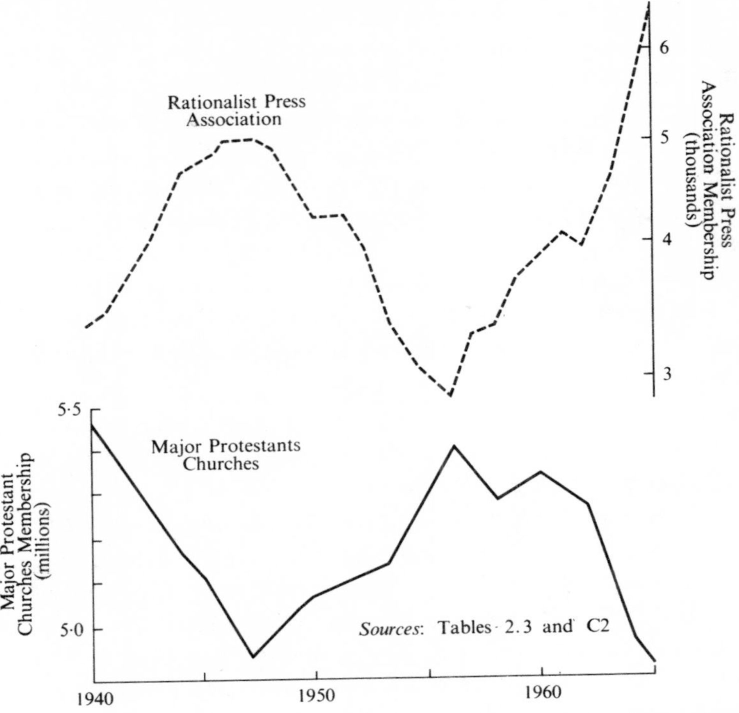

Fig. 5.1: Membership of the Major Protestant Churches in Great Britain and of the Rationalist Press Association at Annual Intervals, 1940-1965 (semi-log).

maximized in a small society, with very close internal ties, and few external connections, where the established authority system – whether it rested upon the squire, the employer or a dominant trade – required or expected all persons to belong to the church.

Within the British context, such communities have arisen especially in agriculture, mining, and fishing, because each of these economic activities tends to occur in isolated and cohesive settlements where habits and traditions, once established, die hard. Wherever squire and parson worked together, there – other things being equal – the Church of England would be strong; where miners or fishermen lived in districts remote from Anglican influence, Nonconformity would be strong. So, too, in certain types of small-scale manufacturing (particularly textiles), the influence of an employer, allied to the internal disciplines of the work force, could perhaps secure high attendance at church or chapel.

But industrialization opened these communities to wider influences and reduced their significance within the population as a whole. Both pre-industrial occupations, such as agriculture, mining, and fishing, and those manufacturing industries, such as textiles, that set the pattern for the earliest and most cohesive, but not the later and more diffuse, factory communities, dwindled as a proportion of the total labour force. Accurate long-term comparisons are almost impossible, given the deficiencies of the census of occupations, but the trend is plain. Males employed in agriculture, fishing, mining and quarrying, and textiles fell, between 1851 and 1871, from 43·8 to 34 per cent of the male labour force; between 1881 to 1911, from 30·9 to 25·8 per cent; and between 1921 and 1951, from 21·3 to 13 per cent. It is reasonable to argue therefore that, while at the beginning of the nineteenth century at least half the population was associated with those economic activities most conducive to organized religion, by the mid-twentieth century, only about a tenth of the population remained in this category.[6]

These occupational changes coincided with developments in the transport system which were at least of comparable significance for the churches. Up to 1800 there was relatively little movement of population between different communities by comparison with more recent periods; larger centres of population had little influence on smaller centres; and news and information travelled slowly. This situation changed drastically and permanently about 1840, that is, about the period in which the growth rates of the most rapidly expanding churches began to fall significantly. In 1838 the railways carried 5·4 million passengers, a number equal to 30 per cent of the British population; in 1850 they already carried 67·4 million passengers, a total equivalent to 327 per cent of population; and by 1900 the total had risen to 1145·5 million or 3121 per cent of population. In other words, the passengers carried on the railways represented in 1838 , 1850, and 1900 respectively, less than a third of, three, and thirty times the total population at these dates.[7]

The effects on church growth of changes in either employment or transport are not readily measurable; but the relationship between population density and church-membership density can be quantified relatively easily. At 30 June 1963, the Church of England diocese of Leicester, with 837 persons per square mile was the median Anglican diocese in terms of population density. In 1962 only two dioceses with a *higher* population density (Blackburn with 1338, and Guildford with 1409 persons per square mile) were among the fourteen dioceses where Easter Day communicants constituted more than 9 per cent of the population aged fifteen and over; and only two dioceses with a *lower* population density (Bradford with 695, and Ripon with 534 persons per square mile) were among the nineteen dioceses where Easter Day communicants constituted less than 7 per cent of the population aged fifteen and over. At one extreme, Easter Day communicants equalled 16 per cent of the over-fifteen population of Hereford, a diocese with 137 persons per square mile; while, at the other, Easter Day communicants equalled 3·6 per cent of the over-fifteen population of London, a

6. B. R. Mitchell and Phyllis Deane, *Abstract of British Historical Statistics*, Cambridge, 1971, pp. 60-1.
7. Ibid, pp. 225, 226.

diocese with 13 893 persons per square mile.[8]

Various measures of urbanization can be devised. In 1801, 1881, and 1951 respectively, the Greater London conurbation and seventy towns listed in the *Abstract of British Historical Statistics* contained 2·5, 12·6, and 22·4 million persons, or 24, 42, and 46 per cent of the total British population. The average population of these urban areas at these three dates was 35 000, 177 000, and 315 000. Much of the British pre-industrial urbanization is attributable to the growth of Greater London, which already had 1·1 million inhabitants by 1801. Only five other towns – Edinburgh, Liverpool, Glasgow, Manchester, and Birmingham – had over 70 000 inhabitants; and these towns, with an average population of 78 000 in 1801, must be accounted true urban areas relatively unfavourable to the churches. Here church membership density was always low. By 1881, a further twenty-seven towns also had populations of over 70 000. These towns had an average population of 32 000 in 1801, when they were still probably fairly homogeneous communities; but by 1881 their average population had risen to 133 000. And among these towns, the northern textile manufacturing centres, the industrial areas where the churches had had most success, grew as rapidly as any urban area: Blackburn, Bolton, Bradford, Halifax, Huddersfield, and Oldham having on average 12 000 inhabitants in 1801 and 109 000 in 1881. Here church membership density, high by urban standards early in the nineteenth century, fell fairly fast as 1900 approached.[9]

Finally, industrialization and urbanization have brought two major shifts of population, both of which have hindered church growth. If a line be drawn round the southern and central counties of England so as to exclude Devon and Cornwall, Wales and Monmouthshire, Shropshire, Staffordshire, Leicestershire, Rutland and Lincolnshire, and all English counties to the north, and Scotland, the region thus enclosed very largely represents the traditional heartland of English (and Anglican) power and prosperity. Early industrialization saw a shift of population away from this area, which fell between 1781 and 1841 from about 44 to 41 per cent of total British population; while later industrialization saw a shift back into this area, which rose between 1891 and 1951 from 41 to 45 per cent of total British population. In the first of these phases, the Church of England lost members and potential members by the movement of population out of the counties where it was strong and into the counties where it was weak; and in the second of these phases, the Nonconformist churches suffered through the reverse migration of population into the counties where Nonconformity had few resources.[10]

While the effects of the earlier population movement are not well documented,

8. Statistical Unit of the Central Board of Finance of the Church of England, *Facts and Figures about the Church of England*, 3, London, 1965, pp. 11, 58.

9. Mitchell and Deane, op. cit., pp. 19, 24-7

10. Ibid., pp. 5, 20-2; Phyllis Deane and W. A. Cole, *British Economic Growth, 1688-1959*, Cambridge, 1962, p. 103.

those of the latter movement are. Between 1891 and 1931 Wesleyan membership in the southern and central area rose from 27·16 to 31·29 per cent of total Wesleyan membership; and while, in 1931, 27·79 per cent of the total membership of the constituent churches of the Methodist Church resided in this area, by 1961 30·8 per cent of members of the Methodist Church did so. Such a movement wasted resources in the north and demanded new investment in the south, if migrant members were to be retained. During 1911-31 Wesleyan chapel accommodation rose over-all by 0·47 per cent, but in the south it increased by 3·74 per cent. Ultimately, a new suburban Methodism was created, in southern and central England, which has proved more successful, since 1945, than the older Methodism elsewhere; but during the late nineteenth and early twentieth centuries migration to the south put severe strains on the Methodists and other Nonconformists.[11]

Beside these long-term developments, there are certain short-term changes in church growth that seem to be associated with economic changes. Roughly speaking, there are two views of the influence of trade fluctuations on the churches. Those who hold what might be termed the 'soup kitchen' theory argue that, in times of economic difficulties, people (and especially city dwellers with small incomes) have attached themselves to churches in order to benefit from religious philanthropy. But it is possible to argue that church membership, like membership of any other association, involves both benefits and costs; and that, in times of economic difficulties, some church members and some potential church members will think the costs outweigh the benefits. If the 'soup kitchen' theory were correct, church growth and trade fluctuations would vary inversely, peaks in church growth tending to coincide with troughs in business activity, and *vice versa*. But if the cost-benefit explanation were correct, troughs in growth would tend to coincide with troughs in business activity.[12]

In practice, economic fluctuations have a rather diffuse influence on church growth. Sometimes this influence may be counterbalanced by other factors such as political developments; and even when this is not so, economic changes will be most readily felt by low-income groups traditionally underrepresented in the membership of most churches. Moreover, net change in church membership is quite largely shaped by the volume of new membership, and most new members are juveniles at least somewhat protected from economic vicissitudes by their parents. A clear pattern of economic influences is therefore not to be expected.

Nevertheless the evidence available suggests that economic difficulties *adversely* affect church growth because members wish to escape, and potential members wish to defer, the burdens of time and money arising from church membership.

11. Robert Currie, *Methodism Divided, A Study in the Sociology of Ecumenicalism*, London, 1968, pp. 104-9; Wesleyan Conference Office, *Returns of Accommodation . . .* London, 1932, pp. 126-7.
12. R. B. Walker, 'The Growth of Wesleyan Methodism in Victorian England and Wales', *Journal of Ecclesiastical History*, 1973, p. 270.

The number of Easter Day communicants of the Church of England for example, having risen every year in the boom conditions that immediately followed the First World War, fell 1·93 per cent in 1922 when unemployment reached 14·3 per cent. Though unemployment remained very high after 1922, it did decline slightly and the number of communicants rose, reaching a peak of 2 390 978 in 1927; but after 1927 unemployment again increased, and the number of communicants again fell, dropping to 2 279 713 by 1932, when 22·1 per cent of the labour force was out of work. Similar falls were experienced by the Nonconformist churches, Baptist, Congregationalist, and Primitive Methodist membership falling 2·35, 1·72, and 1·49 per cent respectively between 1927 and 1932.

During the nineteenth century, falls in Nonconformist membership frequently coincided with economic disturbances. The first recorded fall in Wesleyan membership occurred in 1799-1801, years when, amid considerable distress, wheat prices rose 73 per cent. Economic dislocation after the Napoleonic Wars also inhibited Wesleyan growth. Having increased by 18·31 per cent in 1813-16 Wesleyan membership increased only 2·21 per cent in 1816-19, and fell 2·39 per cent in 1820. This set-back accompanied trade depression and rapidly falling demand, wheat prices decreasing over 50 per cent and cotton prices 60 per cent during 1817-22, and coal and iron prices also reaching very low levels. Both in the 1830s and the 1840s, downturns in trade seem to have caused losses in Nonconformist membership. The Wesleyans decreased in number in 1837, 1842, and 1847; the Primitive Methodists in 1844-7; the Bible Christians in 1837 and 1842-7; and the General Baptists in 1847: years which saw falling prices, declining business activity, and high unemployment.[13]

The period 1876-89 provides particularly clear evidence on the relationship between economic fluctuations and church growth. During these years, the returns of trade unions that published the relevant data show that unemployment reached peaks of 11·4 and 10·2 per cent respectively in 1879 and 1886, but fell as low as 3·7, 2·3 and 2·1 per cent respectively in 1876, 1882, and 1889. Wesleyan membership increased 4·15, 3·39, and 1·24 per cent respectively, in these years of low unemployment, but decreased 0·86 and 0·19 per cent respectively in 1879 and 1886. It seems reasonable to conclude from this evidence that high unemployment has not stimulated recruitment among poor people hoping for economic assistance from the churches but, on the contrary, has weakened the churches' appeal to those who, in reduced circumstances, can no longer afford to go to church. Such circumstances, noted a Primitive Methodist historian, writing about the depression of the mid-1830s, rendered the people 'incapable of assisting the good cause', and had such 'a tendency to cast down the mind and damp the spirits of the people', that it became 'almost impossible to keep up' church work.[14]

13. Mitchell and Deane, op cit., pp. 479 ff.

14. Ibid., p. 64; W. J. Robson, *Silsden Primitive Methodism*, Silsden, 1910, pp. 83-4. We owe this reference to John Walsh.

POLITICAL FACTORS

A church is a group of individuals who have many links with the rest of the church-centred community from which new members tend to be drawn; and in modern times each church very largely belongs to a particular socio-cultural section of the total population. That section will probably have its own characteristic political views; and it is not least by an ability to associate with, and even express, those political views that a church maintains its congruity with its non-member constituency. To this extent, therefore, political factors exert a long-term influence over church growth comparable to the long-term influences of secular economic factors such as the occupational structure and geographical distribution of the population. In addition, just as fluctuations of trade affect church growth in the short run, so changes in the intensity and character of church members' and adherents' political activity and interests will also contribute toward the pattern of membership change.

This must be particularly – but not only – true during periods, such as that between the mid-nineteenth century and the First World War, when religious loyalties coincide with the loyalties of secular politics. Before this period, class and regional rather than partisan alignments had characterized religious groups. Almost all the upper class, whether Whig or Tory in politics, were members of the Church of England, and virtually no one within that class belonged to the Nonconformist churches – most but by no means all of whose members were Liberals. Moreover, while the Church of England enjoyed virtual hegemony in the agricultural areas of the south, it was very weak in northern industrial districts. By about 1850, however, the Nonconformists' allegiance to the Whig-Liberal coalition had become so strong and so uniform that many Church of England members felt powerful pressures to support the Conservative Party. As these pressures increased, a sharp partisan cleavage both in political and religious life produced highly homogeneous and mutually hostile Nonconformist-Liberal and Anglican-Conservative groupings, within each of which political developments came to have great significance for the fortunes of religious organization.

Probably the most widely known concept of the relationship between religious and political activity is that propounded by E. P. Thompson. Thompson argues that social activity is an 'oscillation' between the 'negative' (or religious) and the 'positive' (or political) poles of the social process. When political activity seems possible and fruitful, society, or a certain section of it, takes up politics; but when the limitations of political activity are seen, those that have been engaged in such activity (or those who think with them) take up religion. Thompson's argument is complicated by the assumptions that 'radical' political activity is purposive and good; and that, when those who pursue such activity are thwarted or defeated, they 'despair' – and may express their 'despair' in religious activity, which, since it does not achieve the radicals' political goals, is seen as purposeless and bad.[15]

The argument is not easy to substantiate. Moral judgements on social systems, activities, or institutions do not readily lend themselves to precise sociological analysis. Moreover, while some political crises, such as the collapse of the Balfour government in 1905, seem to have a rather close relationship with contemporary religious developments, others, such as the collapse of the MacDonald government in 1931, do not. In any event, if Thompson is correct in postulating an 'oscillation' between political and religious activity, the form of his argument presupposes a fairly clear chronological sequence, in which distinct and explicit political activity (such as a 'reform movement') first suffers a palpable set-back from the operation of some inimical development (for example, 'political oppression'), and distinct and explicit religious activity then significantly increases. In practice, however, religious and political activity quite often coincide or at least overlap in time; and when heightened religious activity *follows* political activity, the delay may be attributable simply to the time-lag inseparable from the effects of what is, after all, from the point of view of religious organization, an exogenous factor.

Among the cases with which Thompson deals are the radical Corresponding Societies, which were suppressed in 1793-4, and the passage of the First Reform Bill in 1832. Both events were associated with very high church growth: the Wesleyans increasing 13·52 per cent between 1793 and 1794, and 9·23 per cent between 1832 and 1833. If popular 'despair' at the government's attack on the Corresponding Societies, or working-class disillusionment at the limited nature of the extension of the franchise in 1832, had caused 'oscillation' to the 'negative pole' of religion, the Wesleyans might be expected to have enjoyed continued high growth after 1794 and after 1833, since a further occasion for 'oscillation' back to the 'positive pole' of politics did not occur for some time after those dates. Yet 1794 and 1832 proved to be peaks in Wesleyan growth, which fell to 2·83 per cent in 1797-8, and to –0·33 per cent in 1834-5.[16]

In view of these difficulties, it is assumed here that the effect of politics on church growth is to be explained by reference not to the ambitious arguments put forward by Thompson, but to the simpler model of 'mobilization', as loosely defined by J. P. Nettl. Nettl saw 'mobilization' as the process whereby, through creation of 'new referents', a 'commitment to action' is aroused in all or part of a population, which then engages in one or more types of activity in such a way that the actors' cohesiveness and self-consciousness as a group is significantly increased. 'Mobilization' in this sense can be a manifold process in which the 'new

15. E. P. Thompson, *The Making of the English Working Class,* London, 1963, pp. 388, 390-1.
16. See Table 2.4.

referents', through which attitudes are changed, suffice to stimulate differing kinds of organized activity, including organized religious activity. Hence, in certain circumstances, 'political mobilization' becomes 'religious mobilization' – or *vice versa*.[17]

Religious and political mobilization are most likely to come together when the organization for the one is linked with that for the other, and when the 'referents' generated during mobilization have both religious and political associations. In the miners' strike in Northumberland and Durham in 1844, for instance, 'A religious feeling was mixed up in a strange and striking way' with the colliers' union activity, a parliamentary report noted. Primitive Methodist 'local preachers . . . were . . . the chief promoters and abettors of the strike', and they 'made a religious question of it, to induce the men to . . . stand out.' At services in the Primitive Methodist chapels, 'Prayers were offered up for God's blessing and support during the strike, and that He would give them the victory'; and miners claimed 'that they attended their prayer meetings "to get their faith strengthened", *i.e.* to encourage each other in the confidence the strike would succeed.' The strike did not succeed; but such interactions of religious and secular activities did. Primitive Methodist membership increased more than 4 per cent per annum during these years; and much of this expansion must be due to the skill of the Primitive Methodist leaders in making 'a religious question' of what would now be regarded as non-religious issues.[18]

Where such skill was lacking, or could not be applied, religious organization would not enjoy the growth consequent upon a 'mobilization' which involved both political and religious matters, but might suffer the losses consequent upon what might be called, from a church standpoint, a purely secular 'counter-mobilization'. C. G. Finney remarked, in his *Lectures on Revivals of Religion,* that, 'in labouring to promote a revival', church leaders were sometimes confronted with an event that tended to 'counter-act' revival, 'something or other turning up to divert the public attention from religion, which baffles every effort'. Finney's comment might be applied, for example, to the experience of the Wesleyans in north-west England in 1820, a year when Wesleyan Methodist membership throughout Britain decreased 2·39 per cent. Much radicalism followed the Peterloo riot; and, in these circumstances, a Wesleyan wrote, 'politics, with many, are everything, and the cursed spirit of . . . opposition to Government leads them from God'.[19]

Religio-political mobilization may be identified as a factor in the rapid expansion of the communicant membership of the Church of England in the third

17. J. P. Nettl, *Political Mobilization, A Sociological Analysis of Methods and Concepts,* London, 1967, pp. 32-3.

18. 'The Report from the Select Committee on the Operation of the Act 5 and 6 VICT., c. 99, and on the State of the Mining Population in various parts of the Mining Districts', *Pp.,* 1846, I, pp. 8, 16.

19. Charles Grandison Finney, *Lectures on Revivals of Religion,* Cambridge, Mass., 1960, p. 33; W. R. Ward, *Religion and Society in England 1790-1850,* London, 1972, p. 91.

quarter of the nineteenth century. For most of the eighteenth and nineteenth centuries, Anglicanism grew more slowly than Nonconformity. According to the data presented in Table 2.2, it appears that, between 1800 and 1885, Episcopalians and Nonconformists increased at a mean rate of 1·11 and 2·37 per cent per annum respectively. But between 1885 and 1906, Church of England Easter Day communicants and the membership of the major Methodist churches increased at a mean rate of 1·74 and 0·87 per cent respectively. This change is partly attributable to increased Anglican emphasis on participation in the communion, though this emphasis can be interpreted precisely as 'mobilization' of Church of England supporters; but it must also be attributed to the almost uninterrupted run of Conservative governments between 1885 and 1906, and to the contemporary popularity of nationalist and imperialist ideas. During these years, the British Empire seemed to be victorious against heavy odds; within the Empire, Conservative England predominated over Liberal Wales and Scotland and Nationalist Ireland; and inside England the Conservatives were still successful against the growing challenge of urban radicalism and socialism. In these circumstances, Conservatives and Anglicans could scarcely fail to respond to calls to activity and vigilance.

The number of Easter Day communicants increased most rapidly during the Home Rule crisis of 1892 and 1893 when the House of Lords finally defeated Gladstone; but the active membership of the Church of England continued to grow rapidly up to the Boer War. Thereafter Anglican growth slackened, falling from a mean rate of 2·15 per cent per annum for the years 1885-1901 to 0·44 per cent per annum for the years 1901-6. This drop in growth rates can probably be attributed to the damage done to nationalists' and imperialists' confidence by the Boer War, to the unsettling effects of the Tariff Reform controversy within Conservative and Unionist ranks, and to the revival of Liberalism and Nonconformity. The fall of the Balfour government in 1905 and the Liberal landslide in the 1906 election coincide with the only two years between 1902 and 1939 when Easter Day communicants fell below 2 million, a decrease only partly due to changes in the method of measuring the number of communicants.

If political influences can be traced in the growth of the Church of England, they can be seen still more plainly in the growth of Nonconformity, which became very closely associated with politics almost from the onset of industrialization. Between 1828 and 1906 there are virtually no periods of high Wesleyan growth which are not associated in some way with political activity. A simple explanation of each such period is scarcely possible, given the multiplicity of political factors operative at any one time; but the recurrent coincidence of rapid Wesleyan expansion and political crises in which Nonconformists were more or less involved is so pronounced that it can hardly be attributed to chance.

The Reform Acts of 1832 and 1867 were immediately followed by sharp rises in Wesleyan growth rates; as were the Chartist movements of 1839 and 1848;

while the fall of Balfour and the Liberal landslide of 1906 marked the last great expansion of Nonconformity. So, too, the crisis caused by Catholic Emancipation in the late 1820s brought increases to the Wesleyans and probably to other Nonconformists also. The campaign against church rates which reached its height in 1858-9 and was finally successful in 1868, clearly assisted Wesleyan growth; as did the Disestablishment campaign of 1876, and the attacks on the allegedly pro-Anglican educational clauses of the Factory Bill of 1843, and on the Education Act of 1902. And there is much documentary evidence to show that other Nonconformists, who did not publish membership figures for most of this period, grew rapidly when the Wesleyans grew rapidly.

As religious and political structures became sufficiently formalized, and Nonconformist organization reached the necessary level of self-awareness and sophistication, such political crises gave rise to large scale and quite routinized mobilization of members and adherents, during which process church leaders used religious appeals to promote their political ends, and political appeals to increase their membership. When in 1843, Sir James Graham proposed to include in his Factory Bill clauses to establish schools, run by Anglicans only, and supported from rates, to give child workers three hours' education a day, including religious instruction, the Nonconformists raised enough petitions to kill the scheme. During this process, they made many adherents into members, the Wesleyans, the General Baptists, and the Primitive Methodists growing by 3·33, 8·2, and 10·71 per cent respectively between 1842 and 1844.[20]

Similar methods were used by the Nonconformists to secure both their own expansion and the abolition of church rates, that is, of rates levied to maintain the fabric of Church of England churches. The Liberation Society, a disestablishmentarian body, and other Nonconformist individuals and organizations raised 20 000 signatures when a bill to end compulsory church rates was unsuccessfully introduced in the House of Lords in 1858. When a new bill was introduced in 1860, petitions bearing 580 000 signatures were collected, and, during the Lords' debate on this bill, the Nonconformists sent Parliament 150 petitions a day. Although compulsory church rates were not abolished until 1868, through this very large-scale campaign, and by other means, the Nonconformists greatly increased their numbers, the Wesleyans and the Primitive Methodists raising their membership by 14·89 and 17·93 per cent respectively between 1857 and 1860.[21]

By the 1906 election (when the Primitive Methodists postponed their theological students' examinations to enable them to campaign for the Liberals), the religio-political methods developed in earlier years were at their most efficient. But since that date these methods have fallen into disuse. The Liberal Party

20. R. A. Soloway, *Prelates and People, Ecclesiastical Social Thought in England 1783-1852*, London, 1963.

21. W. H. Mackintosh, *Disestablishment and Liberation, The Movement for the Separation of the Anglican Church from State Control*, London, 1972, pp. 68-70.

collapsed in 1916-18, and politics were reconstructed on a virtually secular basis as a debate about economic redistribution conducted by Conservatives and the new Labour Party. The Nonconformists' allegiance to the Liberals began to disintegrate and, once this occurred, Anglican support for the Conservatives also declined. Butler and Stokes found that, while at least 60 per cent of Nonconformists were Liberals before the First World War, only 12 per cent were Liberals by the 1960s. Indeed, they concluded that, though 50 per cent of working-class Anglicans and only 19 per cent of working-class Nonconformists supported the Conservatives before 1914, by the 1960s 'no significant religious difference' was 'associated with the incidence of working class Conservatism'.[22]

Since 1960 'mobilization' appears to have been replaced as a factor in church growth by what may be called 'de-mobilization'. Most churches have suffered losses unprecedented in peacetime conditions. Between 1960 and 1968, Church of England Easter Day communicants decreased by 16·88 per cent; Baptist, Congregationalist, and Methodist membership by 12·2, 14·46 and 10·63 per cent respectively; and the Catholic adult conversions in England and Wales by 50·41 per cent. These losses accompanied a general and continuing disintegration of the party system in Britain which has given rise to the growth of nationalism and extremist organizations, to the revival of Liberalism, and to frequent changes of government. These political changes indicate the weakening of traditional positions and established authority, and the emergence of new commitments and convictions. The latter process has probably been obscured or modified by an increasing 'privatization' of individual and social activities; yet the formation of new structures far from compensates for the collapse of the old, since the new movements and new allegiances are quite weak by comparison with the old. The chief tendency of recent years is, then, a de-mobilization, in which the old 'referents' decreasingly evoke the 'commitment to action' hitherto expected by an established elite: and this over-all 'de-mobilization' is also to be found in the religious sphere where, despite emergence of new movements and new beliefs, the new is incommensurable – in purely quantitative terms – with the old.

Contemporary political changes can be attributed to various causes, but are so widespread that they cannot be due to *religious* changes which directly affect at most a fifth of the population. Current religious changes might, on the other hand, be affected by these political developments which, by analogy so to speak, cast doubt on established ecclesiastical authorities and symbols. It cannot be entirely coincidental, for example, that the peak of confidence in the post-war political system, and the post-war peak of church membership, both occurred in 1959. Since that date, just as traditional political loyalties have decayed, so church

22. David Butler and Donald Stokes, *Political Change in Britain, Forces Shaping Electoral Choice*, London, 1969, pp. 133-4.

members' loyalty to their organizations has declined; and that decline has been a major feature in the churches' recent experiences.

WAR

The twentieth-century Protestant church-membership curve presented in Table 2.4 and Figure 2.3 is dominated by the falls of 1913-17, 1939-47, and 1960-70. Two of these falls coincide with periods of war, which must be counted the most significant exogenous factor in church growth in Britain since 1900. The impact of war can be stated thus. According to the data presented in this Table and Figure, between 1900 and 1967 Protestant church membership fell 6 per cent throughout: but between 1913 and 1919 it feel 4 per cent, and between 1939 and 1947, 13 per cent. Both 1920 and 1948 saw church membership rising once more, yet much of the effect of war appears to be relatively short-term. During 1925-7, Protestant church membership increased at much the same rate as in 1911-13, while during 1956-60 it decreased at much the same rate as in 1927-39; and it would appear that by 1925 and 1956 respectively a great deal of the reaction to, and recovery from, war was complete, and that, from these dates onwards, a pre-war trend reasserted itself.

Of war's many influences upon organized religion, probably the most serious is its disruptive effect. Church growth is maximized in a church-centred community responsive to recruitment and free from other attractions. The world wars physically and psychologically disrupted such communities. In both wars, the United Kingdom engaged forces totalling nearly 6 million men and women, very largely concentrated in the age-group 18-45. Many women entered employment for the first time, and many men changed their employment and often their residence. And in the Second World War very many children were evacuated from their homes.

Contrary to received opinion, there is little evidence of a flight to the churches on the outbreak of war. In 1914-15 Easter Day communicants of the Church of England fell 1·03 per cent in number, and 'active' communicants of the Church of Scotland fell 2·5 per cent. There is no Church of England return available for 1940, but 'active' communicants of the Church of Scotland fell 6·82 per cent in number between 1939 and 1940. From the onset of war, recruitment fell in almost all churches; and this can most clearly be seen in the data for the Second World War. Between 1939 and 1941, those admitted to the Church of Scotland communicant roll for the first time fell from 2·65 to 1·98 per cent of the total number of communicants; and Methodist new members fell from 4·28 to 2·79 per cent of the membership roll. Because these falls represented decreases in allogenous growth, membership retention rose: those who terminated Church of Scotland communicant membership otherwise than by death or certificated transfer falling to a low point of 1·69 per cent, and those who 'ceased to be members' of the Methodist Church declining to 1·53 per cent, by 1944.

After 1941, churches began to recover from the first years of war. Armies had been recruited and were, in large part, based in Britain rather than abroad. The losses of church leaders that arose from military recruitment at the outset of hostilities were now made good. Recruitment rates therefore rose from 1942 onwards, and loss rates from 1945 onwards. The established churches, but probably not the Nonconformists, regained by the mid-'fifties much of the ground they had lost in the early 'forties. Confirmations and church membership, deferred, like marriages and births, during the war, rose sharply immediately after it and continued to rise for some years.

Yet, despite the post-war rise in recruitment, war seems to have shaken certain loyalties permanently. The percentage of the Church of Scotland communicant roll which participated in the communion at least once a year fell from 76·78 to 65·36 per cent in 1939-40, and thereafter continued to fall to a low point of 56·73 per cent in 1943. From 1943, communicants' participation rate slowly rose to 58·29 per cent in 1945, and jumped to 72 per cent in 1946. But 1946, which of course did not regain the level of 1939, proved to be a high point, since the participation rate did not exceed 70 per cent again until 1959, when it reached 71·36 per cent. After 1959, the Church of Scotland ceased publishing the number of those who communicated at least once a year, but it is very unlikely to have exceeded the 1959 total. Thus, very many Church of Scotland communicants ceased receiving the communion during the early years of the Second World War, returned to this practice especially in the atmosphere of the months immediately after the War, but thereafter reverted to their wartime habits. Whether this pattern occurred in the Church of England is unknown. But, though the number of Anglican confirmees was almost certainly smaller in 1939 than in 1960, there were in the former year 2 245 102 Easter Day communicants, and in the latter only 2 159 356: in other words, it seems probable that a smaller proportion of Anglican confirmees communicated in 1960 than in 1939.

From the Methodist evidence, the disturbance of existing customs and practices due to war seems to have affected the crucial mid-teens age-group more than any other. Methodist full members, Sunday-school pupils, and junior members decreased in number 1·28, 5·11, and 10·92 per cent respectively between 1939 and 1940, and 5·27, 28·42, and 37·53 per cent respectively between 1939 and 1943. The high losses in Sunday-school pupils and junior members are probably due, above all, to evacuation; and, from 1943 onwards, as conditions stabilized, the Sunday schools recovered in strength, increasing the number of their pupils 16·78 per cent between 1943 and 1952. That increase did not of course permit Methodist Sunday schools to equal their intake of 1939 in any post-war year:

and to this extent, the war broke pre-war customs of Sunday-school attendance. Yet junior membership fared still worse, *falling* by 31·44 per cent between 1943 and 1952. It would seem therefore that, though parents partly re-established Sunday-school attendance among their younger children after 1943, older children never regained ties with the church lost after 1939. In consequence, full membership also continued to fall after 1943, despite slight increases in 1949-50 and 1952-4.

If wartime disturbance of established religious practices did thus break certain habits of religious observance permanently, the effects of war would, to this extent at least, make themselves felt over the long-term. But the significance of the generation that grew up in the war years must diminish as the churches seek to recruit the generations born in the post-war years, and the effects of war must therefore decrease over time as other exogenous factors become more powerful.

VI
Conclusions

During the last three centuries an ever smaller number of inhabitants of the British Isles have been subjected to social, cultural, or legal pressure to adopt active membership of a church not of their choosing. In this geographical and historical context, therefore, churches have come to be voluntary associations whose members join and leave them at will. Associations of this type must confer upon their members real or apparent benefits commensurate with the cost of membership; and this is as much true of churches as, for example, of sports clubs, insurance societies, or trade unions.

Yet the benefits conferred by church membership depend, to a degree unusual among voluntary associations, upon factors *external* to the organization. Even the most characteristic activity of a church, the exercise of its primary, religious functions, depends upon the existence, favour, and efficacy of supernatural agencies other than itself. If these conditions do not, or cease to, obtain – or, indeed if church members and potential members think that they do not, or cease to, obtain – then membership must fall. Moreover, the churches' secondary or cultic, and tertiary or organizational, functions are little less dependent than their primary functions upon variables beyond their control. The appeal of a religious cult largely presumes the absence of secular opportunities for education and entertainment; the attractions of the church as a community rely very much upon the absence of satisfactory alternative social structures; and, since 1800, these deficiencies have generally been remedied by the development of new social and cultural forms, forms often based on new industrial techniques. From time to time, churches appear to wield power in the secular world, and such an appearance plainly favours church growth; yet the adventitious nature of such power was amply demonstrated at and after the Reformation, and has since been proved again by secular authorities' and secular organizations' successive withdrawals from the churches. Hence the great emphasis placed by Christian apologists – according to the audience being addressed – upon the tendency of church membership to make people happy, law-abiding, or rich.

The utility of church membership therefore appears problematical. It may in truth always be very great; but in many social and historical situations it will seem rather small. For this reason individuals will most easily accept the utility of church membership not when it is put to the test, or held up to close scrutiny, but when it is deemed to be self-evident. Such an assumption is most likely to be made by those whose parents, teachers, or friends are already church members, and whose personal relationships thus encourage them to think church membership an ordinary, desirable, or necessary element of their world and identity. In the British Isles during recent generations few individuals have joined a church with whose members they were not thoroughly acquainted in their everyday lives, and few churches have made significant gains outside the community or communities centred upon them.

A church-centred community may be formed in many ways. Sometimes an apparently random vicissitude of history leads to the building and filling of a church or chapel in a settlement geographically isolated from influences inimical to membership; and in these circumstances, the activities of a few individuals, and the spatial location of a small group of people, may suffice to explain church growth. More often, however, the establishment and expansion of a church is caused by complex social factors. In general, these factors have operated, at least since the Reformation, when objective social divisions have occurred in very large aggregates of individuals. Social and political power may be divided and contested between different sections; national differences especially of a cultural or linguistic character, may gain new significance; trades may arise which distinguish themselves from rival occupational groups or from society at large. In all such cases, the whole is divided into parts and the parts, being smaller, more homogeneous, and more prone to organized loyalties, can the more readily be recruited by the churches.

To recruit such groups or sections successfully a church must enjoy certain advantages. The church's basic claim to activate supernatural agencies on its members' behalf must seem credible to those it seeks to recruit, whatever the precise circumstances and motives of those recruited, for little can be done if such credibility is lacking. No other organization beside the church must be able to recruit the section as a whole without reference to special characteristics of individuals such as economic status, occupation, political convictions, or sex, because it is the ability to recruit a community *without discrimination* among its members, and without rivalry from any other body, that most readily identifies a church with a community. The church itself must be able to distribute through the population recruited a supply of buildings and professionals such that no member needs to travel more than about a mile to meet and worship with his fellow members. And above all, the church's professionals, part-time leaders and members must be culturally and socio-economically congruous with the population recruited.

Given these conditions, a church can maintain a *constituency* of individuals, linked to itself by various ties, who are or could become adherents to the church, and who, as such, could then be recruited to full membership. A church's appeal to its constituency is quite general in character – all men, regardless of qualification or distinction being eligible for membership; and, indeed, despite the special social or historical conditions which may be needed to bring a constituency into existence, the group or groups to which a church appeals are almost invariably a sample *biologically* representative of the total population. In other words, a church's growth is much less influenced than that of a more specialized organization (such as an occupational association) by sectoral or structural changes, and much more influenced by demographic changes, in the population.

In the long run, few churches' membership will grow faster than the total population, because few churches have a constituency whose fertility sufficiently exceeds, and whose mortality falls sufficiently short of, that of the total population to allow a permanently higher rate of growth. In any event, every church will suffer from wastage of its constituency, quite regardless of over-all fluctuations in the size of the constituency, as individuals migrate or become less convinced of the utility of membership, owing to changes either in attitudes or in life circumstances. Such wastage will of course inhibit growth and tend to press the expansion of churches farther behind the expansion of the total population. A church is therefore most likely to grow faster than population when its constituency is relatively very large, or is itself growing, whether through an increase in the attractions of church membership or through the operation of larger social forces tending to raise the number of persons disposed toward membership.

A church-centred community is, however, far from uniform. Some of its members will be too young for recruitment to full or communicant membership; and once they are old enough for membership they will rapidly pass those years in the middle teens in which most individuals take up membership. Most churches require a period of formal instruction before receiving persons as members and at any one time few adherents will have undergone such instruction. Responsiveness to recruitment varies markedly, not merely from time to time in one individual's life, but as between different persons and – according to the events of the day, both within the church-centred community and in the larger world – among the stock of recruitable individuals as a whole. Thus, even if a church's constituency could be quantified with perfect accuracy, the quality of that constituency as a group recruitable to church membership could not easily be determined.

Perhaps the crucial distinction within the church-centred community is that between families of church members and families of non-members. If one or both parents in a family are already members, the children in the family will be very strongly disposed to regard membership as an ordinary, desirable, or necessary element of their world and identity. Furthermore, once they have become members, pressures toward integration of the family will strongly encourage them to retain their membership. And, though the particular circumstances of non-members' families will obviously vary, those circumstances are highly unlikely so to stimulate the acquisition and retention of church membership.

If a church is to grow as fast as the population it must be able to recruit an expanding constituency; and if it is to grow at all, it must, given wastage, be able to recruit persons other than its own members' children. A church which can rely only on such *autogenous* growth — such recruitment from within 'church' families, so to speak — must decline, unless those families are increasing very much faster than the total population, simply because no church can expect to recruit *all* its members' children. To achieve a net increase of membership, however small, a church must be able to secure *allogenous* growth through recruitment outside 'church' families. Yet the more rapidly a church grows, the more it must recruit members who have little commitment to a membership which they receive little encouragement from their family and friends to retain. The shift from autogenous to allogenous growth, however necessary for expansion, will therefore bring a later contraction, as many of the new recruits leave.

Membership turnover is thus directly related to membership growth. Rapid expansion can be achieved only through allogenous growth, and such growth means a flow of individuals into and out of membership. But, provided high losses are associated with high gains, they should not be unacceptable to a church. For a substantial turnover of membership, beside indicating successful recruitment, has the effect of increasing the proportion of the population which has been educated into the churches' ways and concerns and is therefore able to spread that knowledge. To an expanding church each lost member is, therefore, not merely a potential restored member but a potential unpaid instructor preparing others for membership.

Of course churches do not expand at a uniform rate throughout their history, and they may well shrink in unfavourable conditions. Although various patterns can be seen in the fluctuations of church growth, two types of movement seem particularly significant, one lasting some decades, the other lasting about five or six years. The first of these can most clearly be seen in long-term variations in the *density* of church membership in the total population. A church newly formed will often increase its density rapidly over many years, then maintain a more or less constant density, and later lose ground until it becomes a relatively small, if fairly stable, fraction of the population; and this pattern may be repeated from time to time in the history of an older church.

Movements of this type arise to a great extent from quantitative and qualitative changes in a church's constituency. It can be argued that a church's very existence is the product of demand for it, however unconsciously and incoherently expressed, by a part of a population. Once formed, a church that is able to appeal to a large or expanding constituency will itself grow rapidly, and will, in particular, experience a high level of allogenous growth. The opportunities for such growth are unlikely to continue indefinitely; and almost all churches appear to move from the rapid expansion characteristic of this early, progressive phase to a marginal phase in which growth is very similar to the growth of the population. This tendency may be attributed to the narrowing of the church's appeal as it does acquire a membership and leadership, and that necessarily of a specific kind congruous only with a particular population; or simply to the slackening of an earlier historical impetus to expansion.

Sooner or later too, a church's constituency will decrease as exogenous factors which caused the social cleavage from which the church first benefited give way to new factors producing new cleavages. In these circumstances, membership density will fall as membership recedes. It is this recessive phase that is generally exemplified by the Nonconformist membership series, because most of these series do not begin until the very late nineteenth century; but similar movements can probably be traced in the history of the Church of England and Church of Scotland since the First World War. During such a phase allogenous growth rapidly diminishes and membership retention therefore rises; but in recent years churches' losses have risen, suggesting that, even when membership density falls to a residuum, the trend is still downward until some new factor may introduce a further progressive phase in part or all of the organization.

Major phases in a church's membership density take many years to complete; yet both membership and membership density fluctuate quite widely in the short-term. It appears that these short-term fluctuations about the trend are caused by the interaction between the attitudes and expectations of full- and part-time church leaders, members, and adherents on one hand, and the forces determining loss and recruitment rates on the other. Two such forces predominate. First, each new member gained is an adherent lost; and, since it seems to be easier to make members than to gain adherents, there is a time lag between making an adherent into a member and replacing him with a new adherent. Secondly, any increase in recruitment means acquisition of less committed members; and any decrease in recruitment generally means acquisition of more committed members. Thus, a rise in the recruitment rate reduces the possibility of further rises, while also raising the loss rate; and a fall in the recruitment rate reduces the possibility of further falls, while lowering the loss rate. At the end of a rise in recruitment, the pool of adherence is depleted; at the end of a fall in recruitment, the pool is replenished.

The results of different recruitment policies naturally influence church leaders, members, and adherents. Quite apart from any external influences, falling losses and a large pool of adherence will ultimately stimulate demands for higher recruitment, but rising losses and a small pool of adherence will ultimately reduce such demands. Some types of religious organization, notably the established churches, will be relatively unconscious of (though certainly more exempt from) the operations of this mechanism. Among churches more closely and more consciously involved in proselytizing, however, the cyclical element in church growth is readily identified as 'revivalism', and strong views and strong emotions are roused by events to some seemingly arbitrary and to others seemingly miraculous.

Typically, churches of this latter type manifest many spontaneous 'revivals' during the progressive phase of their history; but, as the progressive is succeeded by the marginal phase, revivals tend to be routinized by means of special recruiting campaigns often dominated by a well-publicized 'revivalist'. Such routinization is partly due to the bureaucratic development of the organization, partly to heightened anxieties about the church's future as allogenous growth begins to decline. But just as the cyclical fluctuations of membership growth, which are the substance of 'revivals', are usually beginning to decrease in frequency and amplitude when such routinization commences, so they continue to decrease to a point at which the returns from revivalist campaigns cease to be commensurate with the effort. Such campaigns are, therefore, virtually abandoned during the recessive and residual phases in a church's history.

In the long run, then, church growth is most assured among a section of the population to which church membership is a normal and acceptable part of life; and those sections are most often formed by a cleavage which defines separate or opposing cultural or socio-economic groups. This tendency may assist church growth in the short run also: for periods of high recruitment often arise from a further intensification of the section's self-consciousness through some crisis – and often some political crisis – in which it feels itself threatened by, or about to triumph over, its rivals.

Political crises are sometimes explicitly religious in character, but in Britain at least this is generally not so. Such crises are, therefore, exogenous factors which influence short-term changes in church growth, just as the formation of a constituency for church membership is itself a very long-term exogenous factor in growth. The significance of certain political crises for the churches is that they so mobilize a section of the population that its members' loyalty to their community can most readily be expressed in church membership. In these circumstances, even the most casual adherent of a church will become more responsive to the church's recruiting activity which is, in any event, likely to be increased at such times.

The continued secularization of British culture has restricted the churches' opportunities to profit from political crises. For the churches' fundamental problem during recent generations has been to demonstrate the utility of church membership; and the spread of secular attitudes and assumptions has made this problem ever less soluble. We have argued that, though secularization is a very long-term, gradual, and cumulative inhibition on church growth, different phases can be seen in the effects of secularization on the church. In the early and middle nineteenth century, secularization may have done no more than check growth which otherwise would have been higher. Later in the nineteenth century, and during much of the twentieth century, however, the secularist critique of churches and church membership appears to have reduced both recruitment and membership retention, so that churches, themselves now relatively highly secularized, have suffered substantial net losses of membership. And in recent years, the fortunes of the churches and of secularist associations are inversely related over short enough periods to suggest that church growth is now highly sensitive to slight fluctuations in attitudes toward secularist and religious claims.

The most striking effect of secularization, so far as churches are concerned, is simple disbelief in the supernatural. Plainly once such disbelief becomes widespread, individuals need unusual qualities to be sure of the utility of churches' religious functions. But churches do have other functions, and these may be perceived to have a utility more or less independent of that of strictly religious functions. A church might therefore attract many recruits even in a highly secularized atmosphere, were it not for a less dramatic but very important effect of secularization, namely the tendency of a population that does not accept the existence of the supernatural to lose interest in, and even knowledge of, the churches' ideas and concerns. Since new church members cannot be made of persons quite ignorant of a church and its teaching, the *preparation* of a secularized population for church membership becomes a very lengthy process.

In the eighteenth century, and in part of the nineteenth, churches could still directly recruit a population sufficiently educated in religious and Christian things to know at least the outlines of the Bible, the doctrines associated with Jesus, and the significance of the churches' concept of salvation. By 1800, however, the number of people so educated was rapidly decreasing; and the churches were obliged to turn from direct recruitment to a process of indirect recruitment, in which recruiting activity proper was preceded by a period of religious socialization designed to instruct those who underwent it in the practices, attitudes, and beliefs of the church. By lengthening the recruitment process, the churches necessarily lowered their rate of recruitment over time; while the system of religious socialization which they adopted (namely, the Sunday schools) ultimately proved unable either to command the support of an adequate proportion of the population or to bring enough of those instructed to an adequate responsiveness to recruitment. In recent years many Sunday schools have virtually collapsed, and there is no evidence that the churches have found a satisfactory means of reorganizing their methods of indirect recruitment.

The churches' recent difficulties arise not merely from the problems of recruiting members but also from the problems of retaining members once made. Membership termination may be said to arise from two sources. On the one hand, a church member is likely to surrender his membership if he ceases to believe in its utility, or if he regards the costs of membership as greater than the benefits. On the other hand, he is also likely to relinquish membership if he ceases to belong to the church-centred community in which membership was regarded as normal and acceptable. The clearest example of membership termination arising from a calculation of the costs and benefits of membership is that afforded by the tendency for church membership to decline during years of bad trade. Economic downturns are unlikely to affect the members' assessment of the existence of the supernatural, but they do leave members with less resources to meet the cost of membership.

But economic downturns are less dangerous to church growth than the manifold social and personal factors conducive to a dissolution of the church-centred community. As the special connection between migration and membership termination shows, individuals often leave churches at the same time as they leave their homes or the area in which they have long lived; and the effect on membership retention of a change in *personal* life-circumstances is similar to that of historical and social changes which tend to disturb the settled life of the section of the population into which any given individual may have been born. In the present century war has been the most noticeable cause of such disturbance; but greater geographical and occupational mobility, as well as the spread of further education must also be included among the influences making for the churches' increased losses: while these losses themselves, from whatever cause they may arise, produce further losses simply by depleting church-centred communities and increasing churchless communities.

Appendix

Abbreviations

Adherts	Adherents
Adult Convsns	Adult Conversions
BCs	Bible Christians
BHA	British Humanist Association
Ches	Churches
Ches of Christ	Churches of Christ
Ch of the Nazarene	Church of the Nazarene
Chpls	Chapels
Chrstn Science	Christian Science
C of E	Church of England
C of I	Church of Ireland
C of S	Church of Scotland
Commcts	Communicants
Ep C in S	Episcopal Church in Scotland
Free C of S	Free Church of Scotland
GBNC	General Baptist New Connexion
Latter Day Saints	Church of Jesus Christ of Latter Day Saints
Lay Ps	Lay Preachers
LPs	Local Preachers
MC	Methodist Church
Mems	Members
Mins	Ministers
MNC	Methodist New Connexion
New Ch	New Church
Orig Sec C of S	Original Secession Church of Scotland
Other Denoms	Other Denominations
PMC	Primitive Methodist Church

Pres C of E	Presbyterian Church of England
Pres C in I	Presbyterian Church in Ireland
Pres C of W	Presbyterian Church of Wales
Ref Pres C of I	Reformed Presbyterian Church of Ireland
Ref Pres C of S	Reformed Presbyterian Church of Scotland
Reg Clergy	Regular Clergy
Relig Soc of Friends	Religious Society of Friends
RPA	Rationalist Press Association
Salv Army	Salvation Army
Sec Clergy	Secular Clergy
Sun Sch Scholars	Sunday School Scholars
UF C of S	United Free Church of Scotland
UMC	United Methodist Church
UMFCs	United Methodist Free Churches
Unitns	Unitarians
UP C of S	United Presbyterian Church of Scotland
WMA	Wesleyan Methodist Association
WMC	Wesleyan Methodist Church

A1 EPISCOPALIAN COMMUNICANTS AND MEMBERS

	Church of England		*Church in Wales*	*Episcopal Church in Scotland*	
	Easter Day Communicants[1]	Electoral Rolls[3]	Communicants[4]	Communicants[5]	Permanent Members[6]
1877					56 200
1878					58 904
1879					63 963
1880					68 653
1881					70 847
1882					66 819
1883				25 460	71 656
1884				28 628	76 939
1885	1 384 000		86 087	29 744	80 073
1886				31 559	81 091
1887				31 356	84 782
1888				31 762	82 932
1889				33 694	86 668
1890				34 459	87 441
1891	1 490 000		111 249	35 593	91 740
1892	1 582 000		118 595	36 800	94 257
1893	1 650 000		122 521	37 714	96 251
1894	1 705 000		126 344	39 664	99 971
1895	1 746 000		131 107	40 805	103 291
1896	1 793 000		130 613	42 135	106 304
1897	1 824 000		134 477	43 335	109 130
1898	1 845 000		134 569	44 805	113 036
1899	1 875 000		137 005	45 571	114 315
1900	1 902 000		141 008	46 181	116 296
1901	1 945 000		144 319	46 922	
1902	2 012 000		151 794	47 821	119 391
1903	2 037 -00		152 583	47 929	124 081
1904	2 084 000		160 191	48 468	
1905	1 939 000[2]		125 234[2]	49 117	131 232
1906	1 988 000		138 964	50 499	133 122
1907	2 023 000		138 782	51 289	136 263
1908	2 108 000		144 411	50 949	139 816
1909	2 158 000		146 407	52 029	140 249
1910	2 212 000		152 654	53 246	141 732
1911	2 293 000		159 252	54 751	142 464
1912	2 195 000		155 191	55 095	142 909
1913	2 304 000		164 601	55 383	142 871
1914	2 226 000		155 532	55 756	146 073
1915	2 203 000		157 069	55 597	144 159
1916	2 097 000		148 455	55 722	144 853
1917	2 095 000		145 718	56 034	146 053
1918	2 122 000		152 286	55 778	142 911
1919	2 153 000		159 316	56 212	144 867
1920	2 171 619		159 957	56 979	144 489
1921	2 213 620		157 614	59 246	147 518
1922	2 170 880		157 457	59 623	145 349
1923	2 290 662		166 715	59 349	145 687
1924	2 315 495	3 537 020	171 626	59 719	145 141
1925	2 388 419	3 601 782	176 271	60 286	144 670

Table A1: Continued

	Church of England		*Church in Wales*	*Episcopal Church in Scotland*	
	Easter Day Communicants[1]	Electoral Rolls[3]	Communicants[4]	Communicants[6]	Permanent Members[6]
1926	2 372 610	3 620 881	184 568	60 495	142 605
1927	2 390 978	3 636 422	187 178	59 657	138 833
1928	2 339 283	3 641 536	183 179	59 731	138 515
1929	2 304 482	3 627 104	187 534	59 325	135 579
1930	2 261 857	3 655 630	184 604	59 538	134 066
1931	2 288 076	3 648 729	185 484	59 977	133 752
1932	2 279 713	3 652 424	185 045	60 797	134 619
1933	2 328 436	3 634 480	194 225	61 821	132 753
1934	2 319 093	3 568 273	196 736	61 456	130 891
1935	2 299 573	3 598 522	195 744	61 151	130 028
1936	2 241 825	3 559 926	195 494	60 333	127 151
1937	2 225 880	3 507 760	194 084	62 059	129 771
1938	2 249 718	3 463 668	196 389	62 375	128 322
1939	2 245 102	3 390 125		61 486	124 936
1940	1 997 820	3 388 859		61 583	124 498
1941				59 130	119 508
1942				58 600	117 270
1943				57 113	115 668
1944				57 071	114 559
1945				55 597	110 673
1946				55 471	108 558
1947	1 728 940	2 989 704		55 270	108 844
1948				56 070	110 284
1949				56 572	110 802
1950	1 847 998	2 958 840		56 382	108 502
1951				56 121	103 598
1952				56 298	105 791
1953	1 941 000	2 922 627		54 382	106 112
1954				55 601	107 342
1955				56 528	108 127
1956	2 167 503	2 894 710	176 723[5]	56 132	106 069
1957		2 944 222		55 764	108 241
1958	2 073 369			55 957	107 344
1959		2 887 671		56 027	101 500
1960	2 159 356	2 861 887	182 369[5]	56 725	97 038
1961				56 460	97 508
1962	2 158 521	2 793 191		56 759	97 894
1963				55 576	98 029
1964	1 957 452	2 739 023		55 070	96 950
1965			168 900[5]	54 584	97 175
1966	1 899 469	2 682 181		53 585	94 476
1967				52 959	94 364
1968	1 794 817	2 636 412	154 500	51 919	94 332
1969				50 967	90 066
1970	1 631 506	2 558 966	123 925[5]	48 967	85 816

NOTES AND SOURCES

1. Statistics for 1885 and 1891-1919 are taken from the Statistical Unit of the Central Board of Finance of the Church of England, *Facts and Figures about the Church of England,* 1962. Because the early returns published in the *Church of England Yearbook* were incomplete, the Statistical Unit adjusted each year's figures. The population of the parishes containing the churches for which no returns were received was related to the population of the parishes containing churches for which returns were received, and the ratio between the two, diocese by diocese, was used to estimate the missing information. Statistics for the four dioceses which later constituted the Church in Wales were excluded in order to enable comparisons between pre- and post-1920 figures.

Since 1920, the number of non-returning congregations has been very small (less than 0·1 per cent of the total), and post-1920 statistics have therefore been drawn directly from the *Church of England Yearbook,* with the exception of the figure for 1953. The *Yearbook* for that year gives only the total number of Easter Day plus Easter Week Communicants, and the estimate published in *Facts and Figures* has been used instead.

From 1922 onwards the *Church of England Yearbook* has published figures for the number of 'Easter' communicants: that is, for those who receive the sacrament on Easter Day and during Easter week. This series, which is reprinted in *Facts and Figures,* involves a certain element of double counting, since many persons receive the sacrament more than once during Easter week. The number of Easter week communicants was 2 317 000 in 1922; 2 416 000 in 1939; and 2 347 000 in 1962.

2. The sharp decline in the number of communicants between 1904 and 1905 may be partly due to a discontinuity in the series caused by revision of the Form of Inquiry on which the returns were made. In 1905 and subsequent years, the figures represent only the number of those actually communicating on Easter Day. In previous years an estimated total had been given, since the earlier inquiry form allowed clergymen to provide an approximate figure. The "uncorrected" returns for England and Wales published in the *Yearbook* are: 2 223 207 communicants in 1904 and 2 053 455 in 1905, an over-all decline of 7·6 per cent. But since the decline was proportionately much greater in Wales (6·9 per cent in England, 21·9 per cent in Wales), the fall in the number of communicants in Wales may be partly due to the effects of the Welsh Revival.

3. The *Church of England Yearbook* first included electoral-roll figures in 1924. The figures show the number of electors on the electoral rolls of all Dioceses (except Sodor and Man) as certified to the various Diocesan Secretaries in 1924, and at the revisions of the rolls in 1929, 1934, 1939, 1949, 1954, 1959, 1964, and 1969. The figures recorded for the intervening years are based on incumbents' annual statistical returns. Lay members of the Church of England of either sex, aged seventeen or over, who are baptized and are resident in the parish or, if not resident, have habitually attended public worship in the parish during a period of six months prior to enrolment, are entitled to have their names entered on the roll of the parish.

4. The Church in Wales was disestablished by an Act of Parliament of 1914, which came into force on 31 March 1920, when four dioceses were separated from the province of Canterbury. There are now six dioceses in the Church in Wales, Monmouth having been formed in 1921, and Swansea and Brecon in 1923.

Figures for 1885 and 1891-1938 are taken from the *Church of England Yearbook.* Some adjustment has been made for non-reporting congregations in the years 1885-98: there were 129 in 1885, 10 in 1898, 5 in 1899, and one or less from 1905 onwards. Non-reporting congregations have been assumed to have the average number of communicants per reporting congregation.

5. In recent years the Church in Wales has published few aggregate statistics. The diocesan *Directories* and *Calendars* of the Church of Wales contain parochial returns of Easter communicants which have been summed for 1956, 1960, 1965, and 1970. In the absence of returns for Swansea and Brecon, it has been assumed that communicants in these dioceses constitute the same proportion of total Church in Wales communicants as they did in 1936-8, for which returns are available. The 1971-2 *Church of England Yearbook* gave an estimate of the number

of Church in Wales communicants; and it has been assumed that this, like other statistics in the same *Yearbook*, relates to 1968.

6. Statistics of members and communicants of the Episcopal Church in Scotland are from *The Episcopal Church in Scotland: Annual Report of the Representative Church Council*, except those for 1901 and 1904, which are taken from the *Scottish Episcopal Church Yearbook and Directory*. Church statistics are revised by the Synod Clerk and sometimes marginally altered before publication in the *Annual Report;* and some recent decreases apparently derive from the Synod Clerk's alterations. Both series relate to the twelve months ending 31 December of the year cited.

The *Scottish Ecclesiastical Journal* for December 1856 and June 1857 estimates that there were 38 113 members and 14 234 communicants in 1855 and about 12 000 in 1792.

A2 PRESBYTERIAN COMMUNICANTS

	Church of Scotland		*Free C of S*[6]		*UP C of S*[9]	*UF C of S*[10]	*Ref Pres C of S*[11]	*Orig Sec C of S*[12]	*Pres C of E*[13]	*Pres C in I*[14]		*Ref Pres C of I*[15]
	Number on Roll	Active Commcts	Commcts	Members/ Adherts	Commcts	Commcts	Commcts	Commcts	Commcts	Commcts	Active Commcts	Commcts
1840	367 000[2]								10 000	185 000		
1844	252 000[3]		127 000[3]									
1856			188 707[a]		142 956		5866					
1857					141 422		5642					
1858				234 953[f]	146 386							
1859					150 011							
1860					150 969				27 000			
1861					154 037							
1862					154 106		5981					
1863				245 210[f]	154 676		6729					
1864					155 041		6208			122 790		
1865					156 450		6338					4500
1866					158 220		6535			126 000		
1867				249 351[g]	159 457		6609					
1868	˙422 357[4]			250 499[h]	160 491		6516					
1869					160 823					126 858		
1870					161 791		6609		38 000	123 441		4628
1871	436 147			253 830[h]	163 030		6729	3100		115 495		
1872					163 553		6969			111 889		
1873	460 464		226 000[b]	258 996[h]	164 279		6940	3200		110 393		
1874					167 290		7134			109 395		
1875					170 298					109 336		5033
1876	483 537				172 170				46 540	108 264		
1877					173 554				50 739	107 262		
1878	515 786		238 000[b]		175 066				54 135	106 110		
1879				308 337[i]	174 134		1197	5450	54 487	106 776		
1880					173 982				55 286	104 769		4802
1881	528 475		248 200[c]	312 160[i]	174 557				56 399	103 548		
1882	530 292			315 244[i]	176 299		1120	5500	57 402	102 825		
1883	543 969		259 350[c]	322 926[j]	178 195				58 423	102 340		
1884	555 622			324 920[j]	179 891				59 690	101 403		
1885	564 435	359 857		330 464[j]	181 146				61 021	102 241		4633

Table A2: Continued

	Church of Scotland		*Free C of S*[6]		*UP C of S*[9]	*UF C of S*[10]	*Ref Pres C of S*[11]	*Orig Sec C of S*[12]	*Pres C of E*[13]	*Pres C in I*[14]		*Ref Pres C of I*[15]
	Number on Roll	Active Commcts	Commcts	Members/ Adherts	Commcts	Commcts	Commcts	Commcts	Commcts	Commcts	Active Commcts	Commcts
1886	571 029	361 260		331 242[j]	182 063				61 781	102 027		
1887	579 002	343 468	263 113[d]	333 098[j]	182 170		1171	5000	62 566	102 057		
1888	581 568	422 393		336 335[j]	182 963				64 024	103 499		
1889	587 954	435 617		338 978[k]	184 354				65 019	103 415		
1890	593 393	437 772		340 953[j]	184 820		1185	3617	65 941	102 678		4176
1891	599 531	438 260	271 981[d]	337 331[i]	185 298				66 774	102 735		
1892	604 984	440 788		338 274[17]	187 075				66 971	102 175		
1893	612 411	450 498			188 706				67 585	102 710		
1894	620 376	457 356	279 639[e]	344 273[k]	190 950		1176	3837	68 997	104 578		
1895	626 771	463 048	283 659[e]	393 113[m]	191 881				69 632	104 769		4085
1896	633 408	474 650	287 689[e]	398 050[m]	194 463			3797	70 639	104 838		
1897	641 803	476 192	290 789[e]	402 135[m]	195 631		1040	3769	71 444	106 104		
1898	648 476	476 081	293 684[e]	404 828[m]	197 476				73 249	106 602		
1899	656 112	477 128	296 085[e]	407 626[m]	199 089				75 541	106 424		
1900	661 629	474 929	4008[8]			492 964			76 071	106 630		3709
1901	668 335	486 892				495 259			78 087	106 070		
1902	674 293	491 308				498 476	1040	3611	79 620	106 121		
1903	678 821	497 608				501 835			81 555	106 053		
1904	686 698	499 526				503 301			83 113	106 665	68 668	
1905	692 914	504 123	6429			504 853			85 215	106 366	70 177	3894
1906	698 566	508 395				505 774			85 755	106 342	69 083	
1907	702 075	512 248				506 088	1020	3000	85 774	106 516	68 212	
1908	706 653	509 711				506 573			86 421	105 982	68 590	
1909	711 211	512 264				507 408			86 808	106 472	68 441	
1910	714 039	513 758				506 693			86 828	106 481	68 422	3973
1911	714 915	504 495	8000			504 672	1000	3424	86 848	105 962	68 296	
1912	713 849	507 722				504 901			86 783	105 118	66 475	
1913	713 782	507 167				507 075			87 667	104 849	67 063	
1914	718 719	508 653				512 003			88 166	104 569	66 638	
1915	721 137	495 932				516 075			87 424	104 077	66 378	3649

Table A2: Continued

	Church of Scotland		*Free C of S*[6]		*UP C of S*[9]	*UF C of S*[10]	*Ref Pres C of S*[11]	*Orig Sec C of S*[12]	*Pres C of E*[13]	*Pres C in I*[14]		*Ref Pres C of I*[15]
	Number on Roll	Active Commcts	Commcts	Members/ Adherts	Commcts	Commcts	Commcts	Commcts	Commcts	Commcts	Active Commcts	Commcts
1916	721 158	474 261				518 747			86 525	104 306	65 877	
1917	722 246	463 945				522 028			86 078	103 760	64 185	
1918	722 750	455 224				523 808			85 551	104 194	65 679	
1919	728 239	489 537	8192			528 084	930	3561	84 232	104 033	65 102	
1920	739 251	509 541				529 680			83 710	104 778	65 854	3619
1921	745 783	517 361				531 849			84 375	105 462	65 286	
1922	751 870	529 504				534 232			84 462	106 483	66 224	
1923	756 167	535 811	8500			534 210	930	3142	84 638	108 636	69 705	
1924	760 173	540 497				534 950			85 054	109 578	69 197	
1925	762 774	549 012				536 407			85 109	109 224	68 853	3440
1926	761 946	527 142				536 409			84 729	109 748	68 411	
1927	759 797	542 930				536 380	850	3022	84 764	110 161	68 485	
1928	759 625	541 489				538 192			84 598	109 274	67 050	
1929	1 284 449[5]					13 791			83 989	109 370	67 220	
1930	1 271 095					16 577			84 146	108 986	67 835	3461
1931	1 280 620					18 531	800	2905	84 298	110 330	68 390	
1932	1 287 438	892 300				19 440			83 413	111 760	78 179[14]	
1933	1 289 145	919 248				20 016			82 724	112 700	79 347	
1934	1 290 271	928 053				21 142			82 453	113 658	79 992	
1935	1 288 648	919 313	5542			21 826	790	2753	81 715	113 811	80 013	3535
1936	1 288 571	906 901				22 497			80 420	113 697	80 684	
1937	1 280 620	902 831				22 827			79 902	114 581	81 397	
1938	1 286 519	923 563				23 066			79 642	115 304	82 345	
1939	1 285 011	896 610				23 328			78 359	116 822	83 472	
1940	1 278 297	835 432				23 574			76 815	118 203	83 090	3469
1941	1 268 839	752 357				23 375			74 575	117 402	79 562	
1942	1 261 890	728 958				23 256			71 280	116 407	78 447	
1943	1 262 678	716 341				23 448			69 510	117 348	78 992	
1944	1 264 125	730 516				23 541			68 747	118 126	79 247	
1945	1 259 927	734 405				23 863			67 563	118 606	80 918	3496
1946	1 261 646	908 414				24 164			67 236	119 582	82 464	
1947	1 256 167					24 338	800	1953	66 998	121 126	82 048	
1948	1 263 423	841 068				24 606			70 297	121 989	85 675	
1949	1 268 315	848 085				24 440			70 774	123 989	85 066	
1950	1 271 247	863 174				24 556			69 676	125 775	86 066	3322

Table A2: Continued

	Church of Scotland		Free C of S[6]		UP C of S[9]	UF C of S[10]	Ref Pres C of S[11]	Orig Sec C of S[12]	Pres C of E[13]	Pres C in I[14]		Ref Pres C of I[15]
	Number on Roll	Active Commcts	Commcts	Members/ Adherts	Commcts	Commcts	Commcts	Commcts	Commcts	Commcts	Active Commcts	Commcts
1951	1 273 027	864 480				24 528			68 562	126 902	86 822	
1952	1 278 468	889 042				24 588			68 867	128 041	86 467	
1953	1 283 305	894 985				24 618	600	1813	68 599	129 229	90 273	
1954	1 292 127	901 361				24 688			69 513	130 461	91 250	
1955	1 307 573	917 848				24 856			69 651	133 422	93 842	3389
1956	1 319 574	914 031				24 783			70 567	134 446	96 253	
1957	1 315 630	908 464	5909			24 039			70 940	135 685	95 986	
1958	1 315 466	878 430				24 021			70 940	136 432	96 473	
1959	1 306 661	932 456				23 482	617		71 039	137 701	97 694	
1960	1 301 280					23 157	589		71 329	136 554	99 084	3327
1961	1 290 617					22 815	575		71 100	138 596	99 909	
1962	1 281 559					22 780	548		70 298	140 395	100 794	
1963	1 268 887					21 779			69 852	141 238	101 380	
1964	1 259 162					21 355			68 937	142 182	103 050	
1965	1 247 972					20 710			67 619	143 559	102 734	3314
1966	1 233 808					20 396			66 187	144 284	103 182	
1967	1 222 023					19 752			65 066	144 156	102 767	
1968	1 201 833					18 834			63 091	142 768	101 020	
1969	1 178 334					17 812			61 187	142 498	99 912	
1970	1 154 211		5726			17 248	548		59 473	141 072	98 504	3250

NOTES AND SOURCES

1. Unless otherwise stated, the source for Church of Scotland data is the *Yearbook of the Church of Scotland.* Both the number on the communicant rolls, and the number of 'active' or practising communicants (that is, of Church members who communicated at least once during the year) are given.

2. This estimate is based on the assumption that, before the Disruption, Church of Scotland communicants did not number more than 14 per cent of the total population. See Alexander Hugh Bruce (Lord Balfour of Burleigh), *An Historical Account of the Rise and Development of Presbyterianism in Scotland,* Cambridge, 1911, p. 158.

3. The 'Disruption' took place in May 1843. Between 451 and 474 ministers left the Church of Scotland, and it has been estimated that the church lost nearly 38 per cent of its members to the new Free Church of Scotland. (W.L. Mathieson, *Church and Reform in Scotland: a History from 1797-1843,* Glasgow, 1916, p. 371). The 1844 estimate assumes that the two bodies still had between them approximately 14 per cent of the total population as Communicant Members.

4. The 'Report to the General Assembly of the Committee on Statistics', in *Church of Scotland Assembly Papers,* states that there were 269 955 communicants on the rolls of 715 (out of 1254) congregations: the estimate given assumes non-returning congregations to have three-quarters of the average number of communicants. The same source reports 259 861 communicants on the rolls of 717 (out of 1250) congregations in 1867.

5. From 1929 the figures include that part of the United Free Church of Scotland which amalgamated with the Church of Scotland.

6. Variations in the method of calculating Gaelic adherents and the defective nature of the returns inhibit any attempt to construct a consistent series of Free Church membership figures. Since a large proportion of those attached to the Free Church were not communicants, it was usual for nineteenth-century Free Church statisticians to estimate 'members and Gaelic adherents'. But the proportion and ages of 'adherents' included in the official lists published were frequently altered, and it is difficult to draw any comparisons between the returns. The best available statistics are included here, with notes on the various sources and the different means of calculating adherents. Estimates of communicant membership are also given, but these are only reliable from 1894 to 1900. The sources are as follows:

a) *Free Church of Scotland General Assembly,* 1858: 'Abstract showing for the year 1855 the number of Communicants and sitters in the several classes of Congregations. . . .' The total number of 'sitters' is given as 303 007; but it is difficult to know what proportion of this total would have been classified as 'members and adherents'.

b) Lowland communicants (215 136 in 1873 and 225 040 in 1878, according to *The Facts about the Scottish Kirks* [1887] have been added to one-sixth of the estimated *total* number of Highland 'members and sitters', a ratio commonly used by the Church statisticians of the period.

c) *Free Church of Scotland Proceedings and Debates,* 'Report of Committee on Statistics' for 1897 and 1898. The reports do not explain the basis of these estimates but imply that they are comparable with later returns of communicant membership. R. Howie, *The Churches and Churchless in Scotland: Facts and Figures,* Glasgow, 1893, p. 115, gives an estimate of 239 712 communicant members in 1881.

d) Estimates of 'membership alone' supplied by Howie, op.cit., pp. 115-16. The 1887 figure was drawn from J. Rankin's *Handbook of the Church of Scotland,* Edinburgh, 1888; the 1891 figure was compiled by Howie 'directly from the schedules put into his hands'.

e) *Proceedings and Debates:* total members on the roll at 31 December of each year.

f) *Proceedings and Debates:* three-quarters of the 'ordinary Sabbath attendance' in the Highlands and Islands has been included.

g) Howie, op.cit.: the estimate includes two-thirds of the reported average Sabbath attendance of Gaelic congregations.

h) Howie, op.cit.: the estimates include two-thirds of the adherents of Gaelic congregations aged 14 and over.

i) Howie, op.cit.: the estimates include all the adherents aged 18 and over in a certain number of Gaelic-speaking congregations.

j) These figures appear to constitute a consistent series: those for 1884-8 are drawn from the *Original Secession Magazine;* other years are from Howie, op.cit., whose estimates include all adherents aged 18 and over in a certain number of Gaelic-speaking congregations and about 6000 Gaelic adherents aged 18 and over in twenty-six additional Gaelic congregations, chiefly in Lowland presbyteries. Where they overlap, Howie's series and that published in the *Original Secession Magazine* closely coincide.

k) *Report of Proceedings of the General Presbyterian Council,* 1892 and 1896. The figures appear to be consistent with (j).

l) *Proceedings and Debates:* a simple aggregation of the figures for each presbytery, as given in the official lists. Since no correction has been made for non-reporting congregations, this is probably an under-estimate.

m) *Proceedings and Debates*: presumably higher than earlier estimates because all members and adherents aged 18 and over have been included.

7. The Free Presbyterian Church of Scotland separated from the Free Church in 1892. No official statistics are published, but the following estimates have been supplied by the Revd. R. Sinclair, Free Presbyterian Manse, Wick:

	Full Communicants	Members and Adherents
1893		9500
1930	1180	7000
1951	650	4750
1959		4650
1971		5000

8. The majority of the Free Church joined with the United Presbyterian Church of Scotland to form the United Free Church of Scotland in 1900. About twenty or thirty ministers and a considerable body of members, chiefly in the Highlands, refused to enter the Union, formed themselves into a separate ecclesiastical community, and retained the name 'Free Church'. The Free Church continuance does not publish official membership statistics; the estimates included here are drawn mainly from the *Report of Proceedings of the General Presbyterian Council.* In addition figures have been taken, for 1900, from *Proceedings and Debates;* for1905 from *United Free Church of Scotland: Reports to the General Assembly;* for 1957, from John Highet, *The Scottish Churches,* London, 1960; and for 1970, from 'Free Church of Scotland, Synopsis of Statistical Schedule, 1971'. Estimates of 'members and adherents' range from 60 000 in 1905 to 25 000 in 1970 when the total number actually returned was 22 493.

9. All statistics are published in *Proceedings of the Synod of the United Presbyterian Church.* The United Presbyterian Church was formed in 1847 by the union of the United Secession Church with the Relief Church of 1761. Figures given are for Scotland only: they do *not* include the English congregations which withdrew from membership in 1876 to form the Presbyterian Church of England. (See note 13.)

10. The United Free Church of Scotland was formed by the union of the majority of the Free Church with the United Presbyterian Church. Statistics for 1900-28 are taken from *United Free Church of Scotland: Reports to the General Assembly.* In 1929, the majority of the United Free Church rejoined the Church of Scotland. A minority continued in separate existence: statistics for this 'continuance' are published in the *Handbook of the United Free Church of Scotland.* Both series relate to the twelve months ending 31 December of the year cited.

11. The Reformed Presbyterian Church claims continuity with those Societies of Dissenting Covenanters who remained in being when, in 1690, Presbyterianism was restored to the Church of Scotland. In 1876 the majority of the 'Modern Covenanters' joined the Free Church. About

eight ministers and some 500 members, who in 1864 separated and formed a second body, also called the Reformed Presbyterian Church, did not enter into union with the Free Church: and membership figures for this body are given after 1876. Statistics for the years 1856-74 are taken from the *Reformed Presbyterian Magazine;* for 1879-1953, from *Report of Proceedings of the General Presbyterian Council;* and for 1958-62, from the *Reformed Presbyterian Witness.*

12. The Original Secession has its origin in the Secession Church of 1733 and the Associate Presbytery (later, Synod) formed by the 'Original Seceders'. This body was split by various disputes. In 1820 most descendants of the 'Original Seceders' were reunited in the Synod of United Original Seceders, the majority of whom joined with the Relief Church in 1847 to form the United Presbyterian Church. The 'Auld Lichts' stood apart from this union, but joined with the Free Church in 1852. A minority of 'Auld Lichts' maintained a separate existence after 1852, as the (United) Original Secession Church, which was only reunited with the Church of Scotland in 1956. The totals of communicants in 1871 and 1896 were given in the *Original Secession Magazine,* 1895-6; the figure for 1873 is taken from J. Elder Cumming, *The Numbers of the Churches* (1874); other figures are from *Report of Proceedings of the General Presbyterian Council.*

13. The Presbyterian Church of England was established in 1876 by a union between those Presbyterian churches in England that had been formed in association with the Church of Scotland and the English Synod of the United Presbyterian Church of Scotland. These bodies, which had been set up in the 1830s, mainly by Scottish migrants, had attracted remnants of the earlier indigenous English Presbyterianism which had virtually disappeared by the early nineteenth century. The source for statistics from 1876 onwards is *Minutes of the Synod of the Presbyterian Church of England;* and earlier figures are very approximate estimates of the combined membership of the two bodies.

14. Statistics are taken from the *Annual Reports of the Presbyterian Church in Ireland,* except the figure for 1840, which is an estimate provided by J. M. Barkley in *A Short History of the Presbyterian Church in Ireland,* Belfast, 1959. The figures for 'Communicants' refer to communicants on the roll; those for 'Active Communicants' refer to the largest number of communicants present at any one communion for the years 1904-31, and to the 'Number on the roll who have attended at least one communion', during the year specified, for the years 1932 onwards. *Local* variations in the proportion of members who become communicants have caused the Presbyterian Church in Ireland to assess the size of its membership by the number of church families; although *national* fluctuations in the number of families do not vary greatly from *national* fluctuations in the number of communicants. Since 1870 the number of familes has increased as follows:

1870	83 403	1910	85 779	1950	111 866
1880	79 214	1920	90 431	1960	125 603
1890	80 444	1930	94 536	1970	131 414
1900	84 247	1940	100 587		

15. Figures supplied by the Clerk to the Synod of the Reformed Presbyterian Church of Ireland.

A3 METHODIST MEMBERSHIP[1]

	England[2]								Wales[2]	Scotland[2]	Ireland[2]
	WMC	MNC	BCs[3]	PMC[4]	WMA	UMFCs	UMC	MC	Methodists[5]	Methodists[6]	MC[7]
1767	22 410								232	468	2801
1768	23 856								300	485	2700
1769	24 306								250	527	3180
1770	25 400								346	536	3124
1771	26 119								379	892	3632
1772	26 580								409	703	3792
1773	27 161								370	730	4013
1774	28 052								340	1045	4341
1775	29 675								416	669	4237
1776	30 875								435	570	4798
1777	31 922								468	673	5211
1778	33 642								497	614	5336
1779	35 383								531	632	5940
1780	36 667								499	555	6109
1781	37 131								454	701	6175
1782	38 294								458	459	6512
1783	38 932								487	523	6053
1784	41 753								454	533	6429
1785	43 597								530	487	7817
1786	46 559								495	757	10 345
1787	49 350								497	928	11 313
1788	52 585								548	1029	12 213
1789	54 359								638	1198	
1790	55 705								566	1356	14 106
1791	56 605								534	1079	14 158
1792	58 451								585	1284	14 958
1793	59 065								583	1303	13 964
1794	67 563								549	1079	14 077
1795	73 336								547	1048	15 266
1796	77 402								822	918	16 764
1797	80 536	3000							1018	1159	16 806
1798	82 942	6000							1054	1059	16 657
1799	89 213	5700							1195	1117	16 227
1800	88 334	5459							1244	1041	19 292

Table A3: Continued

	England[2]								*Wales*[2]	*Scotland*[2]	*Ireland*[2]
	WMC	MNC	BCs[3]	PMC[4]	WMA	UMFCs	UMC	MC	Methodists[5]	Methodists[6]	MC[7]
1801	87 010	4815							1178	1341	24 233
1802	90 112	4760							1744	1091	26 706
1803	92 401	4960							2569	1199	24 605
1804	92 931	4689							3078	1109	22 962
1805	96 443	4947							4149	1323	23 321
1806	103 549	5586							5879	1375	23 773
1807	110 576	5988							6469	1470	24 560
1808	117 735	6692							7442	1418	24 550
1809	122 765	7130							7867	1448	25 835
1810	128 657	7213							7834	1506	27 801
1811	135 863	7448							8017	1734	28 149
1812	145 314	7977							7772	2038	27 823
1813	152 011	7567							7709	2283	28 770
1814	163 537	7756							7835	2513	29 388
1815	171 179	7870							7801	2729	29 357
1816	181 631	8146							6934	3102	28 542
1817	183 045	8746							7278	3347	21 031
1818	184 122	9127							7323	3656	19 052
1819	184 998	9672							7821		22 580
1820	179 902	9353		7842					8088	3227	23 800
1821	188 668	10 404		16 394					8514	2892	23 538
1822	198 852	10 440		25 066					9442	3098	22 718
1823	206 568	10 363		29 472					9520	3310	22 039
1824	213 743	10 378		33 450					9727	3469	22 047
1825	215 270	10 385		33 582[10]					9853	3523	22 077
1826	217 486	10 233	6433						10 131	3428	22 514
1827	223 449	10 464	8054						10 342	3648	22 599
1828	230 444	11 524	7854	31 610					10 797	3953	22 760
1829	231 695	11 777	7599	33 720					11 857	3977	22 846
1830	232 074	11 624	6297	35 535					12 615	3903	22 896
1831	232 883	11 433	6650	37 216					12 842	3962	22 470
1832	239 478	11 840	6548	41 301					12 707	4087	22 899
1833	260 491	13 883	6881	48 421					15 065	4374	24 403
1834	272 169[9]	14 383	7382	51 877					15 429	4341	25 614
1835	271 416	16 737	7804	56 649					15 262	4310	26 037

Table A3: Continued

	England[2]								Wales[2]	Scotland[2]	Ireland[2]
	WMC	MNC	BCs[3]	PMC[4]	WMA	UMFCs	UMC	MC	Methodists[5]	Methodists[6]	MC[7]
1836	273 588	18 248	10 499	62 306					15 437	4107	26 434
1837	273 450	19 899	9479	64 277	21 262[9]				15 362	3881	26 023
1838	277 240	20 742	9532	67 666	23 361				16 053	3508	26 244
1839	286 568	20 694	10 279	70 396	23 493				17 034	3466	26 383
1840	301 743	20 484	10 629	73 990	23 152				17 795	3640	27 047
1841	305 682	20 506[11]	11 353	75 967	22 074				19 287	3823	27 268
1842	303 817	16 158	12 897	78 862	21 928				19 024	3868	27 630
1843	308 162	15 803	12 825	84 660	21 670				18 847	4015	28 004
1844	314 871	15 812	12 776	87 308	20 597				18 387	4340	28 409
1845	318 289	15 382	12 361	86 338	19 806				18 004	4485	27 926
1846	319 770	15 610	12 181	85 500	19 177				17 275	4423	27 546
1847	318 129	15 236	11 611	84 929	18 901				17 053	4197	24 633
1848	317 522[8]	15 562	12 435	87 400	19 744				17 163	4176	23 142
1849	325 691[8]	16 119	12 852	93 344	20 538				18 409[8]	4174	22 221
1850	334 458[9]	17 656[9]	13 758	102 222	21 192[9]				19 720	4099	21 107
1851	280 054[8]	16 962	13 324	106 074	20 557				18 352[8]	3803	20 815
1852	258 929	16 535	14 095	106 767	19 548				18 699	3635	20 040
1853	249 221	16 070	13 242	105 662	18 272				18 185	3559	19 608
1854	242 231	16 001	12 989	104 118	17 518				18 306	3631	19 233
1855	239 136	16 863	12 369	101 779	17 424				18 143	3579	18 749
1856	242 296	18 380	13 894	104 178	18 136				18 038	3501	18 952
1857	248 338	19 247	13 977	105 937		38 767[9]			18 103	3654	19 287
1858	255 173	20 351	15 265	110 840		41 443			18 267	3651	19 406
1859	269 485	21 344	17 417	118 229		45 583			19 508	3802	19 731
1860	282 783	22 036	17 255	124 932		50 798			23 397	4131	22 860
1861	291 288	22 732	16 866	127 772		52 970			24 025	4469	23 551
1862	297 173	24 271	18 370	132 728		56 934			23 598	4485	22 741
1863	301 825	24 510	18 619	137 225		59 745			23 348	4531	21 953
1864	301 879	24 112	18 594	139 118		60 442			23 077	4712	20 996
1865	303 077	24 289	18 694	140 750		60 790			22 679	5071	20 031
1866	303 132[8]	24 064	18 758	140 905		60 386			22 840	5211[8]	19 835
1867	308 624	24 125	18 751	143 845		62 538			23 020	5426	19 657
1868	314 220	24 757	19 238	146 906		63 043			22 469	5691	19 591
1869	319 012	24 126	18 852	149 225		62 928			20 760	5754	19 659
1870	320 685	23 521	18 182	149 716		62 837			22 064	5722	19 963

Table A3: Continued

	England[2]								*Wales*[2]	*Scotland*[2]	*Ireland*[2]
	WMC	MNC	BCs[3]	PMC[4]	WMA	UMFCs	UMC	MC	Methodists[5]	Methodists[6]	MC[7]
1871	319 495	22 870	18 050	148 597		61 924			22 139	5456	20 005
1872	319 292	22 037	18 438	148 655		61 354			22 155	5403	19 886
1873	321 155	22 149	18 059	147 813		60 678			22 224	5201	19 977
1874	323 619[8]	21 955	17 890	151 354		61 259			22 857[8]	5169[8]	
1875	329 166[8]	22 127	18 324	155 530		62 379			23 707[8]	5189	20 294
1876	342 612	23 055	19 665	160 737		64 777			25 148	5178	20 405
1877	351 129	24 071	20 925	165 401		66 134			26 177	4983	20 148
1878	349 812	24 661	20 629	166 607		65 614			26 115	4949	19 950
1879	346 614	25 060	20 043	166 172		65 137			26 093	4905	25 487
1880	345 332	25 241	20 664	166 108		64 712			26 324	5022	24 463
1881	349 695	25 797	21 209	169 422		65 067			26 365	4896	24 237
1882	362 412	26 584	23 238	173 635		66 297			26 367	4975	24 475
1883	374 700	27 218	23 655	177 442		67 528			27 032	5353	24 384
1884	376 910	27 220	23 455	179 478		67 081			27 748	5708	24 866
1885	378 958	27 167	23 323	181 128		67 290			28 384	5821	24 971
1886	378 518	27 720	23 614	179 901		66 964			28 112	5754	24 644
1887	378 154	27 878	24 389	179 835		66 619			28 243	5901	24 983
1888	381 656	28 326	24 676	180 682		66 869			28 069	6096	25 246
1889	386 158	28 642	25 112	181 863		67 235			28 646	6178	25 306
1890	387 847	28 644	25 213	181 124		67 510			29 387	6381	25 365
1891	387 779	28 756	25 769	181 167		67 200			29 762	6679	
1892	388 161	29 027	25 330	180 278		67 667			29 919	6879	25 553
1893	390 466	29 364	25 863	181 444		67 915			30 321	6913	25 984
1894	395 266	29 635	26 336	181 941		68 017			30 923	7161	26 219
1895	398 910	29 748	26 652	182 279		68 873			31 621	7191	26 443
1896	395 588	29 932	26 306	182 262		69 506			32 187	7645	26 817
1897	398 278	30 291	27 066	183 393		70 602			32 864	7827	27 164
1898	401 042	30 863	27 270	184 710		71 155			33 273	7933	27 180
1899	405 302	31 450	27 625	186 108		71 910			33 855	8119	27 461
1900	410 384	31 782	27 572	186 466		72 085			33 926	8191	27 745
1901	412 194	32 324	28 315	188 683		72 568			34 411	8377	27 924
1902	419 684	33 510	28 462	191 828		74 943			35 025	8516	28 181
1903	424 343	34 085	29 201	194 418		76 254			34 958	8797	28 304
1904	429 562	34 934	29 960	196 836		77 096			35 602	8989	28 351
1905	435 031	35 852	32 062	201 122		78 411			40 600	9248	28 511

Table A3: Continued

	England[2]								Wales[2]	Scotland[2]	Ireland[2]
	WMC	MNC	BCs[3]	PMC[4]	WMA	UMFCs	UMC	MC	Methodists[5]	Methodists[6]	MC[7]
1906	447 474	37 017[12]	32 317[12]	205 182		80 323[12]			41 472	9518	28 992
1907	446 368			206 445			148 988[12]		40 525	9537	28 826
1908	441 768			206 834			148 224		40 582	9656	28 884
1909	441 493			206 543			148 072		39 636	9733	29 246
1910	439 230			206 016			146 715		39 563	9770	29 357
1911	436 356			205 086			144 888		39 359	9820	29 361
1912	433 789			205 045			143 018		39 265	9795	28 863
1913	433 281			204 133			143 029		39 276	9846	28 298
1914	432 370			204 033			143 096		39 118	9651	28 007
1915	430 488			203 119			142 230		38 721	9561	27 795
1916	425 525			201 345			141 336		38 530	9618	27 696
1917	421 542			200 401			140 210		38 728	9623	27 366
1918	420 388			200 539			140 230		39 011	9679	27 302
1919	416 513			200 347			139 238		39 258	9668	27 173
1920	413 206			200 175			138 921		39 751	9668	27 247
1921	414 928			198 806			138 110		40 398	9619	27 288
1922	417 832			198 471			138 947		40 796	9912	27 480
1923	424 088			199 920			140 127		41 311	10 199	27 867
1924	431 708			200 986			140 940		42 034	10 392	28 703
1925	436 875			201 902			141 619		42 588	10 655	29 062
1926	441 419			202 533			142 151		42 945	10 749	29 322
1927	444 015			202 577			142 145		42 595	10 877	29 590
1928	445 584			202 591			141 949		42 705	10 996	29 645
1929	445 548			201 947			141 270		42 128	11 133	29 974
1930	445 735			201 491			140 957		42 118	11 161	30 087
1931	446 746			200 816			140 458		42 024	11 240	29 971
1932	447 122[13]			199 549[13]			139 019[13]		41 868	11 176	30 018
1933								769 101[13]	52 614	13 622	30 218
1934								763 051	52 276	13 710	30 431
1935								759 835	52 065	13 698	30 757
1936								753 221	51 580	13 679	30 786
1937								744 178	51 095	13 727	30 788
1938								740 395	50 798	13 739	30 908
1939								738 061	50 622	13 772	31 033
1940								728 470	49 879	13 843	31 053

Table A3: Continued

	England[2]								Wales[2]	Scotland[2]	Ireland[2]
	WMC	MNC	BCs[3]	PMC[4]	WMA	UMFCs	UMC	MC	Methodists[5]	Methodists[6]	MC[7]
1941								715 345	49 370	13 997	31 062
1942								704 000	48 913	14 018	30 775
1943								697 339	48 837	13 953	30 947
1944								693 236	48 786	14 043	31 212
1945								690 088	48 735	13 836	31 193
1946								684 957	48 124	13 676	31 411
1947								681 717	47 679	13 607	31 437
1948								679 795	47 590	13 487	31 820
1949								682 668[13]	47 276	13 530	31 924
1950								683 823	47 033	13 959	31 933
1951								681 181	46 509	13 906	31 906
1952								683 880	45 730	13 980	32 086
1953								684 496	45 495	13 992	32 392
1954								685 437	45 125	14 097	32 782
1955								684 992	45 009	14 320	32 724
1956								683 691	44 395	14 358	32 386
1957								681 766	43 630	14 284	32 609
1958								679 682	42 865	14 234	31 899
1959								677 055	42 457	14 146	31 864
1960								672 916	41 721	13 952	31 909
1961								668 452	41 461	13 616	31 730
1962								665 051	40 843	13 392	31 763
1963								657 787	39 676	13 311	31 558
1964								649 038	39 056	13 212	31 275
1965								639 028	38 543	12 776	30 996
1966								628 600	37 592	12 574	30 650
1967								617 587	36 809	12 317	30 507
1968								603 100	36 015	12 024	30 173
1969								588 359	34 719	11 634	
1970								571 883	33 714	11 421	

NOTES AND SOURCES

1. Sources: The *Minutes* or *Agenda* of the Conference or Assembly of the (Wesleyan) Methodist Church (or Connexion), the Methodist New Connexion, the Bible Christians, the Primitive Methodist Church (or Connexion), the Wesleyan Methodist Association, the United Methodist Free Churches, the United Methodist Church, and the Methodist Church in Ireland. For a discussion and chronology of Methodist history, see R. Currie, *Methodism Divided*, London, 1968.

The Table contains no data for the Independent Methodists or the Wesleyan Reform Union (see note 9). The Independent Methodists commenced about 1800, remained confined to England, numbered 9614 in 1898, and have since then decreased. The Wesleyan Reform Union has also remained confined to England. It numbered 11 355 in 1862; 7678 in 1895; 8074 in 1913; 9034 in 1930; and 4874 in 1970. See Wesleyan Reform Union *Minutes*. For Wesleyan and Methodist membership in the whole of Great Britain, see Table A7.

2. Great Britain totals have been disaggregated by *circuits*. Each circuit consists of one or more chapel and is named after the town in which the chief (or 'circuit') chapel is situated. It has been assumed that the whole of each circuit is in the country in which the circuit chapel is situated. See also note 5.

3. The series refers to England and Wales since the Bible Christians had no chapels in Scotland. Welsh membership increased as follows:

1851	195	1891	2050
1871	535	1901	3062

See also notes 5 and 6.

4. The series refers to Great Britain. Primitive Methodism reached Wales about 1820 and Welsh membership increased as follows:

1861	3573	1911	8682
1871	4293	1932	8234
1891	6434		

There were a few Primitive Methodists in Scotland from the 1820s onwards, and membership in Scotland increased as follows:

1851	418	1911	2607
1871	738	1931	2429

See also notes 5 and 6.

5. The series for Welsh Methodists refers only to Wesleyans during the years 1766-1932 inclusive; and to members of the Methodist Church from 1933 onwards. Throughout, the series includes all circuits of which the circuit chapel was situated in Wales or Monmouthshire. (See note 2.) Combined Bible Christian, Primitive Methodist, and Wesleyan Methodist membership increased in Wales as follows:

1871	26 967	1911	51 539
1881	34 537	1921	52 596
1891	39 176	1931	53 824
1901	44 576		

Almost all Welsh Bible Christians and Primitive Methodists were English speaking. Welsh-language Wesleyan preaching began in Wales in 1800. In 1871 13 543 or 61 per cent of Welsh Wesleyan membership belonged to Welsh speaking circuits; in 1968 13 645 or 38 per cent of Welsh Methodist membership belonged to such circuits. See also notes 3 and 4.

6. The series refers to Wesleyans during the years 1767 to 1932 inclusive, and to members of the Methodist Church from 1933 onwards. See also notes 4 and 9.

7. Wesley established a separate Irish Conference in the 1750s, and from this a separate Methodist Church gradually developed in Ireland. The Primitive Methodists in Ireland, who numbered 6650 in 1879, united with the Methodist Church in Ireland in that year.

8. This figure is an estimate. When summed, the estimates amount to the exact disaggregated totals from which they have been calculated.

9. In 1796 some hundreds of members left the Wesleyan Connexion and formed the Methodist New Connexion, which remained confined to England. In 1834-5 many members left the Wesleyan Connexion and formed the Wesleyan Methodist Association. This body was virtually confined to England, having, in 1851, 345 Welsh and 283 Scottish members. The Association merged into the United Methodist Free Churches in 1857. The United Methodist Free Churches series refers to Great Britain. Scottish Free Methodist membership never reached 300 and ceased in the 1880s. Welsh Free Methodists numbered 771 in 1861 and 823 in 1901.

From 1849 onwards about 100 000 members left the Wesleyan Connexion. A few of these joined the Methodist New Connexion or the Wesleyan Methodist Association. Many affiliated to the loosely organised body of 'Wesleyan Reformers' who numbered 47 598 in 1852; 49 177 in 1854; 46 240 in 1855 and 46 609 in 1856. Nineteen thousand Wesleyan Reformers joined the United Methodist Free Churches in 1857, and other Reformers joined later. Many Reformers probably returned to the Wesleyan Connexion. Others formed the Wesleyan Reform Union. (See note 1.)

10. The Primitive Methodist Connexion published no membership figures for 1826-7, when many members left or were expelled.

11. About 3000 or 4000 members left the Methodist New Connexion during the Barkerite schism of 1841-2.

12. In 1907 the Bible Christians, the Methodist New Connexion, and the United Methodist Free Churches formed the United Methodist Church.

13. In 1932 the Primitive Methodist Church, the United Methodist Church, and the Wesleyan Methodist Church formed the Methodist Church. Up to and including 1949, all series for the Methodist Church refer to March of each year; but from 1950 onwards the series refer to December of each year.

A4 OTHER NONCONFORMIST MEMBERSHIP

	England			*Wales*			*Scotland*		*Ireland*	
	GBNC[1]	Baptists[1]	Congregationalists[2]	Baptists[3]	Congregationalists[4]	Pres C of W[5]	Baptists[6]	Congregationalists[7]	Baptists[8]	Congregationalists[9]
1772	1221									
1773	1377									
1774	1445									
1775	1464									
1776	1659									
1777	1663									
1778	1730									
1779	1725									
1780	1800									
1781	1850									
1782	1865									
1783	1879									
1784	2055									
1785	2090									
1786	2357									
1787	2463									
1788	2600									
1789	2792									
1790	2843		26 000[2]							
1791	2748									
1792	2966									
1793	2931									
1794	2906			7000						
1795	2804									
1796	3237									
1797	3330									
1798	3438			9000						
1799	3385									
1800	3403		35 000[2]	10 000[3]	15 000					
1801	3594									
1802	3685									
1803	3812									
1804	3910									
1805	4145									
1806	4436									
1807	4766									
1808	4902									
1809	5227									
1810	5322									
1811	5471									
1812	5446									
1813	5988									
1814	6081									
1815	6295				23 600					

Table A4: Continued

	England			*Wales*			*Scotland*		*Ireland*	
	GBNC[1]	Baptists[1]	Congre-gation-alists[2]	Baptists[3]	Congre-gation-alists[4]	Pres C of W[5]	Baptists[6]	Congre-gation-alists[7]	Baptists[8]	Congre-gation-alists[9]
1816	6624									
1817	6833									
1818	7157									
1819	7428									
1820	7673									
1821	7944									
1822	8264									
1823	8615									
1824	9041									
1825	8934									
1826	9251									
1827	9510									
1828	9940									
1829	10 474									
1830	10 869									
1831	10 964									
1832	11 099									
1833	11 358									
1834	11 763									
1835	12 295									
1836	12 844									
1837	13 377									
1838	13 947		127 000	25 000	43 000	37 576				
1839	14 377									
1840	14 905									
1841	15 657									
1842	16 237									
1843	17 076									
1844	17 569									
1845	17 913									
1846	18 084									
1847	18 018									
1848	18 282			35 000	60 000	52 600				
1849	17 991									
1850	18 277									
1851	18 277		165 000[2]							
1852	18 727									
1853	18 218									
1854	18 244									
1855	18 179									
1856	18 135									
1857	18 574									
1858	18 760									
1859	19 038									
1860	19 298									

Table A4: Continued

	England			Wales			Scotland		Ireland	
	GBNC[1]	Baptists[1]	Congre-gation-alists[2]	Baptists[3]	Congre-gation-alists[4]	Pres C of W[5]	Baptists[6]	Congre-gation-alists[7]	Baptists[8]	Congre-gation-alists[9]
1861	19 817			50 903	97 647	90 560				
1862	20 465									
1863	20 714		180 000		94 898					
1864	21 031			51 085			5731		1162	
1865	20 996									
1866	20 775									
1867	20 399					91 462				
1868	20 691					93 044	6855		1354	
1869	20 907					92 448				
1870	20 541					92 735	7053		1389	
1871	20 628					93 276	8873		1434	
1872						95 195	7096		1492	
1873						97 147	6865		1388	
1874	22 070					101 575	7903		1450	
1875	22 655			72 500[3]		106 742	8155		1610	
1876	23 464					112 471	8766		1542	
1877	23 736					116 016	9096		1358	
1878	23 999					116 386	9234		1251	
1879	24 003					118 251	9234		1251	
1880	24 489			80 500		118 970	9466		1395	
1881	25 062					119 355				
1882	25 466			81 378	116 618	122 107	9875		1521	
1883	25 431					124 505	10 096		1544	
1884	25 594					128 374	10 666		1647	
1885	25 826			87 000		129 401	10 905		1639	
1886	25 763					129 458	11 050		1660	
1887	26 326					130 617	11 581		1579	
1888	26 500					132 234	12 120		1608	
1889	26 728					134 239	11 773		1602	
1890	26 805			91 479	130 112	136 051	12 209		1525	
1891		197 403		92 394		137 415	12 304		1847	
1892		204 603		94 895		139 648	12 721		1946	
1893		208 728		98 122		141 964	13 208		2200	
1894		213 923		100 534		145 094	12 572		2326	
1895		216 650		99 627		147 297	14 907		2491	
1896		221 778		101 791		150 442	15 698		2487	
1897		226 290		101 699	143 760	151 882	15 901		2513	
1898		231 713	236 616	104 511	143 428	153 712	16 034		2666	
1899		232 248	247 811	101 057	145 772	156 058	16 905		2719	
1900		239 114	257 435	106 566	147 513	158 114	16 899	30 170	2696	2234
1901		243 534	258 434	109 149	149 778	160 333	17 266	30 270	2649	2298
1902		245 628	268 653	110 955	151 282	162 284	17 954	31 764	2727	2291
1903		252 666	271 883	113 597	165 218	153 350	18 809	33 847	2759	2324
1904		255 516	276 511	116 310	167 181	173 310	19 570	34 647	2909	2421
1905		261 999	278 649	140 443	180 482	189 164	20 647	35 558	2988	2310

Table A4: Continued

	England			*Wales*			*Scotland*		*Ireland*	
	GBNC[1]	Baptists[1]	Congre-gation-alists[2]	Baptists[3]	Congre-gation-alists[4]	Pres C of W[5]	Baptists[6]	Congre-gation-alists[7]	Baptists[8]	Congre-gation-alists[9]
1906		266 699	285 301	143 584	176 632	187 768	20 962	36 785	3013	2193
1907		267 737	288 292	137 507	173 289	185 935	21 142	36 714	2980	2256
1908		266 619	291 102	133 287	171 009	185 366		35 920		2262
1909		267 169	290 616	130 681	169 314	184 588	21 240	34 831	2903	2380
1910		266 224	287 952	128 038	168 693	183 862	20 997	35 660	2935	2368
1911		267 289	288 075	126 863	168 814	183 647	21 025	35 266	2936	2300
1912		266 026	286 963	125 522	167 439	183 932	21 459	35 434	2884	2242
1913		265 781	288 375	125 402	167 951	184 690	21 592	35 478	2881	2160
1914		264 923	289 545	124 795	164 526	184 843	21 871	35 336	2871	2108
1915		263 080	291 128	124 713	165 137	185 278	21 057		2640	2084
1916		260 641	288 784	122 992	162 445	185 377	21 268		2680	2133
1917						186 784				
1918						187 834				
1919		255 469		124 888		187 575	21 875		2758	
1920		254 908		125 068		187 220	21 783	36 498	2785	
1921		254 366		123 798		187 260	21 260	36 331	2759	
1922		255 163		124 511		187 746	21 793	37 682	2816	
1923		258 002		126 933		188 412	22 907	37 862	2967	
1924		258 690		129 009		188 970	22 485	36 038	3145	
1925		257 845		129 734		189 323	22 760	37 270	3358	
1926		259 527		130 098		189 727	23 097	37 610	3430	
1927		258 553	290 934	129 758	163 513	189 132	22 664	37 716	3595	
1928		255 613	290 208	128 747	163 606	187 892	22 839	37 538	3662	2105
1929		253 907	288 155	126 203	164 310	186 194	22 699	37 882	3603	2198
1930		253 614	286 716	125 704	162 781	185 827	22 841	38 337	3649	2305
1931		254 618	286 277	124 891	161 737	185 239	22 499	38 688	3678	2231
1932		254 599	284 884	124 134	159 485	184 257	22 582	39 230	3632	2238
1933		253 584	282 828	123 068	159 283	183 044	22 954	39 327	3842	2195
1934		252 543	280 446	122 840	159 006	182 608	23 188	40 618	3853	2224
1935		251 025	275 247	122 375	159 693	182 221	23 311	39 530	3927	2249
1936		248 295	272 798	120 595	159 565	180 999	23 292	39 351	3802	2159
1937		246 525	267 688	118 580	157 086	179 880	23 157	39 567	3737	2170
1938		244 187	262 985	117 018	156 576	179 386	22 990	39 695	3660	2164
1939		241 915	259 876	116 813	156 566	177 448	22 692	39 949	3759	2078
1940		239 241		115 833		176 245	23 024	39 309	3743	
1941						175 036		39 522		
1942						174 670		39 137		
1943						174 664		38 987		
1944		225 926		116 858		174 005	21 170	38 991	3799	
1945			230 163		155 382	172 954		37 283		1876
1946		218 727	223 634	110 328	151 169	171 185	21 106	35 680	4234	1741
1947		214 775	221 380	110 490	150 990	166 599	21 563	35 314	4241	1720
1948		210 316	214 880	108 386	147 079	164 621	20 223	36 082	4407	1635
1949		208 888	211 865	107 817	146 293	162 538	20 059	34 872	4576	1680
1950		207 101	209 590	105 922	144 078	159 627	19 704	35 030	4476	1731

Table A4: Continued

	England			Wales			Scotland		Ireland	
	GBNC[1]	Baptists[1]	Congre-gation-alists[2]	Baptists[3]	Congre-gation-alists[4]	Pres C of W[5]	Baptists[6]	Congre-gation-alists[7]	Baptists[8]	Congre-gation-alists[9]
1951		205 634	207 152	105 214	143 613	157 124	19 593	35 140	4644	1752
1952		205 013	202 589	102 550	141 746	155 613	19 400	35 139	4679	1821
1953		202 361	203 048	101 370	141 458	154 135	19 393	34 906	4971	1823
1954		200 967	201 607	100 195	140 530	152 305	19 235	35 157	4961	1823
1955		202 239	200 583	99 750	140 049	150 077	19 235	35 467	5045	1885
1956		203 674	199 793	98 500	136 859	147 132	20 146	35 190	5164	1834
1957		203 848	199 538	97 241	130 531	143 530	20 339	35 027	5284	
1958		202 659	195 691	95 593	129 500	140 489	20 290	34 694	5350	
1959		200 100	193 969	94 548	128 388	138 655	20 367	34 495	5421	
1960		198 597	193 341	93 114	127 242	136 716	20 067	34 537	5582	
1961		196 777	192 280	91 802	126 500	133 795	19 321	33 993	5661	
1962		194 951	189 714	89 855	123 877	131 316	19 423	33 227	5889	
1963		187 402	187 239	87 660	120 663	127 814	18 952	32 194	6068	
1964		189 200	185 109	86 421	119 603	125 269	18 732	30 763	6235	
1965		185 641	181 710	83 886	115 437	122 646	18 459	30 133	6374	
1966		183 149	179 865	82 105	111 231	119 276	18 230	29 521	6524	
1967		180 750	175 001	79 214	109 803	116 674	18 098	28 502	6620	
1968		179 829	165 089	77 270	108 108[4]	113 468	16 651	27 515[7]	6761	
1969		176 222	154 313	74 681	106 317[4]	110 155	16 716	26 527	6922	
1970		173 350	151 212	72 097	105 522	108 064	16 074	25 284	7186	

NOTES AND SOURCES

1. The General Baptist New Connexion was formed in 1770 to organize evangelical Baptists, the congregations of the Original Connexion of Baptists either becoming defunct or joining the Unitarians. In 1891 the New Connexion (which was almost entirely confined to England) amalgamated with the Particular Baptists to form the Baptist Union of Great Britain and Ireland. The New Connexion series is from the *General Baptist Hand Book;* the Baptist Union series from the *Baptist Hand-Book.*

In 1750 there were about 10 000 Particular or exclusive Baptists in England. Thereafter numbers grew as follows:

1790	17 000	1851	122 000	1875	169 000
1800	24 000	1863	132 000	1880	176 000
1838	86 000	1870	149 500	1885	194 000

The figure for 1838 is taken from the *Record,* 26 September 1839; those for 1863-85 inclusive from the *Baptist Hand-Book.* The other figures are estimates: that for 1750 is based on data cited in A.S. Langley, 'Baptist Ministers in England about 1750 A.D.', *Transactions of the Baptist Historical Society,* 1918-20; those for 1790 and 1800 are derived from the *Baptist Annual Register,* 1798, and the *General Baptist Year Books;* and that for 1851 is obtained from a comparison of the attendance data in the Census of Religious Worship (*Pp.* 1852-53, LXXXIX) with membership data in the *Baptist Hand-Books.*

For Baptist Union membership in the whole of Great Britain see Table A. 7.

2. In 1750 there were about 15 000 Congregationalists in Engand. This figure (and those given in the Table for the number of English Congregationalists in 1790 and 1800) are estimates derived from E. R. Bebb, *Nonconformity and Social and Economic Life, 1600-1800,* London, 1935; *Transactions of the Congregational Society,* 1911-12; and the sources discussed in these

works, especially the 'Evans Census' (1716), 'Thompson's List' (1773), D. Bogue and J. Bennett *History of the Dissenters from the Revolution in 1688 to the Year 1808*, Vol. IV, London, 1812; and *Pp.* 1852-3, LXXXVIII.

The figure for 1838 is taken from the *Record*, 26 September 1839; that for 1851 is an estimate based on the Census of Religious Worship (*Pp.* 1852-3, LXXXIX); and that for 1863 is taken from the *Baptist Hand-Book*, 1885. From 1898 onwards all figures for English Congregationalists are from the *Congregational Yearbook for England and Wales.*

In 1972 the Congregational Union of England and Wales and the Presbyterian Church of England united to form the United Reformed Church.

For the Congregationalist membership in the whole of Great Britain see Table A. 7.

3. The figures refer to Welsh Particular Baptists before 1891 and Welsh members of the Baptist Union thereafter. (See note 1.) The figures are derived from: the *Baptist Annual Register*, 1798; *Pp.* 1910, XIX, 153; the *Record*, 26 September 1839; the *Protestant Dissenters' Almanack*, 1849; T. Rees, *History of Protestant Nonconformity in Wales*, 2nd edn., London, 1883; and the *Baptist Hand-Book.* The figure for 1800 is an estimate based on the *Baptist Annual Register*, 1798. The figures for 1875-85 inclusive have been adjusted to allow for non-Associated churches excluded from the statistics of the Baptist Union.

4. The figure for Welsh Congregationalists in 1848 is taken from the *Protestant Dissenters' Almanack*, 1849; those for 1861 and 1882 are from T. Rees, *History of Protestant Nonconformity in Wales*, 2nd edn., London, 1883; and all other figures are from the *Congregational Yearbook for England and Wales*, and the Union of Welsh Independents. The figures for 1968-9 are estimated.

Most Welsh Congregationalists belong to the Welsh-speaking congregations which, in 1871, formed the Union of Welsh Independents. In 1900 these congregations had 126 265 members, or 86 per cent of all Welsh Congregationalists. Separate statistics on the Union of Welsh Independents were first published in the *Congregational Yearbook for England and Wales* in 1927. The membership of the Union of Welsh Independents totalled 137 299 (or 84 per cent of all Welsh Congregationalists) in 1927, and 117 981 (or 86 per cent of all Welsh Congregationalists) in 1956. See also note 2.

5. The first Association of the Presbyterian Church of Wales, a Welsh-speaking church known until 1933 as the Welsh Calvinistic Methodist Connexion, was formed in 1742. The figure for the membership of the Presbyterian Church of Wales in 1838 is taken from the *Record*, 26 September 1839; that for 1848 from the *Protestant Dissenters' Almanack*, 1849; that for 1861 from T. Rees, *History of Protestant Nonconformity in Wales*, 2nd edn., London, 1883; and all other figures from *Y Blwyddiadur, neu, Lyfr swyddogol y Methodistiaid Calfinaidd.*

6. All Scottish Baptists were Particular Baptists before the formation of the Baptist Union. (See note 1.) Figures for Scottish Baptists have been derived from the *Baptist Hand-Book.*

7. These figures are derived from the *Congregational Yearbook for England and Wales;* the *Yearbook of the Congregational Union of Scotland;* and the Congregational Union of Scotland. The figure for 1968 is estimated.

8. Most Irish Baptists were Particular Baptists before the formation of the Baptist Union. (See note 1.) Figures for Irish Baptists have been derived from the *Baptist Hand-Book.*

9. These figures are from the *Congregational Yearbook of England and Wales.*

A5 ESTIMATED CATHOLIC POPULATION[1]

	England and Wales[2]	*Scotland*[3]
1887	1 354 000	326 000
1888		
1889	1 360 000	327 000
1890		
1891		
1892	1 357 000	343 000
1893		
1894	1 500 000	365 000
1895		
1896		
1897		
1898		
1899		413 400
1900		
1901		
1902		513 400
1903		
1904		514 000
1905		
1906		514 400
1907		515 625
1908	1 661 375[4]	518 625
1909	1 671 031[4]	518 969
1910		
1911	1 710 000	
1912		
1913	1 793 038	546 000
1914		
1915	1 891 006	
1916	1 885 655	548 000
1917	1 894 243	
1918	1 890 018	
1919	1 903 844	
1920	1 898 843	603 094
1921	1 915 475	601 304
1922	1 931 991	600 000
1923	1 965 787	
1924	1 997 280	
1925	2 030 855	
1926	2 042 630	
1927	2 055 860	
1928		
1929	2 156 146	
1930	2 174 673	
1931	2 206 244	607 000
1932	2 235 237	607 900
1933	2 244 580	
1934	2 278 830	612 330
1935	2 321 117	612 177
1936	2 335 890	614 205
1937	2 353 589	614 021
1938	2 361 504	614 420
1939	2 375 196	614 469
1940	2 406 419	
1941	2 414 002	
1942		
1943	2 334 427	621 398
1944	2 372 074	
1945	2 392 983	
1946	2 415 428	
1947	2 443 600	678 538
1948	2 528 200	
1949	2 648 900	721 200
1950	2 754 249	745 125
1951	2 808 596	748 463
1952	2 837 700	753 434
1953	2 878 400	764 831
1954	2 939 000	774 320
1955	3 031 600	768 420
1956	3 169 700	757 130
1957	3 292 000	772 330
1958	3 343 000	787 170
1959	3 422 500	
1960	3 553 500	792 640
1961		799 180
1962	3 660 000	799 150
1963	3 726 500	812 460
1964		
1965	3 956 500	809 680
1966	4 000 695	827 410
1967	4 004 840	824 800
1968	4 087 949	818 930
1969	4 143 854	820 000
1970	4 010 210	818 500

NOTES AND SOURCES

1. The only available sources of data on the Catholic population of Ireland are the Irish censuses, material from which is summarized in Tables G1 and G2.

The significance and the interpretative difficulties of estimated Catholic population series are discussed in *Catholic Education,* 1967. The following series which refer to England and Wales, are derived either from this periodical, or directly from the Catholic Education Council for England and Wales, which publishes *Catholic Education:*

	Mass Attendance	Estimated Catholic Population A	B
1960	1 941 500		
1961		3 803 000	5 690 000
1962	2 092 667	3 905 000	
1963		4 017 000	
1964		4 001 000	5 900 000
1965		4 048 000	
1966	2 114 219	4 088 000	
1967	2 091 856	4 144 000	
1968	2 055 254	4 090 000	
1969	1 987 880	4 085 000	
1970	1 934 853	4 114 000	

Estimate A is based on parish priests' returns, estimate B on baptisms and demographic data.

2. The series for England and Wales for 1886-1970 is taken from the *Catholic Directory* and is based on local clergy's estimate of the number of Catholics living in their parishes. Since 1955 the introduction of standard parish returns has modified these estimates in some respects and introduced some anomalies. The over-all effect of this change has been a substantial increase in estimated Catholic population.

Some very approximate estimates of Catholic population in England and Wales before 1887 are:

c. 1603	1 500 000
c. 1640-77	540 000
1715-20	115 000
1780	69 376
1840	700 000
1851	900 000
1861	1 353 575

The sixteenth-, seventeenth-, and eighteenth-century figures are based on Brian Magee, *The English Recusants,* London, 1938. The estimate for 1840 was published in the *Catholic Directory* for 1840. In 'The Demography and Sociography of the Roman Catholic Community of England and Wales', in L. Bright and S. Clements (eds.), *The Committed Church,* London, 1966, A.E.C.W. Spencer discusses several early estimates of the size of the Catholic population. Using marriage and baptism data, he estimates the Catholic population of England and Wales in 1851 to be 800 000 – 1 000 000. The 1861 figure, originally given in *Missiones Catholicae,* 1886, published by the Sacred Congregation of Propaganda, is discussed in 'The Leakage of the Catholic Church in England: its Remedy', *The Month,* February 1887. This figure compares quite closely with estimates based on baptisms or school attendances.

3. The figures for Scotland for 1887-94 are taken from the *Catholic Directory;* subsequent figures from the *Catholic Directory for the Clergy and Laity in Scotland.* Estimates are returned on a diocesan basis; but since some dioceses do not revise their estimates from year to year, the figures are approximations only. Where published totals for the estimated Catholic population of Scotland are the same for consecutive years, duplicated figures have been omitted: thus, for example, the estimate of 600 000 first published for 1922 is not revised until 1931.

Fr. Leslie, sent by Propaganda Fide to make a visitation of Scotland in the 1660s, found only 14 000 Catholic *communicants* in that country, of whom 12 000 resided in the Highlands (James E. Handley, 'Scotland', in *A History of Irish Catholicism,* Vol. VI, Dublin, 1968, p.5). Estimates of the Catholic population of Scotland before 1887 are:

1755	16 490
1779	30 000
c. 1790	50 000
1841	190 000
1876	310 789
1882	321 008

The 1755 figure is the 'number of papists' given by Alexander Webster in his *Account of the Number of People in Scotland,* 1755 (see *Scottish Population Statistics,* ed. J. G. Kyd). 'Less than' 20 000 Scots were reported to be Catholics at the General Assembly of the Church of Scotland in 1779; but, according to the *Irish National Almanack for 1851,* Dublin, 1852, statistics prepared by Bishop Hay indicate the number of *communicants* in the Scottish Mission to be about 16 000, 'which would raise the total number of Catholics to some 30 000'.

Sir John Sinclair's *Analysis of the Statistical Account of Scotland,* Edinburgh, 1825, provides the estimate for about 1790. According to the 1841 census, the Irish in Britain amounted to 126 000, but James E. Handley, *The Irish in Scotland 1798-1845,* Cork, 1945, suggests that, as the census gave only the Irish born, there were probably nearly twice that number of persons in Scotland who were either Irish born or of Irish extraction, at least 75 per cent of whom would have been Catholic. This larger estimate is consistent with G. C. Lewis, *Report on the Irish Poor in Great Britain* (Appendix G of the *First Report for Inquiring into the Condition of the Poorer Classes in Ireland*, 1835), which estimated that 'a large part' of the population of Ayrshire, 'at least two-thirds of the population of Wigtownshire' and 'a large part of that of Kirkculdbright', plus about 70 000 people outside of south-western Scotland, were Irish or of Irish extraction. The figure for 1876 is from Robert Howie, *The Churches and Churchless in Scotland: Facts and Figures*, Glasgow, 1893. The 1882 figure is from the *Catholic Directory for the Clergy and Laity in Scotland.*

4. Figures for England and Wales in 1908-9 were obtained by subtracting the estimated Catholic population in Scotland from totals for Great Britain published in the *Catholic Directory*.

A6 OTHER CHURCHES

	Ches of Christ[1]	*Latter Day Saints*[2]	*Ch of the Nazarene*[3]	*Jehovah's Witnesses*[4]	*Moravians*[5] *Commcts*	*Moravians*[5] *Mems*	*New Ch*[6]	*Relig Soc of Friends*[7]	*Seventh Day Adventists*[8]
1821								18 040	
1822									
1823									
1824					2596	4673			
1825							1463		
1826							1428		
1827							1498		
1828							1488		
1829							1609		
1830							1694	17 160	
1831							1606		
1832							1641		
1833							1659		
1834									
1835					2698	5000			
1836							1703		
1837		600					1964		
1838		1310					2186		
1839		1500					2488		
1840		3626					2490	16 277	
1841		5814					2487		
1842	1300	8467							
1843		8848					2479		
1844		8057					2599		
1845		10 956					2534		
1846		11 573					2525		
1847	2300	13 993					2664	15 345	
1848	2057	20 212			2764	4862	2798		
1849	2029	27 912					2742		
1850	1816	30 747			2838	4957	2798		
1851		32 894			2868	4955	2805		
1852	2081	32 339			2828	4841	2736		
1853	1913	30 828			2865	4914	2789		
1854	1998	29 441			2823	4949	2845		
1855	1823	26 001			2921	5061	2672		
1856	2103	22 502			2956	5133	2731	14 530	
1857	2065	15 220			2978	5138	2952		
1858	2275	14 186			2980	5184	2954		
1859	2475	13 027			3053	5196	3020		
1860	2326	13 853					3138	13 862	
1861	2528	14 893					3293	13 844	
1862	2782	14 327					3243	13 809	
1863	3148	13 851					3449	13 761	
1864	3400	13 301					3449	13 755	
1865	3869	12 403					3605	13 756	
1866	3616	10 782					3534	13 786	
1867	3971	10 872				5520	3660	13 815	
1868	4023	10 710			3208	5448	3698	13 894	
1869	4040	10 980			3262	5471	3724	13 955	
1870	3988	8804			3236	5423	3871	14 013	

Table A6: Continued

	Ches of Christ[1]	*Latter Day Saints*[2]	*Ch of the Nazarene*[3]	*Jehovah's Witnesses*[4]	*Moravians*[5] *Commcts*	*Mems*	*New Ch*[6]	*Relig Soc of Friends*[7]	*Seventh Day Adventists*[8]
1871	3776	8246			3190	5372	4098	14 021	
1872	4053	6842			3249	5548	4207	14 050	
1873	4115	6061			3289	5646	4019	14 085	
1874	4394	5423			3302	5673	4388	14 199	
1875	4936	5411			3322	5712	4497	14 253	
1876	4903	5408			3301	5604	4685	14 441	
1877	5764	5188			3324	5705	4765	14 604	
1878	6166	4842			3361	5808	4849	14 710	
1879	6003	5257			3302	5706	4987	14 894	
1880	5844	5112			3220	5645	5100	14 981	
1881	6451	5180			3140	5515	5192	15 101	
1882	6638	4790			3094	5610	5490	15 113	
1883	7112	4402			3256	5682	5409	15 219	
1884	7327	4173			3261	5726	5622	15 381	
1885	7654	3991			3164	5465	5741	15 380	
1886	7872	3588			3211	5647	5730	15 453	
1887	8306	3493			3213	5408	5619	15 531	
1888	8608	3193			3188	5385	5822	15 574	
1889	9137	3142			3178	5336	6078	15 836	
1890	8985	2770					6239	15 961	
1891	9511	2875			3113	5541	6102	16 102	
1892	9954	2604			3135	5765	6063	16 244	
1893	9944	2628			3171	5729	6157	16 369	
1894	10 249	2932					6287	16 412	
1895	10 559	3079			3198	5714	6190	16 476	
1896	10 834	2726			3269	5866	5933	16 674	
1897	10 932	3043			3321	5957	6053	16 854	
1898	11 124	3483			3364	6030	6212	17 031	
1899	11 117	3812			3371	6095	6334	17 153	
1900	11 789	4183					6335	17 346	
1901	12 224	4487			3314	5950	6337	17 476	
1902	12 537	4929			3458	6058	6330		
1903	12 814	4025			3515	6211	6390	17 700	1160
1904	13 063	3893			3607	6230	6448	17 796	1364
1905	13 958	4437			3604	6203	6517	18 466	1515
1906	14 265	4743	80		3656	6258	6635	18 677	1727
1907	14 326	5268			3718	6343	6686	18 860	1812
1908	14 500	6220			3770	6457	6666	19 019	1674
1909	14 440	6481			3782	6473	6665	19 348	1811
1910	14 822	6864			3803	6487	6684	19 522	1939
1911	14 725	7050			3857	6515	6725	19 612	2045
1912	14 788	6956			3885	6525	6723	19 785	2355
1913	15 256	7073			3941	6556	6694		2422
1914	15 228	6885			3991	6618	6705	19 942	2671
1915	15 182	6651	665		3959	6574	6666	19 069	2798
1916	15 191	6757			3735	6129	6579	19 218	2874
1917	15 101	7044			3680	5870	6459	19 166	2982
1918	16 437	7117			3587	5646	6583	19 137	3253
1919	16 243	7084			3590	5539	6398	19 130	3343
1920	16 011	6797			3484	5279	6486	19 049	3487

Table A6: Continued

	Ches of Christ[1]	*Latter Day Saints*[2]	*Ch of the Nazarene*[3]	*Jehovah's Witnesses*[4]	*Moravians*[5] *Commcts*	*Mems*	*New Ch*[6]	*Relig Soc of Friends*[7]	*Seventh Day Adventists*[8]
1921	16 068	6981			3437	5127	6292	19 071	3622
1922	16 306	5658			3425	5041	6304	19 027	3672
1923	16 465	5682			3489	4187	6426	19 076	3815
1924	16 382	5670			3491	4111	6425	19 039	4054
1925	16 349	5592			3477	4063	6372	19 081	4206
1926	16 283	5697			3512	4040	6277	19 147	4450
1927	16 447	5672			3520	4020	6432	19 044	4546
1928	16 576	5826			3511	3983	6295	19 065	4473
1929	16 595	5912			3481	3932	6179	19 063	4545
1930	16 596	6491			3365	3801	6096	19 117	4656
1931	15 991	6640			3336	3765	6030	19 151	4743
1932	16 126	6885		3079	3341	3820	6024	19 119	4868
1933	16 018	7012		3897	3345	3806	6043	19 215	5038
1934	15 527	7139		4007	3315	3728	5968	19 279	5195
1935	15 327	7069		3676	3239	3640	5959	19 301	5358
1936	15 838	6229		4067	3291	3691	5890	19 257	5525
1937	15 823	6364		4137	3254	3641	5758	19 295	5457
1938	15 482	6393		4601	3210	3579	5557	19 424	5921
1939	15 229			5945	3239	3604	5509	19 673	5966
1940	14 948		1001	8823	3206	3555	5461	19 827	5915
1941	14 303	6364		9741	3201	3558	5367	20 153	5955
1942	13 511	6041		10 948	3166	3524	5227	20 269	6085
1943	13 107	6068		11 174	3124	3466	5130	20 363	6184
1944	12 764	5939		11 227	3165	3521	5095	20 472	6353
1945	12 101	5933		11 622	3161	3502	5035	20 534	6372
1946	11 660	5898		11 395	3132	3484	4973	20 661	6268
1947	10 628	5883	993	12 149	3043	3395	5080	20 704	6167
1948	10 359	5609		12 186	3029	3399	5048	20 730	6367
1949	10 001	5846		17 312	3040	3432	4992	20 797	6493
1950	9811	6357	1141	20 936	3015	3440	4852	20 795	6666
1951	9598	7457	1248	23 080	2957	3337	4695	20 839	6797
1952	9511	8397	1321	24 847	2904	3263	4695	21 018	6936
1953	9334	8750	2294	26 104	2873	3223	4628	21 105	7257
1954	8950	8602	1243	27 145	2876	3266	4484	21 194	7535
1955	8761	9209	1324	28 073	2911	3247	4347	21 343	7813
1956	8741	9691	1977	30 342	2933	3255	4268	21 454	8081
1957	8462	10 566	2021	34 004	2885	3196	4243	21 521	8252
1958	8239	12 480	2021	37 416	2824	3119	4215	21 643	8681
1959	7854	13 814	2086	40 884	2842	3132	4150	21 627	8921
1960	7821	17 332	2096	43 650	2843	3107	4081	21 222	9277
1961	7617	29 382	2052	44 974	3012	3269	3899	21 170	9561
1962	7529	45 206	2029	46 842	2998	3263	3832	21 179	9882
1963	7257	55 719	3501	47 053	2936	3186	3815	21 126	10 084
1964	6823	62 138	3524	48 849	2793	3030	3815	21 090	10 314
1965	6585	63 005	3565	48 982	2817		3772	21 062	10 502
1966	6398	65 907	3646	49 073	2773		3556	21 007	10 884
1967	6091	69 052	3633	50 154			3491	20 980	11 210
1968	5615	71 342	3625	52 805	2687		3413	20 909	11 666
1969	5356	72 899		55 876	2838		3242	20 857	11 901
1970	5134	68 217		59 705	2740		3104	20 752	12 145

NOTES AND SOURCES

1. Source: *Churches of Christ Year Book and Annual Report.* The series refers to members in the United Kingdom. The Churches of Christ were formed in 1827.

2. Data supplied by the Church of Jesus Christ of Latter Day Saints. The series refers to members in Great Britain, where the Church first made members in 1837. Losses during the second half of the nineteenth century resulted largely from migration to the United States.

3. Source: The Church of the Nazarene, which was formed in 1906. The figures for 1954-62 cover membership in England and Wales only; all other figures refer to the United Kingdom and the Republic of Ireland. Part of the increments for 1953 and 1954 is due to amalgamations between the Church of the Nazarene and the International Holiness Mission and the Calvary Holiness Church respectively.

4. Sources: *Yearbook of the International Bible Students' Association* and *Yearbook of Jehovah's Witnesses.* The Witnesses first made members in Britain about 1914. The series refers to *publishers,* a strictly defined category also called 'active workers'. For 1932-66 the series covers Great Britain and Northern Ireland; from 1967 onwards, it covers Great Britain only, and in 1967, therefore, the series is reduced by approximately 500 publishers.

5. The first Moravian Society in Britain was established in 1738. The membership and communicant figures for 1824 are from J. T. and K. G. Hamilton, *History of the Moravian Church: The Renewed Unitas Fratrum, 1722-1957,* Bethlehem, Pennsylvania, 1967; those for 1835, 1848, and 1850-9 are from the *Fraternal Messenger,* Bradford, 1850-57 and the *Fraternal Record,* Bradford, 1858-60; those for 1867-1956 are from the *Moravian Almanack;* those for 1957 onwards are from *Reports and Financial Statement* of the Moravian Church, British Province (except for the 1965 and 1966 communicant figures, which are taken from *Whitaker's Almanack*).

Both series cover the United Kingdom and the Republic of Ireland. During the period 1867-86, there is some uncertainty about the years to which statistics refer, since the *Almanacks* are not wholly consistent in the dates they give.

6. Source: *Minutes of the General Conference of the New Church.* The series refers to Great Britain. The New Church was formed in 1787. The figures given are for 'registered members over 20 years of age'. In addition, since 1892 the New Church has enumerated 'isolated receivers', that is, receivers of New Church doctrines not resident in an area served by a New Church Society. There were 330 in 1892. Isolated receivers were most numerous in the period 1908-21, when their numbers ranged from 975 to 1126, and in recent years they have numbered about 700.

7. Quakerism arose in the mid-seventeenth century and may be regarded as a significant movement from 1652 in the north of England, and from 1654 in London and the south. The estimates for membership in 1821 (1820), 1830, 1840, 1847, and 1856, which refer to England only, are taken from J. S. Rowntree, *Quakerism: Past and Present,* London, 1859. The 1840 and 1847 figures were based on actual enumerations while other estimates were based on birth and marriage data, as were two earlier estimates given by Rowntree, namely, 19 800 members in 1800, and 18 920 members in 1810. Rowntree accounts for the fall in membership between 1800 and 1856 in the following way:

Excess of disownments, &c., over admissions	2400
Excess of deaths over births	2336
Emigration	700
Total	5436

The Protestant Dissenters' Almanack and Political Register, London, 1858, puts total membership of the Society of Friends in Great Britain at 24 000 in 1800, and 18 733 in 1847. The

1847 membership figure is disaggregated as follows:

England	15 345
Wales	3421
Scotland	147

The source for membership figures from 1860 onwards is *Extracts from the Minutes and Proceedings of the Yearly Meeting of Friends.* This series refers to Great Britain.

8. Sources: The Seventh Day Adventist Church and *Seventh Day Adventist Church Yearbook;* and *Whitaker's Almanack.* The Seventh Day Adventist Church was founded in 1844 but first began to attract members in Britain in 1878. The series refers to Great Britain.

A7 GREAT BRITAIN TOTALS: SELECTED CHURCHES

	Baptists[1]	*Catholics*[2]	*Congregationalists*[3]	*Methodists*[4]	*WMC*[5]
1767				23 110	23 110
1768				24 641	24 641
1769				25 083	25 083
1770				26 282	26 282
1771				27 390	27 390
1772				27 692	27 692
1773				28 261	28 261
1774				29 437	29 437
1775				30 760	30 760
1776				31 880	31 880
1777				33 063	33 063
1778				34 753	34 753
1779				36 546	36 546
1780				37 721	37 721
1781				38 286	38 286
1782				39 211	39 211
1783				39 942	39 942
1784				42 740	42 740
1785				44 614	44 614
1786				47 811	47 811
1787				50 775	50 775
1788				54 162	54 162
1789				56 195	56 195
1790				57 657	57 657
1791				58 218	58 218
1792				60 320	60 320
1793				60 951	60 951
1794				69 191	69 191
1795				74 931	74 931
1796				79 142	79 142
1797				85 713	82 713
1798				91 055	85 055
1799				97 225	91 525
1800				96 078	90 619
1801				94 344	89 529
1802				97 707	92 947
1803				101 129	96 169
1804				101 807	97 118
1805				106 862	101 915
1806				116 389	110 803
1807				124 503	118 515
1808				133 287	126 595
1809				139 210	132 086
1810				145 210	137 997
1811				153 062	145 614
1812				163 101	155 124
1813				169 570	162 003
1814				181 641	173 885
1815				189 579	181 709

Table A7: Continued

	Baptists[1]	*Catholics*[2]	*Congregationalists*[3]	*Methodists*[4]	*WMC*[5]
1816				199 813	191 667
1817				202 416	193 670
1818				204 228	195 101
1819				205 577	195 905
1820				208 412	191 217
1821				226 872	200 074
1822				246 898	211 392
1823				259 233	219 398
1824				270 767	226 939
1825				272 612	228 646
1826				280 636	231 045
1827				288 224	237 239
1828				296 173	245 194
1829				300 625	247 529
1830				302 048	248 592
1831				304 418	249 119
1832				315 961	256 272
1833				349 115	279 930
1834				365 581	291 939
1835				372 178	290 988
1836				384 185	293 132
1837				407 610	292 693
1838				418 102	296 801
1839				431 930	307 068
1840				451 433	323 178
1841				458 692	328 792
1842				456 572	326 727
1843				465 982	331 024
1844				474 091	337 598
1845				474 665	340 778
1846				473 936	341 468
1847				470 056	339 379
1848				474 002	338 861
1849				491 127	348 274
1850				518 156	358 277
1851				504 126	302 209
1852				485 806	281 263
1853				472 599	270 965
1854				463 971	264 168
1855				455 533	260 858
1856				465 032	263 835
1857				448 023	270 095
1858				464 990	277 091
1859				495 368	292 795
1860				525 332	310 311

Table A7: Continued

	Baptists[1]	*Catholics*[2]	*Congregationalists*[3]	*Methodists*[4]	*WMC*[5]
1861				540 122	319 782
1862				557 559	325 256
1863				569 863	329 704
1864				571 934	329 668
1865				575 350	330 827
1866				575 296	331 183
1867				586 329	337 070
1868				596 324	342 380
1869				600 657	345 526
1870				602 727	348 471
1871				598 531	347 090
1872				597 334	346 850
1873				597 279	348 580
1874				604 103	351 645
1875				616 422	358 062
1876				641 172	372 938
1877				658 820	382 289
1878				658 387	380 876
1879				654 024	377 612
1880				653 403	376 678
1881				662 451	380 956
1882				683 508	393 754
1883				702 928	407 085
1884				707 650	410 366
1885				712 071	413 163
1886				710 583	412 384
1887		1 680 000		711 020	412 298
1888				716 372	415 821
1889		1 687 000		723 834	420 982
1890				726 106	423 615
1891	302 101			726 951	424 220
1892	312 219	1 700 000		727 255	424 959
1893	320 058			732 286	427 700
1894	327 029	1 865 000		739 279	433 350
1895				745 274	437 722
1896	331 184			743 426	435 420
1897	343 890			750 321	438 969
1898	352 258			756 246	442 248
1899	350 210			764 369	447 276
1900	362 579		435 118	770 406	452 501
1901	369 949		438 482	776 872	454 982
1902	374 537		451 699	791 968	463 225
1903	385 072		459 080	802 056	468 098
1904	391 396		478 339	812 979	474 153
1905	423 089		494 689	832 326	484 879
1906	431 245		498 718	853 303	498 464
1907	426 386		498 295	851 863	496 430
1908	421 931	2 180 000	498 031	847 064	492 006
1909	419 090	2 190 000	495 125	845 477	490 862
1910	415 259		491 476	841 294	488 563

Table A7: Continued

	Baptists[1]	*Catholics*[2]	*Congregationalists*[3]	*Methodists*[4]	*WMC*[5]
1911	415 177		492 549	835 509	485 535
1912	413 007		489 668	830 912	482 849
1913	412 775	2 339 038	491 760	829 565	482 403
1914	411 589		489 549	828 268	481 139
1915	408 850			824 119	478 770
1916	404 901	2 433 655		816 354	473 673
1917				810 504	469 893
1918				809 847	469 078
1919	402 232			805 024	465 439
1920	401 759	2 501 937		801 721	462 625
1921	399 424	2 516 779		801 861	464 945
1922	401 467	2 531 991		805 958	468 540
1923	407 842			815 645	475 598
1924	410 184			826 060	484 134
1925	410 339			833 639	490 118
1926	412 722			839 797	495 113
1927	410 975		492 057	842 209	497 487
1928	407 199		491 530	843 825	499 285
1929	402 809		490 347	842 026	498 809
1930	402 159		487 834	841 462	499 014
1931	402 008	2 813 244	486 702	841 284	500 010
1932	401 315	2 843 137	483 599	838 734	500 166
1933	399 606		481 438	835 337	
1934	398 571	2 891 160	480 070	829 037	
1935	396 711	2 933 294	474 470	825 598	
1936	392 182	2 950 095	471 714	818 480	
1937	388 262	2 967 610	464 341	809 000	
1938	384 195	2 975 924	459 256	804 932	
1939	381 420	2 989 665	456 391	802 455	
1940	378 098			792 192	
1941				778 712	
1942				766 931	
1943		2 955 825		760 129	
1944	363 954			756 065	
1945			422 828	752 659	
1946	350 161		410 483	746 757	
1947	346 828	3 122 128	407 684	743 003	
1948	338 925		398 041	740 872	
1949	336 764	3 370 100	393 030	743 474	
1950	332 727	3 499 374	388 698	744 815	
1951	330 441	3 557 059	385 905	741 596	
1952	326 963	3 591 134	379 474	743 590	
1953	323 124	3 643 231	379 412	743 983	
1954	320 397	3 713 320	377 294	744 659	
1955	321 224	3 800 020	376 099	744 321	

Table A7: Continued

	Baptists[1]	*Catholics*[2]	*Congregationalists*[3]	*Methodists*[4]	*WMC*[5]
1956	322 320	3 926 830	371 842	742 444	
1957	321 428	4 064 330	365 096	739 680	
1958	318 542	4 130 170	359 885	736 781	
1959	315 015		356 852	733 658	
1960	311 778	4 346 140	355 120	728 589	
1961	307 900		352 773	723 529	
1962	304 229	4 459 150	346 818	719 286	
1963	294 014	4 538 960	340 096	710 744	
1964	294 353		335 475	701 306	
1965	287 986	4 766 180	327 280	690 347	
1966	283 484	4 828 105	320 617	678 766	
1967	278 062	4 829 640	313 306	666 713	
1968	273 750	4 906 879	300 712	651 139	
1969	267 619	4 963 854	287 157	634 712	
1970	261 521	4 828 710	282 018	617 018	

NOTES AND SOURCES

1. The series refers to the total Great Britain membership of the Baptist Union. For sources and further details, see Table A4.

2. The series refers to the total estimated Catholic population of Great Britain. For sources and further details, see Table A5.

3. The series refers to the combined membership of the Congregational Union of England and Wales, the Union of Welsh Independents, and the Congregational Union of Scotland. For sources and further details, see Table A4.

4. The series refers to the membership of the Methodist Church and its constituents. For the years 1767–96, the series refers to the Wesleyan Methodist Church only. For the years 1797–1819, the series refers to the Wesleyan Methodist Church and the Methodist New Connexion. For the years 1820–5, the series refers to the Wesleyan Methodist Church, the Methodist New Connexion, and the Primitive Methodist Church. For the years 1826–36, the series refers to the Wesleyan Methodist Church, the Methodist New Connexion, the Primitive Methodist Church, and the Bible Christians. Since no returns are available for the membership of the Primitive Methodist Church during the years 1826–7, values of 32 925 and 32 267 have been included in the totals as estimates of that Church's membership in 1826 and 1827 respectively.

For the years 1836–49, the series refers to the Wesleyan Methodist Church, the Methodist New Connexion, the Primitive Methodist Church, the Bible Christians, and the Wesleyan Methodist Association. For the years 1850–6, the series refers to the Wesleyan Methodist Church, the Methodist New Connexion, the Primitive Methodist Church, the Bible Christians, the Wesleyan Methodist Association, and the Wesleyan Reformers. Since no returns are available for the Wesleyan Reformers' membership during the years 1850–1 and 1853, values of 5000, 45 000, and 48 388 have been included in the totals as estimates of that group's membership in 1850, 1851, and 1853 respectively. For the years 1857–1906, the series refers to the Wesleyan Methodist Church, the Methodist New Connexion, the Primitive Methodist Church, the Bible Christians, and the United Methodist Free Churches. For the years 1907–32, the series refers to the Wesleyan Methodist Church, the Primitive Methodist Church, and the United Methodist Church.

No values are included in the series to indicate Primitive Methodist or Bible Christian membership during the years 1800–19 and 1800–25 respectively. In 1819, therefore, the series may fall short of the true total British membership of the constituents of the Methodist Church by 8000.

No values are included in the series to indicate the membership of the Wesleyan Reformers, or the Wesleyan Reform Union, from 1857 onwards. Since some Wesleyan Reformers joined the United Methodist Free Churches during 1857, or later, the series understates the true total British membership of the constituents of the Methodist Church by an unknown amount during the years 1857–60. In no year of this period would this amount exceed 5000.

For sources and further details, see Table A3.

5. For sources and further details, see Table A3.

B1 CHURCH OF ENGLAND

	Baptisms	*Sun Sch Scholars (thousands)*	*Confirmations*		*Baptisms*	*Sun Sch Scholars (thousands)*	*Confirmations*
				1916	495 134	2167	214 209
1872			120 781	1917	434 460	2100	220 718
1873			137 115	1918	412 575	1999	213 381
1874			154 907	1919	451 697	2011	183 214
1875			133 796	1920	603 947	2010	199 377
1876			134 904	1921	550 351	1994	203 233
1877			156 375	1922	516 563	1976	218 196
1878			146 899	1923	499 003	1966	233 427
1879			157 894	1924	483 049	1948	226 766
1880			173 782	1925	470 281	1915	219 091
1881			169 854	1926	459 693	1880	209 565
1882			177 428	1927	436 811	1860	209 451
1883			195 940	1928	437 769	1829	200 838
1884			191 730	1929	421 385	1807	191 677
1885	525 361		195 303	1930	424 483	1802	196 570
1886			201 184	1931	412 542	1798	180 377
1887			201 971	1932	399 279	1801	178 789
1888			212 906	1933	384 913	1778	184 646
1889			212 690	1934	384 288	1715	195 430
1890			189 812	1935	385 476	1645	197 477
1891	510 184	2155	204 067	1936	386 710	1562	182 738
1892	521 118	2185	210 065	1937	386 404	1506	173 709
1893	538 762	2217	211 575	1938	391 702	1471	183 662
1894	550 429	2262	205 659	1939	388 842	1434	157 627
1895	553 321	2276	205 435	1940	365 075		144 323
1896	563 680	2302	218 748	1941			
1897	560 647	2320	208 416	1942			
1898	563 004	2306	208 303	1943			
1899	569 085	2298	201 586	1944			
1900	564 364	2302	181 154	1945			
1901	566 221	2333	208 426	1946			
1902	578 018	2355	198 421	1947	525 835		
1903	580 542	2341	213 883	1948			137 747
1904	587 076	2353	208 032	1949			144 132
1905	576 703	2398	215 477	1950	441 320		142 294
1906	571 675	2337	213 736	1951			139 431
1907	580 403	2334	217 410	1952			148 982
1908	578 701	2380	225 792	1953	387 711	1318	154 548
1909	559 206	2400	229 683	1954			159 957
1910	572 920	2437	227 135	1955			162 848
1911	556 617	2433	244 030	1956	398 280	1308	167 403
1912	543 217	2415	222 470	1957			172 288
1913	571 629	2409	225 117	1958	405 663	1161	173 177
1914	552 198	2350	229 507	1959			182 721
1915	528 017	2255	211 942	1960	411 650	1039	190 713

Table B1: Continued

	Baptisms	*Sun Sch Scholars (thousands)*	*Confirmations*		*Baptisms*	*Sun Sch Scholars (thousands)*	*Confirmations*
1961			191 042	1966	412 961		140 134
1962	422 667		181 623	1967			135 476
1963			162 728	1968	381 000		124 987
1964	437 274		156 265	1969			116 631
1965			145 707	1970	347 167		113 005

NOTES AND SOURCES

1. Sources: *Facts and Figures about the Church of England*, 2, 3. These publications derive the material here used from *The Official Yearbook of the Church of England.*

2. The series refer to the provinces of Canterbury and York: that is, to England (excluding Monmouthshire), the Channel Isles, and the Isle of Man.

3. The number of baptisms and Sunday-school scholars has been adjusted upwards to allow for churches making no returns. See *Facts and Figures*, 2, p. 88 for a discussion of the method of adjustment. Since 1940 only about 85 per cent of churches have made returns.

B2 CHURCH OF SCOTLAND[1]

	Baptisms	Sunday School Scholars	Admissions by[2]			Removals[2]		
			Profession[3]	Certificate	Restoration[4]	By Death	By Certificate	Otherwise
1876		165 471						
1877		170 297						
1878		173 197						
1879		185 796						
1880		187 418						
1881		191 657						
1882	35 760	194 220						
1883	37 601	197 308						
1884	39 611	200 056	20 531					
1885	40 386	206 318	27 059					
1886	43 272	210 197	25 676					
1887	41 393	215 144	26 285					
1888	40 944	216 446	24 821			7628		
1889	40 355	216 980	25 824			7707		
1890	39 178	217 207	24 656			8257		
1891	39 732	218 651	24 389			9999		
1892	39 712	220 462	25 766	30 759	2580	9100	29 416	12 451
1893	40 795	220 866	25 752	30 315	2706	8955	28 856	12 431
1894	39 874	224 703	26 159	29 735	3004	8510	29 217	13 530
1895	40 206	223 827	25 763	29 681	2522	9369	28 039	13 742
1896	40 473	227 986	27 112	30 999	3095	8431	29 821	14 805
1897	40 478	229 302	27 549	31 612	3310	9018	29 845	14 596
1898	40 059	227 452	26 374	31 779	3288	9092	31 105	14 571
1899	39 860	227 665	27 066	31 938	3178	9471	30 657	14 418
1900	39 256	222 944	26 054	31 960	3656	9768	30 532	15 853
1901	38 995	223 140	27 165	33 543	3675	9298	31 435	15 847
1902	38 935	226 363	27 692	31 524	3598	9504	31 453	15 899
1903	38 969	228 343	27 854	31 808	3475	9400	32 830	16 379
1904	37 614	232 546	28 219	31 871	4600	9441	30 888	16 484
1905	37 648	233 814	28 218	31 729	4065	9387	30 498	17 911
1906	37 581	236 068	26 658	31 328	4628	9701	30 988	16 273
1907	34 890	235 964	27 232	30 653	4251	10 064	31 765	16 798
1908	36 148	235 996	26 583	31 298	4242	9612	30 752	17 181
1909	34 867	234 252	26 498	30 593	3998	9830	30 158	16 543
1910	34 411	234 980	26 750	29 312	4364	9592	31 610	16 396
1911	33 390	230 967	26 751	29 260	4129	9653	33 237	16 374
1912	32 182	226 933	26 626	29 007	3774	9849	33 469	17 155
1913	32 165	225 405	26 574	30 780	4261	10 122	34 636	16 924
1914	31 978	218 702	27 099	29 398	4292	9864	29 386	16 602
1915	31 335	211 129	24 529	27 234	4294	11 391	25 801	16 447
1916	29 686	204 264	20 075	23 918	4026	11 119	22 408	14 471
1917	26 384	199 036	20 969	21 252	4408	11 553	19 301	14 687
1918	24 879	190 475	21 734	19 929	4200	12 804	17 972	14 583
1919	25 576	192 496	28 228	24 193	4352	11 379	24 601	15 304
1920	35 812	193 616	32 280	28 338	5264	10 200	28 706	15 964
1921	32 476	194 588	29 543	26 561	5173	10 191	27 269	17 167
1922	30 447	197 352	29 944	25 651	4939	10 653	26 327	17 138
1923	30 618	195 690	30 485	26 191	4606	10 066	29 207	17 225
1924	29 918	196 445	28 942	25 433	5549	10 995	27 256	17 657
1925	28 167	195 952	28 400	25 313	4739	10 453	26 392	18 869

Table B2: Continued

	Baptisms	*Sunday School Scholars*	*Admissions by*[2]			*Removals*[2]		
			Profession[3]	*Certificate*	*Restoration*[4]	*By Death*	*By Certificate*	*Otherwise*
1926	28 337	191 389	25 481	24 101	4436	10 386	26 915	17 605
1927	26 744	188 714	24 713	24 835	5133	10 881	27 504	17 734
1928	26 168	186 713	24 279	25 048[5]	5147	10 796	27 275	16 467
1929	38 244	362 570	41 273	48 775[5]		20 737	46 775	48 057
1930	38 357	355 018	42 480	49 787[5]		19 150	43 851	30 467
1931	38 777	369 115	43 572	50 998[5]		19 243	41 053	27 749
1932	37 694	367 492	42 753	48 442[5]		19 912	39 302	25 163
1933	35 546	363 456	39 230	44 993[5]		20 041	38 300	24 175
1934	36 217	356 541	38 510	44 196[5]		19 669	38 663	23 248
1935	36 083	341 223	35 876	37 943	5282	20 282	39 354	21 088
1936	36 231	325 397	35 878	38 646	5373	20 448	38 281	21 245
1937	35 670	369 115	36 311	39 969	4859	21 031	41 441	22 788
1938	36 615	311 027	37 408	41 288	5551	19 350	40 731	22 107
1939	35 678	259 534	34 038	36 187	4971	19 955	35 699	21 040
1940	35 005	244 494	30 413	34 915	4411	21 356	33 951	21 146
1941	34 627	231 226	25 141	28 767	4034	20 820	26 124	20 456
1942	35 546	234 150	24 942	24 495	4488	19 646	22 380	18 848
1943	39 052	239 481	27 495	25 382	5298	20 257	21 830	15 300
1944	41 240	246 893	29 023	23 597	5115	19 953	21 343	14 992
1945	37 843	247 244	29 469	24 675	5323	19 791	24 967	18 907
1946	43 611	256 424	38 731	34 795	6474	20 041	36 580	21 660
1947	51 103	261 884	38 257	37 022	6426	20 555	39 400	27 229
1948	46 311	269 860	40 730	39 717	7185	19 534	40 514	20 328
1949	44 788	269 488	40 350	39 242	7009	20 352	37 410	23 226
1950	43 266	281 108	38 862	39 318	6354	21 261	37 278	23 063
1951	43 492	291 259	38 114	39 455	7340	21 496	39 692	21 941
1952	43 707	300 951	39 152	41 785	6933	20 558	41 929	19 942
1953	45 004	308 920	38 929	42 391	7413	19 377	42 812	21 707
1954	47 879	310 896	41 314	43 676	7105	20 283	42 369	20 621
1955	50 126	316 769	45 832	44 623	7944	20 623	44 331	17 999
1956	51 185	325 200	41 804	43 493	9329	20 671	42 846	18 591
1957	49 607	307 218	35 315	40 476	7638	20 517	44 291	22 565
1958	49 541	296 601	34 875	41 936	7432	20 889	43 378	20 140
1959	51 383	297 192	35 491	40 652	6990	21 418	44 270	26 250
1960	50 631		33 642	39 703	6568	20 747	43 325	21 222
1961	50 387		32 720	39 626	6151	21 495	42 665	23 000
1962	51 767	273 746	31 344	39 776	6207	21 345	42 713	24 327
1963	48 210	268 257	30 967	38 606	5776	21 643	42 655	23 723
1964	47 960	264 328	32 385	38 649	5738	20 421	42 756	23 320
1965	44 974		30 761	38 174	5867	20 735	44 628	21 489
1966	43 128	253 279	27 625	36 892	5930	21 147	41 776	21 688
1967	42 720	251 602	25 327	36 465	5820	19 836	40 968	20 870
1968	39 699	241 522	23 801	34 756	5545	20 827	40 951	20 926
1969	37 677	232 650	21 135	34 817	6093	21 052	40 251	24 241
1970	35 371	220 873	19 204	32 575	5236	20 908	37 508	22 722

NOTES AND SOURCES

1. Sources: 'Report to the General Assembly of the Committee on Statistics' in *Church of Scotland Assembly Papers; Yearbook of the Church of Scotland.* All series refer to Scotland. In 1929 most of the United Free Church of Scotland united with the Church of Scotland.

2. Communicants admitted to, and removed from, the churches' membership rolls during the period January to December each year. The series for admission and removal 'by Certificate' measure movement, by members already enrolled, between different parishes of the Church of Scotland, each member, on leaving his parish or congregation, being given a certificate of accreditation to be presented on taking up residence in another parish or congregation.

3. Those admitted 'by Profession' are those communicating for the first time.

4. Also called 'by Special Admission' (1900-28).

5. 'By Certificate or Restoration': separate figures showing restorations were not published.

B3 OTHER SCOTTISH AND IRISH PRESBYTERIANS

	Free C of S[1]	*UP C of S*[2]		*UF C of S*[3]		*Pres C in I*[4]	
	Sun Sch Scholars	Baptisms	Sun Sch Scholars	Baptisms	Sun Sch Scholars	Baptisms	Sun Sch Scholars
1851	99 090						
1852	103 945						
1853							
1854							
1855							
1856			62 808				
1857			61 050				
1858		8165	65 972				
1859		9084	67 689				
1860		9416	68 495				
1861	109 113[1]	10 140	71 635				
1862		9325	72 322				
1863		10 667	71 154				
1864		10 756	71 084				54 419
1865		10 619	72 501				
1866		11 327	73 754				
1867		11 608	75 062				
1868		11 624	75 549				
1869	114 138[1]	11 636	79 238				
1870	117 064	11 671	82 440				66 305
1871	119 431	11 850	81 481				68 829
1872	125 801	11 762	84 308				
1873	121 909	11 966	84 754				63 840
1874	127 486	12 222	89 224				66 598
1875	132 284	12 612	92 502				68 158
1876	135 695	11 398	79 101				68 741
1877	139 926	11 171	79 816				69 240
1878	144 652	10 809	81 863				72 909
1879	148 401	10 630	84 075				72 288
1880	155 212	10 363	84 440				69 866
1881	152 101	10 180	86 053				87 047
1882	157 086	10 331	87 474				91 025
1883	156 496	10 081	90 444				92 598
1884	161 210	10 217	92 014				95 460
1885	159 351	9755	94 103				99 303
1886	163 482	9894	97 535			8410	100 156
1887	169 563	9374	97 475			8679	101 230
1888	169 642	9238	103 879			8393	103 507
1889	172 555	8821	104 695			8380	105 960
1890	166 166	8735	103 010			8210	102 958
1891	164 954	8739	103 760			8231	103 255
1892	166 641	8645	104 973			8150	101 285
1893	165 410	8849	105 115			8103	103 801
1894	166 048	8490	106 682			8120	103 257
1895	164 492	8493	107 051			8101	106 010
1896	160 054	8548	106 750				106 342
1897	156 156	8585	105 701			8103	103 816
1898	155 094	8562	106 200				104 754
1899	152 030						105 046
1900				21 230	235 724		102 401

Table B3: continued

	Free C of S[1]	*UP C of S*[2]		*UF C of S*[3]		*Pres C in I*[4]	
	Sun Sch Scholars	Baptisms	Sun Sch Scholars	Baptisms	Sun Sch Scholars	Baptisms	Sun Sch Scholars
1901				21 449	244 339		100 392
1902				21 705	247 461		99 263
1903				21 751	249 312	7798	98 985
1904				20 990	245 364		99 538
1905				20 549	245 713		99 818
1906				20 145	244 513		97 647
1907				18 768	241 160		96 119
1908				18 804	240 303	7759	94 735
1909				18 269	239 049		94 194
1910				17 405	240 619		94 728
1911				16 757	235 929		93 954
1912				16 508	232 720		93 199
1913				16 442	229 292	7647	92 608
1914				16 380	223 599	7457	91 477
1915				16 371	217 011		90 275
1916				15 705	211 031	7222	89 254
1917				13 930	208 559	6869	87 634
1918				12 772		6631	87 071
1919				13 363	201 014	6588	85 586
1920				18 211	197 602	6997	85 831
1921				16 550	197 817	7736	85 117
1922				15 708	197 859	7619	84 894
1923				15 373	196 905	6665	85 163
1924				14 818	192 623	7080	85 093
1925				13 981	190 230	6746	86 171
1926				14 259	187 545	6527	84 343
1927				13 423	185 617	6296	84 168
1928				13 289		5967	81 667
1929					4227	6050	82 673
1930					6379	6042	82 308
1931					7645	5879	80 275
1932						5630	79 659
1933					8184	5726	81 026
1934					8609	5704	80 777
1935					8823	5873	79 989
1936						5970	79 185
1937					8848	5879	76 284
1938					8627	6010	75 872
1939					7257	6183	72 899
1940					7038	6107	70 898
1941					6773	6229	61 720
1942					7115	6891	59 741
1943					7606	7406	60 933
1944					8005	7432	60 549
1945					8224	7254	60 323
1946					8217	7579	61 118
1947					8650	7775	62 307
1948					8632	7292	63 257
1949					8673	6997	63 292
1950					8897	6914	63 938

Table B3: continued

	Free C of S[1]	*UP C of S*[2]		*UF C of S*[3]		*Pres C in I*[4]	
	Sun Sch Scholars	Baptisms	Sun Sch Scholars	Baptisms	Sun Sch Scholars	Baptisms	Sun Sch Scholars
1951					8749	7014	64 118
1952					8756	6876	65 975
1953					8836	6990	66 212
1954					8635	6678	66 362
1955					8724	6866	66 720
1956					8281	6936	67 008
1957					7588	7029	68 476
1958					7756	7115	67 490
1959					7571	7103	66 949
1960					7192	7022	65 589
1961					6999	7286	64 535
1962					6556	7315	64 186
1963					6000	7372	63 364
1964					5703	7725	62 675
1965					5598	8445	61 790
1966					5537	7411	61 645
1967					5538	7181	60 747
1968						7115	59 957
1969						6789	59 426
1970						6284	58 305

NOTES AND SOURCES

1. Source: *Proceedings and Debates* of the Free Church of Scotland. The figures for 1861 and 1869 are estimates.

2. Source: *Proceedings of the Synod of the United Presbyterian Church of Scotland.*

3. Sources: *United Free Church of Scotland: Reports to the General Assembly* (to 1928); *Handbook of the United Free Church of Scotland* (from 1929).

4. Source: *Annual Reports of the Presbyterian Church in Ireland.*

B4 PRESBYTERIAN CHURCH OF ENGLAND

	Baptisms	*Sunday School Scholars*	*Gains*			*Losses*		
			Admitted First Time[1]	Received by Certificate		Transfers	Deaths	Other Losses[2]
1876	2941	45 741	3246	3677		2705	660	2083
1877	3267	49 471	3426	3797		2579	711	2259
1878	3277	53 855	3349	3987		2848	702	2160
1879	3208	60 775	3042	3991		2833	778	2274
1880	3199	61 125	3174	4301		3053	768	2557
1881	3167	64 830	3404	4458		3053	828	2481
1882	3269	67 311	3342	4438		3183	838	2660
1883	3224	74 830	3707	4691		3304	841	2767
1884	3318	73 801	3959	4585		3208	901	2712
1885	3398	75 548	4171	4406		3454	914	2810
1886	3183	75 704	3600	4113		2890	789	2780
1887	3064	77 251	3611	4191		3217	873	2785
1888	3023	77 114	3865	4609		3323	935	2516
1889	2848	78 490	3736	4508		3327	972	3006
1890	3071	79 282	3477	4493		3137	955	2704
1891	2687	79 697	3806	4811		3400	1008	3107
1892	2685	78 542	3952	4226		3313	970	3678
1893	2672	80 018	3862	4422		3286	1029	3355
1894	2471	82 596	4081	4953		3240	898	3484
1895	2603	80 969	3632	4471		3222	1025	3221
1896	2663	80 933	4069	4830		3593	987	3312
1897	2616	81 923	3589	4794		3243	941	3394
1898	2642	83 930	3945	5233		3432	960	2981
1899	2580	82 488	3927	4822		3207	1086	3164
1900	2723	81 078	3895	5359		3515	1025	3184
1901	2586	81 967	4337	5607		3754	997	3227
1902	2625	84 807	4411	5708		3868	1011	3557
1903	2893	87 610	4595	5840		3927	988	3585
1904	2809	88 071	4577	5547		3808	1130	3628
1905	2844	89 558	5028	5275		3598	1075	3520
1906	2601	88 609	4211	5074		3727	1124	3894
1907	2762	87 313	3924	5060		3667	1029	5298
1908	2717	87 087	4163	5232		3813	1053	3828
1909	2801	86 015	4083	5023		3660	1162	3897
1910	2770	86 394	4033	5054		3705	1109	4253
				English[3]	Non-English[3]			
1911	2778	84 180	3827	2572	2365	3870	1112	3753
1912	2750	81 928	3794	2468	2218	3811	1144	3608
1913	2678	81 236	4027	2632	2523	3719	1148	3431
1914	2573	78 586	3672	2211	2452	3355	1224	3257
1915	2510	74 894	3094	1872	1913	2984	1342	3295
1916	2317	70 660	2936	1679	1504	2413	1466	3139
1917	2035	67 181	2789	1629	1623	2082	1462	2944
1918	1820	66 526	3086	1735	1268	2285	1523	2808
1919	1980	67 139	3062	2025	1693	2909	1388	3802
1920	2171	64 064	3424	2155	2270	3185	1234	3952

Table B4: continued

	Baptisms	Sunday School Scholars	Gains			Losses		
			Admitted First Time[1]	Received by Certificate		Transfers	Deaths	Other Losses[2]
				English[3]	Non-English[3]			
1921		65 050	3683	2263	2229	2966	1190	3354
1922		64 466	3350	1998	1979	2740	1265	3235
1923		63 993	3439	1807	2070	2884	1160	3096
1924		63 423	3430	1996	1736	2582	1219	2945
1925		62 588	3291	1965	1806	2598	1240	3169
1926		61 630	3008	1812	1957	2658	1184	3315
1927		59 341	3115	1772	2036	2435	1205	3248
1928		57 484	3099	2000	2037	2562	1191	3549
1929		56 671	2809	1984	1814	2503	1346	3367
1930		55 283	3064	2073	1988	2546	1163	3259
1931		55 158	3078	1889	2211	2419	1198	3409
1932		53 066	2532	2097	1650	2421	1190	3553
1933		50 845	2523	1867	1842	2328	1225	3368
1934		48 953	2589	1948	2026	2359	1211	3264
1935		46 474	2297	1718	2012	2306	1163	3296
1936		43 245	2230	1823	1997	2346	1302	3697
1937		41 923	2262	1865	2173	2550	1240	3028
1938		40 730	2601	1999	1936	2512	1217	3067
1939		35 753	2015	1811	1906	2267	1239	3509
1940		22 997	1947	1408	1374	2027	1282	2964
1941		20 912	1292	1313	912	1672	1230	2855
1942		23 013	1444	1309	898	1584	1176	4186
1943		24 169	1132	1101	779	1372	1188	2222
1944		25 570	1228	852	746	963	986	1640
1945		26 153	1433	1272	1180	1436	1195	2540
1946		27 846	1738	1947	2331	2042	1014	3287
1947		30 968	1907	2065	2396	2009	1144	3453
1948		32 505	2665	2437	3708	1936	1050	3525
1949		33 619	2059	1577	2597	1990	1200	2566
1950		33 699	2038	1738	2605	2185	1310	3984
1951		35 296	1704	1722	2240	1997	1272	3511
1952		36 608	2007	1632	2424	1874	1159	2725
1953		36 811	2062	1530	2587	2233	1073	3141
1954		37 208	2213	1662	2636	2032	1109	2456
1955		37 008	2314	1581	2466	2221	1128	2874
1956		36 558	2399	1650	2975	2191	1179	2738
1957		34 720	2292	1480	2770	2125	1113	2931
1958		33 231	2092	1424	2779	2351	1194	2750
1959		31 022	2139	1523	2671	2245	1175	2814
1960		30 125	2084	1629	2650	2275	1098	2700
1961		29 363	2091	1469	2682	2320	1171	2980
1962		28 885	2069	1374	2398	2450	1237	2956
1963		26 975	2110	1450	2443	2559	1143	2747
1964		25 095	1842	1450	2498	3031	1096	2578
1965		23 818	1496	1327	2522	2794	1115	2754

Table B4: continued

	Baptisms	Sunday School Scholars	Gains			Losses		
			Admitted First Time[1]	Received by Certificate		Transfers	Deaths	Other Losses[2]
				English[3]	Non-English[3]			
1966		24 406	1479	1346	2215	2664	1111	2697
1967		23 968	1369	1314	2214	2618	1010	2390
1968		21 875	1236	1090	2013	2584	1068	2662
1969		20 811	1066	1007	1749	2429	1107	2190
1970		19 900	1133	1091	1618	2223	1107	2226

NOTES AND SOURCES

1. Those 'Admitted First Time' include a small number of 'Restored Members'.

2. 'Other Losses' include removals from membership rolls through lapsing and expulsion, and through certificated transfer (see note 3).

3. Members transferring from one Presbyterian Church of England congregation to another were given a certificate of accreditation. From 1911, entries on churches' membership rolls 'by certificate' were broken down by origin of certificate, the series now distinguishing whether the member was admitted by a certificate showing him to be previously a member of another English, or a non-English (chiefly Scottish), Presbyterian church.

4. The Presbyterian Church of England is now part of the United Reformed Church. See note 2 to Table A4.

5. Sources: *Minutes of the Synod of the Presbyterian Church of England*, 1876-1920; *Minutes of the General Assembly of the Presbyterian Church of England*, 1921-70. All series refer to England.

B5 PRESBYTERIAN CHURCH OF WALES

	Children in Church[1]	*Probationers*	*Sunday School Scholars*	*The Whole Congregation*[2]	*Gains*			*Losses*			
					Children of the Church[3]	Probationers/ from without[4]	Transfers[5]	Deaths	Transfers[5]	Expulsions	Declensions[6]
1895	67 090	2954	169 475	305 890	4441	3778	11 495	2715	11 605	624	2769
1896	67 585	2706	173 920	308 307	4575	3980	13 762	2516	13 444	814	2956
1897	68 717	2569	176 192	312 189	4511	3891	13 914	2566	14 418	788	2892
1898	68 335	2547	176 748	316 053	4273	3740	13 920	2555	14 076	776	2874
1899	69 753	2336	174 702	315 182	4782	3620	14 310	2745	14 155	761	2787
1900	72 740	2363	177 172	319 261	4624	3687	14 326	2643	14 481	747	2878
1901	74 522	2532	180 278	323 951	4446	4750	13 918	2685	13 931	626	3630
1902	74 330	2494	179 190	327 566	4786	4244	13 584	2605	14 379	792	3394
1903	75 453	2477	179 423	332 167	4658	4561	13 402	2640	13 492	718	3166
1904	77 827	5875	187 484	336 997	5392	9404	13 462	2706	13 898	672	3017
1905	80 365	3050	195 227	343 757	6228	20 820	15 093	2927	16 755	1292	5500
1906	82 458	2421	193 599	347 785	3657	4022	15 522	2845	16 331	994	5673
1907	82 760	2152	191 188	342 804	4541	3587	14 960	2830	15 613	933	5444
1908	82 311	2409	189 264	340 858	4717	3174	14 679	2845	14 767	738	4830
1909	83 136	2124	188 489	344 545	4662	3298	13 516	2822	13 696	719	4662
1910	83 503	1920	187 024	340 644	4692	3280	12 853	2857	13 747	579	4427
1911	83 138	2016	185 643	337 096	4665	3280	13 117	2791	13 375	713	4398
1912	78 455	2799	183 698	338 979	4784	3218	12 768	2677	13 312	613	3883
1913	77 578	1874	182 088	339 293	5188	3503	13 356	2817	13 801	614	4198
1914	75 893	1927	177 678	335 203	4480	3165	12 100	2844	12 394	609	3745
1915	75 912	1720	173 444	334 089	5088	3016	12 280	3170	12 403	590	3743
1916	75 069	1485	170 819	327 246	4738	2830	10 547	3328	10 309	524	3847
1917	74 445	1923	168 649	326 372	5185	2984	9192	3446	9007	453	3088
1918	74 031	1372	166 624	326 483	4926	2754	8493	3766	8200	423	2734
1919	72 994	1353	166 876	326 647	4894	2825	10 535	3268	10 812	540	3893
1920	72 010	1592	165 656	326 415	4758	3179	10 773	2869	11 032	744	4420
1921	72 264	1801	163 512	319 484	4697	3380	9637	2802	10 131	709	4032
1922	70 420	1693	161 836	317 354	4726	3707	9650	3151	9452	664	4330
1923	69 175	1556	162 049	316 545	4981	3406	9310	2935	9464	575	4057
1924	68 767	1679	160 721	317 076	4683	3268	8988	3039	8988	501	3853
1925	67 605	1630	159 782	315 296	4704	3047	8640	3041	8931	458	3608

Table B5: Continued

	Children in Church[1]	Probationers	Sunday School Scholars	The Whole Congregation[2]	Gains			Losses			
					Children of the Church[3]	Probationers/ from without[4]	Transfers[5]	Deaths	Transfers[5]	Expulsions	Declensions[6]
1926	65 217	1382	155 941	312 393	4659	3030	8351	2888	8507	429	3802
1927	64 860	1369	155 759	308 144	4322	2852	8272	3088	8484	401	4035
1928	64 036	1162	152 070	305 515	4106	2626	7822	2899	8193	415	4305
1929	62 751	961	146 724	297 741	3999	2650	7335	3217	7583	352	4322
1930	61 057	849	145 294	294 547	4251	2735	7344	2989	7563	355	3865
1931	59 655	867	142 970	288 503	3727	2854	6822	3157	6903	378	3524
1932	58 811	861	139 932	284 505	3687	2674	6168	3151	6380	359	3621
1933	57 208		136 841	279 854	3632	2595	6064	3178	6222	423	3696
1934	55 187		133 399	276 526	3867	2640	6302	2998	6265	357	3625
1935	53 878		128 970	272 935	3960	2667	6415	3116	6255	322	3736
1936	51 773		122 422	266 879	3602	2431	6147	3125	6317	341	3619
1937	49 490		116 612	261 287	3646	2276	6147	3109	6399	290	3390
1938			113 961	257 716	3632	2325	6159	3078	5977	247	3308
1939			108 771	251 218	3125	1937	5658	3189	5589	200	3680
1940			100 839	247 468	3030	1736	5250	3026	5071	174	2949
1941			94 783	243 593	2764	1451	4335	2945	4019	165	2730
1942			90 243	241 302	2885	1412	4395	2694	3729	144	2491
1943			88 618	239 940	2596	1263	3082	2383	2885	111	1568
1944			88 686	237 100	2738	1458	3716	2793	3572	143	2053
1945			85 863	235 470	2518	1363	3741	2897	3767	174	1835
1946			84 940	232 090	2557	1542	4533	2871	4638	117	2775
1947			84 494	227 321	2469	1373	6505	3009	7185	216	4523
1948			83 211	224 851	2441	1675	5012	2564	4604	350	3588
1949			83 254	221 679	2353	1566	4704	2794	4765	186	2961
1950			82 152	217 239	2355	1548	3818	3043	4076	160	3353
1951			80 681	213 399	2301	1747	4349	3138	4470	188	3104
1952			80 920	211 022	2420	1544	3949	2695	4144	164	2421
1953			80 078	208 999	2262	1479	3457	2734	3474	160	2308
1954			79 631	206 847	2267	1328	3387	2773	3608	89	2342
1955			76 646	204 101	2215	1316	3380	2890	3546	52	2651

Table B5: Continued

	Children in Church[1]	*Probationers*	*Sunday School Scholars*	*The Whole Congregation*[2]	*Gains*			*Losses*			
					Children of the Church[3]	Probationers/ from without[4]	Transfers[5]	Deaths	Transfers[5]	Expulsions	Declensions[6]
1956			75 190	201 068	2159	1241	3252	2880	3626	217	2874
1957			72 065	195 936	2036	990	3089	2846	3534	148	3172
1958			68 738	187 651	2217	910	2935	2753	3279		3078
1959			67 063	181 396	2299	949	3282	2548	3486		2548
1960			62 641	177 764	2118	820	3135	2656	3031		2325
1961			59 179	172 870	2008	842	2886	2810	3187		2660
1962			56 875	169 138	2217	715	2808	2621	2967		2631
1963			54 768	164 531	1717	710	2862	2693	3077		3021
1964			53 033	160 405	1844	763	3026	2573	2843		2762
1965			50 885	157 132	1831	742	2624	2566	2751		2503
1966			49 744	153 055	1547	660	2464	2588	2725		2728
1967			46 876	149 149	1608	789	2617	2596	2723		2386
1968	25 901			145 309	1318	598	2270	2511	2450		2448
1969					1259	543	2367	2519	2199		2659
1970					1184	524	2094	2339	2107		1923

NOTES AND SOURCES

1. 'Children in Church' are those regular churchgoers, under the age of 14-15, whose parents are church members.

2. 'The Whole Congregation' includes 'Children in the Church', Probationers, full communicant members (the total of which is given in Table A4), and non-member adherents, of whatever age.

3. 'Children of the Church' are those new members, aged 14-15, whose parents are church members.

4. 'Probationers' and those received as new members 'from without' are those new members, of whatever age, whose parents are not church members.

5. Gains and losses attributable to 'Transfers' indicate changes in the membership of churches of the Presbyterian Church of Wales attributable to entry on, or removal from, the membership roll of members changing their place of residence from the area served by one church to that served by another.

6. 'Declensions' include all losses unattributable to death, transfer, or expulsion.

7. Source: *Y Blwyddiadur, neu, Lyfr swyddogol y Methodistiaid Calfinaidd* . All series refer to Wales.

B6 UNITED METHODIST FREE CHURCHES

	Sunday School Scholars	Junior Members[1]	Members On Trial[1]	Removals[2]	With-drawals	Deaths
1857	67 025		2142			
1858	89 174		2652			
1859	96 197		3642			
1860	104 048		3504			654
1861	112 353		3866			
1862	120 834		7562			
1863	119 134		5283			
1864	133 371		5621			
1865	145 035		5637			851
1866	131 701		4921			906
1867	137 318		5956	3524	2509	1034
1868	143 753		7053	3853	3372	907
1869	148 865		5007	3423	4027	986
1870	150 490		5777	4187	3187	1011
1871	153 684		4537	3894	3464	1022
1872	153 616		4573	3879	3152	977
1873	155 358		4302	3464	3039	1040
1874	160 613		5650	3597	2685	942
1875	164 978		5575	3463	2590	1104
1876	170 849		8225	3538	2889	1013
1877	176 385		6254	4072	3227	1085
1878	178 925		5929	4033	3131	1016
1879	181 971		5468	3920	2999	1123
1880	181 218		6580	4014	3025	980
1881	183 005		6917	3674	3050	1014
1882	186 254		8599	3722	3199	976
1883	186 787		7116	3879	3531	1070
1884	187 729		7063	3717	3530	1035
1885	187 288		7076	3316	3136	1015
1886	188 089		6312	3171	3226	1092
1887	190 072		7049	3392	2759	1054
1888	192 480		7178	3150	2923	1063
1889	193 173		6868	3416	2812	926
1890	191 707		6242	3328	2679	1067
1891	192 066		6383	3107	2739	1125
1892	194 238		6679	2949	2541	1186
1893	194 553		7430	3108	2621	1004
1894	193 464	2067	6653	2880	2506	1128
1895	194 989	3240	6606	2818	2394	1015
1896	193 826	3552	6599	2783	2349	992
1897	192 495	3401	6842	2884	2412	1011
1898	191 484	2600	6331	2950	2225	996
1899	189 795	2235	5806	3025	2435	970
1900	186 238	1968	4639	2723	2183	1145

Table B6: Continued

	Sunday School Scholars	*Junior Members*[1]	*Members On Trial*[1]	*Removals*[2]	*With-drawals*	*Deaths*
1901	185 448	2422	6474	2710	2065	994
1902	188 148	2461	6186	2912	2094	986
1903	191 450	2574	5368	3040	1865	1007
1904	193 346	2382	4914	3179	2083	935
1905	193 362	2901	6993	3084	1958	1067
1906	194 862	3198	5280	3370	1954	996
1907	189 168	3101	4516	3404	1959	1134

NOTES AND SOURCES

1. Junior members were persons aged fourteen or under enrolled in this category of membership. These and any other persons seeking full membership would be enrolled for about six months as 'on trial' members, before being admitted as full members.

2. 'Removals' include all persons who, with the cognizance of the church on whose membership roll they are entered, ceased to reside in the area served by that church (whether to reside in another part of the United Kingdom or to migrate to another country), but indicated an intention to remain church members. The United Methodist Free Churches published no statistics on the number of such persons who did effect a transfer to another church, and were entered on that church's roll. (See also note 2 on Table B7.)

'Withdrawals' include all persons, other than those who so 'removed', and those who died, whose names were deleted from the membership roll.

3. Source: *Minutes of the Assembly of the United Methodist Free Churches.* All series refer to Great Britain.

B7 UNITED METHODIST CHURCH

	Sunday School Scholars	*Junior Members*[1]	*Members On Trial*[1]	*Removed from Circuit*[2]	*Otherwise Ceased to be Members*[2]	*Deaths*
1907	315 723		9871			
1908	315 993	5986	10 8717	6014	4617	1909
1909	314 957	5498	9574	5596	4425	1875
1910	309 649	5141	8949	5392	4268	1851
1911	305 335	5298	9069	5756	4450	1845
1912	299 892	5537	8657	5973	4484	1962
1913	296 354	6379	8319	5441	3682	1836
1914	292 531	7373	8241	5456	3719	1848
1915	285 681	6697	7099	4558	3500	2008
1916	279 348	6871	6270	4111	2707	2109
1917	270 273	6524	6132	3139	2744	2267
1918	268 182	6777	6261	3020	2486	2156
1919	262 593	6408	5588	2812	2098	2719
1920	264 113	6313	5465	3366	3217	1944
1921	262 595	6059	4904	3196	2978	1702
1922	262 583	6215	5825	3258	2951	1947
1923	263 482	6699	6734	3048	2790	1907
1924	259 499	6713	6566	3095	3041	1995
1925	253 242	6834	5769	3042	2827	1857
1926	246 832	6274	5440	2951	2446	1952
1927	242 886	6535	5077	2987	2583	2033
1928	237 269	5995	4853	3103	2696	1858
1929	231 420	5992	4053	2930	2549	2138
1930	224 767	5587	3811	2798	2527	2039
1931	222 430	5494	3401	2639	2606	2030
1932	218 050	5192	3545	2579	3021	2146

NOTES AND SOURCES

1. See note 1 to Table B6.

2. See note 2 to Table B6. It is unclear from United Methodist Free Churches statistics whether 'Removals' included or excluded persons moving from one church to another in the same 'circuit' of churches. The statistics of the United Methodist Church take no account of such transfers, which would, however, constitute a very small proportion of all membership transfers.

3. Source: *Minutes of the Conference of the United Methodist Church.* All series refer to Great Britain.

B8 WESLEYAN METHODIST CHURCH

	Sunday School Scholars	*Junior Members*[1]	*Members On Trial*[1]	*Gains* New Members[2]	From Other Circuits[3]	From Other Churches[4]	*Losses* To Other Circuits[3]	To Other Churches[4]	To Other Countries[3]	Deaths	Ceased to be Members[5]
1855			12 620								
1856			17 839								
1857			17 893								
1858			22 611								
1859			25 541								
1860			30 892								
1861			23 271								
1862			25 608								
1863	536 313		21 646								
1864	532 000		18 080							4703	
1865	537 311		19 091							5557	
1866	543 067		20 819							5850	
1867	556 502		21 987							5817	
1868	582 020		24 926							5471	
1869	601 801		20 596							5513	
1870	622 589		20 433							5861	
1871	638 606		18 126							5800	
1872	654 577		20 058							5618	
1873	666 766		20 844							5633	
1874	688 986		24 794							5199	
1875	700 210		26 719	44 265						6012	
1876	725 312		33 228	53 277						5642	
1877	742 419		28 063	51 878						5461	
1878	760 199		24 096	42 051						5487	
1879	766 757		23 984	40 153						5836	
1880	787 143		25 824	43 201						5572	
1881	810 280	21 431	30 707	46 611	10 837		23 975			5451	23 652
1882	829 666	32 417	40 653	55 382	11 040		24 697			5107	25 205
1883	841 951	38 145	34 399	60 606	10 525		24 802			5135	27 710
1884	852 459	41 821	35 272	51 686	10 792		25 036			5301	28 814
1885	862 279	44 423	30 861	49 554	10 002		23 691			5437	27 609
1886	879 112	45 953	28 531	45 230	9413		22 423			5357	27 135
1887	895 532	52 855	31 470	46 029	10 115		22 320			5495	26 967
1888	908 719	57 100	32 235	47 891	10 038		22 479		977	5622	25 690
1889	928 506	59 887	33 921	47 812	11 018		23 211		988	5232	24 353
1890	932 888	60 801	28 024	47 207	10 779		24 316		755	5372	24 747

Table B8: Continued

	Sunday School Scholars	*Junior Members*[1]	*Members On Trial*[1]	*Gains* New Members[2]			*Losses* To Other Circuits[3]				
				New Members[2]	From Other Circuits[3]	From Other Churches[4]	To Other Circuits[3]	To Other Churches[4]	To Other Countries[3]	Deaths	Ceased to be Members[5]
1891	938 372	62 730	28 082	42 807	10 792		23 290		646	5795	23 297
1892	939 938	65 099	27 540	44 292	10 897		23 923		561	6871	23 136
1893	948 508	68 096	32 364	44 820	10 935		23 425		547	5561	23 839
1894	955 518	70 856	33 229	47 934	10 752		23 418		475	5996	22 999
1895	965 222	72 927	30 050	46 046	10 784		22 694		383	5298	23 819
1896	965 201	71 880	31 291	41 337	10 524		22 776		593	5668	25 105
1897	962 778	73 367	31 876	43 994	10 732		22 630		385	5391	22 645
1898	969 484	76 484	32 005	44 051	11 259		23 055		323	5531	22 896
1899	972 426	77 780	32 905	43 475	11 802		22 856		440	5473	21 210
1900	967 046	79 142	28 560	43 186	11 761		22 638		425	6221	20 121
1901	965 057	81 945	36 915	41 486	11 700		23 520		496	5589	20 926
1902	971 223	86 907	33 469	48 855	11 148		23 519		674	5671	21 597
1903	987 668	91 012	34 020	44 102	11 335		22 987		916	5522	21 168
1904	1 001 448	94 734	34 692	45 403	11 331		23 632		1048	5481	20 570
1905	1 006 515	99 831	40 271	50 021	11 451		23 246		991	5600	20 829
1906	1 013 391	102 897	38 148	56 549	11 784	1116	24 321	1403	1236	5436	23 365
1907	1 000 819	100 850	32 018	42 716	11 801	1219	23 801	1629	1617	5778	24 365
1908	990 264	99 939	30 715	39 509	12 899	1320	23 740	2057	1856	5847	23 519
1909	987 953	100 434	30 006	38 439	10 727	1941	20 447	2785	1185	5856	22 079
1910	980 165	99 380	28 033	36 186	11 656	1810	21 053	2640	1379	6021	20 838
1911	976 752	98 914	29 102	35 049	10 982	1831	20 275	2999	2091	5631	19 843
1912	964 309	99 414	28 326	35 380	11 207	2035	20 437	3135	2625	6036	19 061
1913	951 468	101 595	28 377	36 570	11 272	2139	20 101	3474	2840	5865	18 098
1914	939 619	104 884	27 424	34 619	10 775	2064	19 303	3258	2483	6153	17 495
1915	922 773	106 056	24 139	31 148	9629	1762	17 178	3212	1288	6331	16 900
1916	893 527	100 715	21 320	26 560	9137	1908	16 356	3129	622	6843	15 752
1917	872 674	96 336	21 969	24 369	7608	1656	13 304	2590	469	7687	13 363
1918	863 538	94 816	21 679	23 876	6652	1512	11 145	2479	256	7409	11 566
1919	869 334	90 034	20 094	23 054	6469	1326	11 286	2408	326	8738	11 757
1920	849 861	87 632	21 138	28 398	8997	2055	15 277	3132	961	6775	16 119
1921	850 871	86 668	19 837	29 705	7766	2231	13 191	3192	1081	6038	13 880
1922	854 746	86 589	22 788	30 127	7717	1934	12 794	2959	842	6497	13 091
1923	859 317	89 987	26 417	33 082	7041	1759	11 795	2873	800	6265	13 091
1924	854 312	91 297	26 381	33 886	7263	1714	11 863	2800	1034	6627	12 003
1925	840 205	91 516	25 021	30 949	7321	1942	12 008	2748	814	6585	12 073

Table B8: Continued

	Sunday School Scholars	*Junior Members*[1]	*Members On Trial*[1]	*Gains*			*Losses*				
				New Members[2]	From Other Circuits[3]	From Other Churches[4]	To Other Circuits[3]	To Other Churches[4]	To Other Countries[3]	Deaths	Ceased to be Members[5]
1926	830 318	90 469	24 188	30 819	8615	1849	13 452	2821	745	6407	12 908
1927	825 604	89 254	22 023	29 417	7214	1645	12 098	3041	881	7145	12 737
1928	813 839	86 598	21 088	27 308	8097	1813	12 690	2827	771	6816	12 316
1929	800 292	83 927	18 921	25 672	7325	1516	11 791	2667	729	7665	12 137
1930	763 075	80 387	18 491	26 368	7383	1579	12 431	2419	669	7171	12 435
1931	759 968	79 974	17 798	25 121	8281	1588	12 615	2317	453	6960	11 595
1932	752 855	77 379	17 385	24 661	8000		12 240			7516	11 706

NOTES AND SOURCES

1. See note 1 to Table B6, and note 2 below.
2. The series for 'New members' indicates the number of full members newly entered on the roll *during a twelve-month period,* while the series for 'Members on Trial' indicates the number of such members *on the date* at which the returns were made for the year.
3. The series 'From other Circuits' and 'To other Circuits' indicate those members in good standing who are, respectively, transferred to, and received by circuits, to whose area they move from the area of the circuit where they were earlier accredited members. These series take no account of members known to emigrate outside the United Kingdom, and these members are included in the series 'To other Countries'.
4. The series 'From other Churches' and 'To other Churches' indicate, respectively, those members known to have been, and those members known to have become, members of other churches.
5. The series 'Ceased to be Members' indicates members deleted from the roll for any reason other than transfer to another circuit, joining another church, emigration, or death.
6. Source: *Minutes of the Methodist Conference.* All series refer to Great Britain.

B9 METHODIST CHURCH

	Sunday School Scholars	*Junior Members*	*Members on Trial*	*Gains*			*Losses*				
				New Members	From Other Circuits	From Other Churches	To Other Circuits	To Other Churches	To Other Countries	Deaths	Ceased to be Members
1932		111 130	21 599								
1933	1 297 953	107 626	22 192	39 207	9340	1817	17 321	3352	258	13 131	19 374
1934	1 249 669	99 635	21 178	34 756	10 928	1473	18 465	2835	177	11 744	19 387
1935	1 187 056	93 104	21 810	33 211	10 266	1306	17 574	2530	221	11 226	19 430
1936	1 138 795	85 256	21 098	33 920	10 198	1244	17 352	2514	199	12 361	18 961
1937	1 056 175	78 853	19 812	33 395	10 864	1531	18 694	2483	212	12 846	20 050
1938	1 006 800	75 048	19 078	34 981	11 109	1376	17 620	2450	178	12 451	18 376
1939	980 005	65 999	18 330	34 370	11 936	1464	16 817	2471	214	12 672	17 773
1940	929 942	58 795	15 515	26 848	10 015	1090	16 130	2031	209	13 880	15 788
1941		50 632	13 884	21 729	10 069	937	15 563	1765	113	12 896	15 735
1942		44 681	12 642	22 252	9394	832	12 556	1667	75	11 985	16 823
1943	701 493	41 231	11 576	21 935	8055	931	10 629	1425	40	11 485	13 976
1944	706 237	38 867	11 190	22 345	6920	892	8971	1196	66	12 314	11 589
1945	717 021	37 013	10 881	23 486	8312	921	10 498	1233	66	12 258	12 043
1946	739 470	34 964	9995	24 510	10 041	1119	13 836	1689	215	12 192	14 163
1947	765 184	33 823	9708	25 992	12 421	1401	15 609	1861	372	12 064	13 694
1948	788 930	33 333	9737	27 885	12 832	1666	15 034	2073	435	11 639	14 843
1949	794 340	32 953	9654	30 794	12 620	1625	14 724	1887	500	11 905	13 341
1950	799 873	31 843	8479	28 401	11 852	1511	13 649	1983	360	12 624	12 705
1951	805 659	30 002	8800	27 023	13 954	1579	15 780	2076	422	12 118	13 379
1952	819 198	28 267	8319	28 404	11 940	1748	13 705	2142	489	12 314	11 448
1953	816 718	25 676	8180	28 222	13 018	1766	14 705	2228	461	13 134	12 085
1954	802 654	24 200	8164	28 259	18 065	1771	19 592	2390	454	12 917	12 036
1955	769 733	22 831	7509	28 257	17 175	1862	19 211	2479	429	13 395	12 123
1956	742 592	21 178	7120	25 907	15 276	2154	16 653	2532	572	13 385	12 088
1957	699 494	20 633	6510	23 898	18 188	1972	19 392	2552	730	12 917	11 232
1958	665 560	19 036	6003	25 133	14 863	2120	16 314	2735	653	13 376	11 970
1959	629 080	18 589	5870	24 675	18 127	2139	19 366	2868	591	13 398	11 824
1960	587 276	17 361	5557	23 753	16 139	2162	17 504	2738	567	13 439	12 799
1961	557 839	14 582	5557	23 780	17 033	2258	18 319	2957	568	14 021	12 232
1962	529 230	11 534	5221	24 188	17 290	2276	18 208	2752	684	14 259	12 044
1963	504 839	11 089		21 322	16 578	2285	18 416	3002	774	14 278	12 344
1964	495 696	9489		19 212	20 242	2489	22 264	3029	794	13 175	12 257
1965	482 420	8113		17 654	18 551	2563	20 131	2927	854	13 252	12 625

Table B9: continued

	Sunday School Scholars	*Junior Members*	*Members on Trial*	*Gains*			*Losses*				
				New Members	From Other Circuits	From Other Churches	To Other Circuits	To Other Churches	To Other Countries	Deaths	Ceased to be Members
1966	476 436			17 390	19 888	2668	21 439	2769	879	13 737	12 740
1967				15 898	17 611	2627	19 256	3092	890	12 809	12 228
1968				14 481	16 019	2667	18 070	3140	843	13 465	13 333
1969				12 847	15 943	2676	17 931	2838	813	13 071	13 345
1970				11 806	17 070	2512	19 086	2745	719	13 078	13 547

NOTES AND SOURCES

1. See note 1 to Table B6 and note 2 to Table B8.

2. See note 2 to Table B8.

3. See note 3 to Table B8. Since 1963 the Methodist Church has recorded the number of new members received from Methodist Churches in other countries. The figures are as follows:

1963	130	1967	156
1964	124	1968	169
1965	123	1969	197
1966	118	1970	144

4. See note 4 to Table B8.

5. See note 5 to Table B8.

6. Baptismal figures collected for England and Wales only for the years 1961 to 1970 show the Methodist Church to have baptized an average of 44 716 persons per annum during this ten-year period, or approximately 5½ per cent of all live births in England and Wales. Since 1969, the Methodist Church has undertaken an estimate of the 'Methodist community', that is, of the total number of full members, baptized children and adherents. In 1970 the size of the Methodist community in England and Wales was estimated to be 1 232 000, or 2½ per cent of the total population of England and Wales, but this figure is probably an underestimate due to errors in circuit returns.

7. Source: *Minutes of the Methodist Conference;* Agenda of the Methodist Conference; Methodist Membership Committee. All series (other than the data in note 6) refer to Great Britain.

B10 OTHER CHURCHES

	Baptists[1]		*Congregationalists*[2]	*BCs*[3]	*MNC*[4]	*PMC*[5]		*Catholics*[6]	
	Baptisms	Sun Sch Scholars	Sun Sch Scholars	Sun Sch Scholars	Sun Sch Scholars	Sun Sch Scholars	Adherts	Baptisms	Adult Convsns
1851					42 993	112 568			
1852					43 942	118 508			
1853					44 337	121 394			
1854					44 515	123 341			
1855					45 240	126 680			
1856					47 803	133 867			
1857					43 551	139 486			
1858					52 360	148 368			
1859					54 029	159 251			
1860					56 566	167 533			
1861					58 383	180 064			
1862					61 521	189 057			
1863					64 114	202 631			
1864					62 546	208 399			
1865					63 698	215 777			
1866					64 376	227 476			
1867					65 189	234 794			
1868					66 961	247 969			
1869					67 696	258 857			
1870					67 636	271 892			
1871					69 413	281 085			
1872					68 492	290 141			
1873					69 175	296 512			
1874					69 885	306 333			
1875					71 657	316 985			
1876					72 160	334 991			
1877					73 387	347 961			
1878					74 289	359 001			
1879					76 126	365 004			
1880				35 980	76 457	372 570	520 241		
1881				36 335	78 224	383 350	540 454		
1882				37 361	79 697	394 238	550 582		
1883				37 170	81 800	400 597	521 162		
1884				36 704	81 234	397 570	517 412		
1885				36 586	81 401	405 389	521 830		
1886				37 021	82 486	411 935	534 486		
1887				37 615	83 388	410 950	517 993		
1888				38 525	84 981	423 713	530 351		
1889				38 738	87 247	430 641	562 676		
1890				39 262	87 717	431 868	544 148		
1891				39 424	86 446	435 922	551 731		
1892				40 270	83 895	442 895	545 003		
1893				41 085	84 561	450 233	568 944		
1894				41 086	84 474	456 331	534 197		
1895				41 026	83 515	462 856	543 080		
1896				41 387	83 377	466 052	545 363		
1897				41 483	83 251	467 836	551 574		
1898			616 907	41 521	83 216	465 089	554 834		
1899			660 867	43 121	83 481	467 884	579 389		
1900		525 136	687 068	42 485	82 465	460 632	559 673		

Table B10: Continued

	Baptists[1]		*Congregationalists*[2]	*BCs*[3]	*MNC*[4]	*PMC*[5]		*Catholics*[6]	
	Baptisms	Sun Sch Scholars	Sun Sch Scholars	Sun Sch Scholars	Sun Sch Scholars	Sun Sch Scholars	Adherts	Baptisms	Adult Convsns
1901		529 516	687 012	43 401	82 617	460 763	560 841		
1902		539 328	699 623	43 841	83 309	450 396	568 250		
1903		554 337	705 790	44 993	85 795	458 420	595 233		
1904		566 465	734 986	45 540	86 704	466 997	598 590		
1905		577 936	729 711	47 242	88 042	471 855	603 727		
1906		586 601	732 466	46 741	88 522	477 114	601 689		
1907		583 290	723 580		87 741	470 095	600 281		
1908			714 842			465 726	588 338		
1909		575 346	707 823			465 531	564 481		
1910		572 686	697 509			470 839	591 073		
1911		572 083	693 454			466 848	575 193	60 209	3609
1912		567 260	685 692			467 516	595 522	73 302	6511
1913		561 007	674 162			454 095	575 912	85 773	7184
1914		558 570	662 798			453 430	558 220	89 538	9034
1915		544 919	622 985			447 056	565 536	83 361	9367
1916		527 937	605 796			436 077	557 765	80 355	8501
1917						428 404	558 355	72 678	9108
1918						427 013	566 749	71 571	9402
1919		498 460				416 937	544 767	77 133	10 592
1920		508 759				424 452	548 221	100 814	12 621
1921		514 411				419 245	545 324	95 715	11 621
1922		519 933				419 927	551 739	91 485	12 406
1923		526 223				419 632	533 534	88 945	12 796
1924		526 306				414 678	518 433	87 312	12 355
1925		521 219				407 571	527 277	84 851	11 948
1926		520 822				398 923	523 181	86 776	11 714
1927		504 419	552 350			394 050	515 793	83 386	12 065
1928		494 587	541 210			386 412	510 730	84 939	12 372
1929	10 127	483 710	522 051			378 581	502 158	76 002	12 075
1930	11 051	477 929	512 592			368 782	488 424	83 494	11 980
1931	11 986	473 887	506 184			361 307	474 934	82 713	12 162
1932	11 212	471 380	498 356			355 169	460 675	81 909	12 288
1933	11 294	460 079	486 754					80 692	12 206
1934	10 349	448 577	470 213					82 650	12 206
1935	9640	431 592	450 771					82 871	11 648
1936	9286	413 168	436 608					83 270	10 617
1937	9376	396 577	411 448					83 750	10 651
1938	8525	381 794	395 239					87 064	11 049
1939	8796	371 837	382 326					86 871	10 646
1940	6841	372 174							
1941								83 908	9511
1942								83 246	8959
1943								88 284	8319
1944	5895	287 841						89 490	8722
1945			292 700					90 033	9767
1946	6047	297 293	274 642					98 551	10 363
1947	6630	292 665	276 323						10 594
1948	6456	305 837	280 992						11 520
1949	7117	313 434	287 567					109 146	11 517
1950	7048	317 688	291 124					106 767	11 010

Table B10: Continued

	Baptists[1]		*Congre-gation-alists*[2]	*BCs*[3]	*MNC*[4]	*PMC*[5]		*Catholics*[6]	
	Baptisms	Sun Sch Scholars	Sun Sch Scholars	Sun Sch Scholars	Sun Sch Scholars	Sun Sch Scholars	Adherts	Baptisms	Adult Convsns
1951	7501	315 237	290 473					108 762	11 360
1952	7549	320 642	292 032					110 035	11 532
1953	7531	323 011	298 115					111 614	11 900
1954	7563	321 430	300 984					112 756	11 920
1955	9580	319 701	296 825					114 537	13 291
1956	9996	313 367	292 834					123 902	14 077
1957	7992	304 634	234 377						14 581
1958	7038	283 205	222 689					136 296	14 363
1959	6748	273 253	210 506						16 250
1960	7240	259 742	201 192					147 109	14 803
1961	7070	228 554	191 973					155 294	14 351
1962	7562	190 944	181 400						13 630
1963	7089	190 695	172 734						12 941
1964	6658	191 645	166 256						12 348
1965	5675	189 683	160 904					158 366	10 308
1966	5811	191 232	157 613					154 696	9121
1967	5923	191 333	152 641						8293
1968	6356	193 620							7341
1969	5420	192 949							
1970	4660	190 315							

NOTES AND SOURCES

1. Source: *Baptist Hand-Book.* Both series refer to Great Britain. The series for baptisms refers to adult baptisms and indicates the number of new full members during each twelve-month period.

2. Sources: *Congregational Yearbook for England and Wales; Yearbook of the Congregational Union of Scotland;* Congregational Union of Scotland. The series refers to Great Britain, and includes the Sunday-school scholars of the Union of Welsh Independents.

3. Source: *Minutes of the Conference of the Bible Christians.* On the geographical coverage of the Bible Christians, see Table A3, note 3.

4. Source: *Minutes of the Conference of the Methodist New Connexion.* On the geographical coverage of the Methodist New Connexion, see Table A3, note 9.

5. Source: *Minutes of the Conference of the Primitive Methodist Church.* On the geographical coverage of Primitive Methodism, see Table A3, note 4. The series for 'Adherents' excludes full members of the Primitive Methodist Church but includes all other persons deemed by the ministers of that body to be in some way associated with it.

6. Sources: *Catholic Directory of England and Wales; Catholic Directory for the Clergy and Laity in Scotland;* Catholic Education Council for England and Wales. The series for baptisms refers to *Great Britain,* that for adult conversion to *England and Wales* only; the only available statistics for Catholic baptisms in Scotland include adult conversion, whether or not accompanied by baptism. The adult conversion series has been derived from the Directory for *England and Wales* except for the years 1959-68 inclusive, figures for which have been supplied by the Catholic Education Council. The Council breaks down adult conversions by age as follows:

	Ages 7-13	Age 14 and over	Total
1959	2515	13 735	16 250
1960	2617	12 186	14 803
1961	2047	12 304	14 351
1962	1894	11 736	13 630
1963	1781	11 160	12 941
1964	1777	10 571	12 348
1965	1459	8849	10 308
1966	1431	7690	9121
1967	1371	6922	8293
1968	1319	6022	7341

In all, this series includes 119 386 adult conversions, of which 101 175 are conversions of persons aged fourteen and over. Of persons aged 7-13 converted to Catholicism during 1959-68, 8651 were males and 9560 females; of persons so converted aged fourteen and over, 43 671 were males and 57 504 females.

In 1971 there were 5747 adult conversions in England and Wales.

C1 THEOSOPHICAL SOCIETY[1]

		1921	4658	1936	3338	1951	3163	1966	2633
1907	1843	1922[4]	4654	1937	3280	1952	3112	1967	2583
1908	1463	1923	4821	1938	3267	1953	3015	1968	2508
1909[2]	1666	1924	4938	1939	3191	1954	3082	1969	2479
1910[3]	1694	1925	4780	1940	3090	1955	3028	1970	2438
1911	2023	1926	4872	1941	2990	1956	2881		
1912	2280	1927	5056	1942	3061	1957	2753		
1913	2450	1928	4982	1943	3171	1958	2672		
1914	2636	1929	4701	1944	3317	1959	2626		
1915	2833	1930	4206	1945	3496	1960	2550		
1916	3056	1931	3903	1946	3635	1961	2431		
1917	3545	1932	3643	1947	3610	1962	2409		
1918	3946	1933	3450	1948	3295	1963	2482		
1919	4104	1934	3470	1949	3254	1964	2617		
1920	5105	1935	3406	1950	3210	1965	2656		

NOTES AND SOURCES

1. The table shows total membership of the Theosophical Society. Figures for 1907-24 are from the *General Report of the... Theosophical Society;* for 1925-1959, from *Theosophical Society News and Notes;* for 1960-9, from the *Theosophical Journal.* Before 1925 statistics refer to October of each year; from 1925 onwards they refer to December.

The first English Lodge of the Theosophical Society was founded in 1878. By 1893 there were twenty-eight lodges in Great Britain and Ireland. The Society had 160 lodges in England in 1927 and eighty-one in 1969. As membership grew, separate Theosophical Societies were formed in Ireland, Scotland, and Wales. The figures given here for 1922-69 are for England only. Membership of the Theosophical Society does not exclude membership of a church.

2. From 1909 onwards, membership statistics for Ireland were not published with those for Great Britain. No separate figures are available for Ireland, but half-a-dozen Irish lodges had been chartered by 1911.

3. A separate Theosophical Society in Scotland was chartered in 1910. By 1911 Scotland had thirteen lodges and seven centres with a total membership of 296.

4. Fourteen lodges, four centres, and 209 members were transferred in 1922 to the new Theosophical Society in Wales. Over the next three years, the Welsh Society added another hundred members.

C2 RATIONALIST AND HUMANIST ASSOCIATIONS

	RPA[1]	BHA[3]		RPA[1]	BHA[3]		RPA[1]	BHA[3]		RPA[1]	BHA[3]
			1916	2661		1936	4376		1956	2878	
			1917	2695		1937	4287		1957	3337	
			1918	2774		1938	4257		1958	3377	
1899	94		1919	2789		1939	3802		1959	3696	417[4]
1900	192		1920	2908		1940	3367		1960	3864	
1901	234		1921	2717		1941	3518		1961	4035	
1902	307		1922	2692		1942	3891		1962	4019	746[4]
1903	556		1923	2770		1943	4187		1963	4726	918[4]
1904	768		1924	2722		1944	4683		1964	5267[2]	2169[5]
1905	952		1925	2867		1945	4823		1965	6603	3221
1906	1135		1926	2906		1946	4951		1966	5666	3118
1907	1259		1927	3015		1947	5010		1967	4284	4179[6]
1908	1609		1928	3229		1948	4861		1968	4840	4175
1909	1842		1929	3341		1949	4480		1969	4603	4122
1910	2150		1930	3526		1950	4262		1970	4064	3020
1911	2342		1931	3737		1951	4289				
1912	2505		1932	4166		1952	3985				
1913	2748		1933	4222		1953	3460				
1914	2881		1934	4374		1954	3227				
1915	2684		1935	4457		1955	3015				

NOTES AND SOURCES

1. The series (which is derived from the *Annual Reports* of the Rationalist Press Association) indicates members and 'other subscribers'. Until 1965 there were few 'other subscribers': there were 362 subscribers to the *Rationalist Annual* in 1931, but in other years the number was never above 300.

2. Since 1964 the memberships of the Rationalist Press and British Humanist Associations have partly overlapped. In 1964-5, R.P.A. membership was included in membership of the B.H.A.; thereafter B.H.A. members were required to apply separately for membership of the R.P.A., and those who did not apply were treated as non-member subscribers. We are informed that few B.H.A. members have applied separately for R.P.A. membership, but that a larger number have become non-member subscribers of the R.P.A. These B.H.A. members are classed as 'other subscribers' (see note 1) and included in the R.P.A. totals for each year since 1966. The actual membership of the R.P.A. has fallen from 3687 in 1966 to 2076 in 1970. This in part reflects an advertising policy which was aimed at subscriptions to periodicals rather than at recruitment of new members. The following subscribe to:

	Humanist only	*Humanist* and *Rationalist Annual*
1965	990	648
1966	1461	518
1967	1071	578
1968	1343	969
1969	1269	1018
1970	1063	925

After 1967 the *Rationalist Annual* was retitled *Question.*

3. Sources: *Minutes of the General Purposes Committee of the Ethical Union;* and *Minutes of the... Annual Meeting,* 1964-5, and *Annual Reports,* 1966-70, of the British Humanist Association. See also G. Spiller, *The Ethical Movement in Great Britain: A Documentary History,* London, 1934, and Colin Campbell, 'Humanism in Britain: the Formation of a Secular Value-oriented Movement', in *A Sociological Yearbook of Religion in Britain,* Vol. 2, ed. D. Martin, London, 1969.

Spiller provides a list of seventy-four Ethical Societies founded between 1793 and 1927, and gives the following summary of the number of Ethical centres affiliated to the Ethical Union, which was founded in 1896:

1896/97	4	1903/4	17	1910/11	17
1897/98	5	1904/5	25	1911/12	17
1898/99	6	1905/6	26	1912/13	13
1899/1900	6	1906/7	24	1913/14	16
1900/1	6	1907/8	23	1914/15	15
1901/2	10	1908/9	17	1915/16	15
1902/3	14	1909/10			

The strength of the Union continued to decline during and after the war; and by the early 1930's, only ten Ethical centres were affiliated to the Ethical Union.

The earliest of the Ethical Societies, the South Place Ethical Society, which was founded in 1793, has published membership statistics since 1898. Until the opening of Conway Hall in 1929, the Society had 200-300 members; but, since then, the Society has gradually grown in size, reaching a peak of 908 members in 1971.

4. Membership of the Ethical Union (see not 3). New members of the British Humanist Association, which was founded in 1963, were, unless they objected, registered as members of the Ethical Union and the R.P.A.

5. This figure refers to August 1964, but in April 1964 the Association had only 1706 members. Campbell, op. cit., gives the following table, showing the growth in the number of local humanist groups:

1954 (Dec.)	4	1959	24	1964 (May)	45
1955	7	1960	30	1965 (Apr.)	65
1956	9	1961	34	1966 (May)	75
1957	14	1962	31	1967 (Dec.)	91
1958	15	1963	33		

6. The *Humanist News* notes that 1967 was a year of intensive advertising.

D1 THE PROFESSIONALS: THE EPISCOPALIAN CHURCHES[1]

	Benefices	*Total Beneficed Clergy*	*Resident Incumbents*	*Non-resident Incumbents*	*Curates*[4]	*Total Parochial Clergy*	*Total Clergy*[1]
1807				6145[2]			
1808				6120			
1809			3836	6087			
1810	10 261		4421	5435	3694		
1811	10 801		4490	5908	3730		
1812	10 582						
1813	10 558		4183	5644	4327		
1814	10 602		3798	6003	4405		
1815	10 501						
1816							
1817							
1818							
1819							
1820							
1821							
1822							
1823							
1824							
1825							
1826							
1827	10 533		4413	5171	4254		
1828							
1829							
1830							
1831	10 560		4649	4983	4373		
1832							
1833							
1834							
1835	10 571	7190[3]	5146	4975	4435	11 625	
1836							
1837							
1838	10 742		5859	4307	4813		
1839							
1840							
1841	10 987		6699	3736	4743		14 613
1842							
1843							
1844	11 127		7246	3454	4770		
1845							
1846	11 386		7445	3366	4690		
1847[5]			7642	3255	4726		
1848	11 611		7779	3094	4906		
1849							
1850	11 728		8077	2952			
1851							17 621
1852							
1853[5]			8459	2712	4935		
1854							
1855							

Table B10: Continued

	Benefices	*Total Beneficed Clergy*	*Resident Incumbents*	*Non-resident Incumbents*	*Curates*[4]	*Total Parochial Clergy*	*Total Clergy*[1]
1856							
1857							
1858							
1859							
1860							
1861[5]		12 829			5140	17 969	19 195
1862							
1863							
1864[5]					5166		
1865							
1866							
1867							
1868							
1869							
1870							
1871							20 694
1872[5]	13 168	12 626			5500	18 126	
1873[5]	13 185				5858		
1874							
1875[6]		13 300			5765	19 065	
1876							
1877							
1878[7]	13 358				5281		
1879							
1880[7]	13 380						
1881							21 663
1882	13 739	13 528	12 462	1066	6053	19 581	
1883	13 713	13 558	12 495	1063	6150	19 708	
1884	14 034	13 821	12 840	981	6117	19 938	
1885			12 550		6173		
1886	13 918	13 655	12 574	1081	6221	19 876	
1887	13 928	13 654	12 654	1125	6175	19 829	
1888	13 943	13 643	12 592	1051	6146	19 789	
1889			12 728		6407		
1890	14 016	13 547	12 527	1020	6587	20 134	
1891	14 033	13 778	12 770	1008	6557	20 335	24 232
1892	14 055	13 774	12 752	1022	6556	20 330	
1893	14 063	13 695	12 662	1033	6598	20 293	
1894	14 055	13 693	12 717	976	6631	20 324	
1895	14 090	13 725	12 720	1005	6681	20 406	
1896		13 876			7059	20 935	
1897		13 877				20 936	
1898		13 873				20 932	
1899							
1900	14 242	13 894				20 953	
1901		13 881				20 940	25 235
1902		13 881					
1903		14 020					
1904		14 029				20 594	
1905		13 925			6565	20 571	

Table D1: Continued

	Benefices	*Total Beneficed Clergy*	*Resident Incumbents*	*Non-resident Incumbents*	*Curates*[4]	*Total Parochial Clergy*	*Total Clergy*[1]
1906		13 897					
1907		13 904					
1908		13 835					
1909		13 915					
1910		13 964					
1911		13 986					23 918
1912		14 019					
1913		14 057					
1914		14 079				18 180[9]	
1915		14 072					
1916		14 056					
1917		14 040					
1918		14 023					
1919		13 980					
....	....	....	....	....	....	....	....
1920[8]		12 985					
1921		12 967					21 989
1922		12 962				17 162[9]	
1923		12 936					
1924		12 932					
1925		12 908			4652	17 560	
1926		12 906			4478	17 384	
1927		12 890			4305	17 195	
1928		12 864			4287	17 151	
1929		12 824			4224	17 048	
1930		12 807			4135	16 942	
1931		12 773			4083	16 856	19 147
1932		12 743			4189	16 932	
1933		12 715			4266	16 981	
1934		12 698			4394	17 092	
1935		12 698			4495	17 193	
1936		12 681			4559	17 240	
1937		12 645			4527	17 172	
1938		12 595			4544	17 139	
1939		12 558			4555	17 113	
1940		12 556					
1941							
1942							
1943							
1944							
1945							
1946							
1947							
1948							
1949							
1950							

Table D1: Continued

	Benefices	*Total Beneficed Clergy*	*Resident Incumbents*	*Non-resident Incumbents*	*Curates*[4]	*Total Parochial Clergy*	*Total Clergy*[1]
1951[10]	12 838	11 300			2200	13 500	12 377
1952							
1953							
1954							
1955							
1956							
1957		10 594	9491		2496	13 090	
1958	11 533	10 506	9456				
1959	11 497	10 375	9386		2700	13 075	
1960	11 470	10 370	9372		2781	13 151	
1961	11 438	10 390	9386		3039	13 429	
1962	11 390	10 361	9355		2988	13 349	
1963	11 436	10 376			3047	13 423	
1964	11 348	10 362					
1965	11 365	10 298	9321		3210	13 508	
1966	11 314	10 198	9232		3262	13 460	
1967	11 251	10 172	9213		3268	13 440	
1968	11 209	10 071	9110		3317	13 388	
1969	11 162	9903	8945		3347	13 250	
1970							
1971	11 063	9591	8659		3314	12 905	

NOTES AND SOURCES

1. (a) The main sources used are the Census of Occupations (from which the series for 'Total Clergy' is taken); other Parliamentary Papers, for the years 1806-50; and the *Church of England Yearbook* for the years 1882 onwards. Other sources are separately identified in these notes. For the years 1806–1919, during which period roughly 7 per cent of the 'total beneficed clergy' worked in Wales, the Table refers to both England and Wales. From 1920 onward it refers to England only. Separate figures showing incumbents in the dioceses which in 1920 formed the Church in Wales are only available for the years 1883-1920:

1883	920	1896	975	1911	978
1886	927	1901	1002	1916	983
1891	966	1906	968	1920	975

(b) Little statistical information is available regarding clergy of the Church of Ireland. Donald H. Akenson, *The Church of Ireland: Ecclesiastical Reform and Revolution, 1800-1885*, Yale Univ. Press, 1971, pp. 128-9, quotes the following figures from *Pp.* 1807, LXXVIII, and 1820, XCIII; and the 3rd and 4th Reports of the Royal Commission on Ecclesiastical Revenue in Ireland:

	Benefices	Total Parochial Clergy	Resident Incumbents
1806	1175	1253	545
1819	1263		824
1826		1977	
1832	1395		1043

The numbers of Protestant Episcopal Clergymen in Ireland during 1851-1911 are given by the Censuses of Occupations as:

1851	1786	1891	1734
1861	2265	1901	1617
1871	2221	1911	1575
1881	1828		

Since 1926, the following census figures have been given for the Republic of Ireland and Northern Ireland:

	Republic of Ireland	Northern Ireland
1926	788	392
1936	722	
1946	717	
1951	640	378
1961	551	

(c) According to the *Scottish Ecclesiastical Journal* for December 1856 and June 1857 the clergy of the Episcopal Church in Scotland increased from fifty in 1806 to 160 in 1856. The *Annual Reports of the Representative Church Council* have published statistics on clergy since 1877. In that year, the church had 189 active and thirty-seven other clergy. According to the *Reports* the total number of Episcopal Church in Scotland clergy has since changed as follows:

1881	240	1931	316
1891	276	1941	316
1901	321	1951	334
1911	349	1961	367
1921	326	1968	325

(d) Some indication of the growth in the number of livings in Britain between 1371 and 1705 is given by the following data:

	Parishes	Benefices
1371	8600*	
1535	8838	
1585		8803
1603	9244	
*c.*1640		9284
1704/5		9812

*excluding Cheshire

The sources for these estimates are, respectively, A. H. Inman, *Domesday and Feudal Statistics,* London, 1900; Valor Ecclesiasticus; Whitgift, Archbishops' Register (C.S.P.D. 1634-5, p. 381); Archbishops' Report to the King, 1603 (Harleian MSS. 280, f. 157); Spelman, *An Apology of the Treatise De non Temerandis Ecclesiis;* A. Tindal Hart, *The Life and Times of John Sharp,* London, 1949, p. 17. The sixteenth- and seventeenth-century figures are summarized by Christopher Hill, *Economic Problems of the Church,* London, 1956. Hill also discusses the effect of impropriations, which numbered 3347 by 1535, 3845 by 1640, on the state of the livings. The Archbishop's 'Report to the King' in 1603 gives the number of 'Preachers' as 4830.

2. The series for non-resident incumbents during the years 1807-53 includes a substantial proportion of clergymen 'doing duty', that is, performing the duties of their parishes. In some Parliamentary returns, non-residents doing duty are counted as residents, though the extent to which these categories overlap is not entirely clear. In other words, it is not known how many resident incumbents held second benefices the duties of which they performed while residing elsewhere. The numbers given as 'doing duty' are:

1810	622	1838	1184
1811	1159	1841	1059
1813	1641	1844	1061
1814	1990	1846	1177
1827	1590	1848	1119
1831	1684	1850	1137
1835	1646		

3. *Statistics of the Church of England, as Developed in the Reports of the Ecclesiastical Commissioners,* London, 1836, using information from the *Ecclesiastical Directory,* states that 7190 individuals held 11 331 preferments.

4. In the nineteenth century the number of curates includes both assistant curates and curates serving benefices in which the incumbents were non-resident. As non-residency declined, so did the latter category, from 3435 in 1835 to 167 in 1895.

5. The figures for these years are taken from J. J. Halcombe (ed.), *The Church and her Curates,* London, 1874.

6. *Parliamentary Papers,* 1875, XIV: 'Report from the Select Committee on Public Worship Facilities Bill'. The report gives the total number of clergy, including dignitaries, schoolmasters, and foreign chaplains as 23 738.

7. The figures for 1878 and 1880 are taken from *Church Congress,* 1880-8.

8. From 1920 onwards all series except 'Total Clergy' refer to England only.

9. These figures are given by Roger Lloyd, *The Church of England 1900-1965,* London, 1966, p. 340, under the category of 'active clergy'. The same table gives 19 053 active clergy in 1905 and 16 745 in 1930.

10 The 1951 figures are given in Church Information Board, *The Ordained Manpower of the Church of England,* London, 1956, and are discussed in Guy Mayfield, *The Church of England: Its Members and Its Business,* London, 1958. Mayfield notes that, though the 1951 Census shows a total of 14 332 ecclesiastical parishes, 'after the number of united parishes and united benefices has been deducted, there is left a total of 12 838 incumbencies or benefices to be held by clergymen' (p. 19).

11. Since 1957 there has been a very thorough analysis of Church of England manpower, and only a few of the available statistics are reproduced here. The 'Benefices' column contains the total numbers of livings (that is, occupied livings plus vacant benefices and conventional districts). The total number of beneficed clergy is taken to include curates-in-charge of conventional districts as well as ministers, and resident incumbents are defined as holders of single or united benefices. The following categories of clergymen are omitted from this Table: dignitaries without parochial cure of souls (about 2000-3000); a growing number of non-parochial clergymen, totalling 957 in 1957 and 1947 in 1968, who perform ecclesiastical work independently of the parochial system; clergymen in full-time secular appointments; and clergymen awaiting full-time appointments. The Church of England Statistical Unit includes all of these among 'clergymen working full-time in the Provinces of Canterbury and York', who number as follows:

1959	14 745
1963	15 470
1968	15 607

Auxiliary and retired clergymen, though excluded from this series, are included in the Statistical Unit's series on 'Total Clergymen working or residing in the two provinces', who number as follows:

1959	18 148
1963	19 185
1968	19 493

For further data on Church of England clergymen, see Statistical Unit of the Central Board of Finance of the Church of England, *Facts and Figures about the Church of England*, London, 1959 onwards.

D2 THE PROFESSIONALS: THE METHODIST CHURCHES

	WMC		*MNC*	*BCs*	*PMC*		*WMA*	*UMFCs*	*UMC*	*MC*	
	LPs	Mins	Mins	Mins	LPs	Mins	Mins	Mins	Mins	LPs	Mins
1790		228									
1791		235									
1792		259									
1793		272									
1794		297									
1795		293									
1796		283									
1797		314									
1798		318									
1799		330									
1800		345									
1801		334									
1802		338									
1803		363									
1804		399									
1805		417									
1806		452									
1807		510									
1808		535									
1809		547									
1810		593									
1811		648									
1812		661									
1813		702									
1814		685									
1815		736									
1816		727									
1817		719									
1818		708									
1819		707									
1820		700				48					
1821		709	42			104					
1822		725	44			161					
1823		745	44			202					
1824		777	48			232					
1825		811	48			256					
1826		814	47	88		221					
1827		820	49	95		232					
1828		829	53	87		204					
1829		842	59	86		228					
1830		848	56	72		234					
1831		846	53	71		257					
1832		883	52	71		264					
1833		900	53	75		290					
1834		922	57	84		339					
1835		952	65	97							

Table D2: Continued

	WMC		*MNC*	*BCs*	*PMC*		*WMA*	*UMFCs*	*UMC*	*MC*	
	LPs	Mins	Mins	Mins	LPs	Mins	Mins	Mins	Mins	LPs	Mins
1836		998	73	97		413					
1837		1001	83	90		460	57				
1838		1019	87	91		470	63				
1839		1053	89	89		467	66				
1840		1078	89	94		487	81				
1841		1110	87	100		495	85				
1842		1093	82	103		491	85				
1843		1105	79	102		488	86				
1844		1216	74	100		485	87				
1845		1247	74	105		506	87				
1846		1296	75	106		495	88				
1847		1316	79	107		485	90				
1848		1195	82	106		505	89				
1849		1207	77	105		486	90				
1850		1217	77	110		491	90				
1851		1225	83	118		518	91				
1852		1210	85	115		526	92				
1853		1184	84	111		530	88				
1854		1186	87	105		528	87				
1855		1182	90	104		527	93				
1856		1188	101	111		536	90				
1857		1178	112	110		538		110			
1858		1212	114	117		549		127			
1859		1243	116	115	10 838	541		150			
1860		1296	118	131	11 384	585		174			
1861		1323	129	127	11 887	634		190			
1862		1368	129	136	12 414	674		196			
1863		1402	131	139	12 777	722		208			
1864		1448	141	145	13 176	722		234			
1865		1494	142	152	13 578	745		245			
1866		1514	150	132	13 727	746		255			
1867		1539	150	135	13 865	751		262			
1868		1565	151	137	14 020	761		267			
1869		1528	155	133	14 169	780		265			
1870		1611	149	131	14 322	791		268			
1871		1649	148	133	14 406	790		274			
1872		1674	143	127		788		278			
1873		1715	141	132		820		286			
1874		1762	148	136	15 111	833		292			
1875		1806	150			860		283			
1876		1863	148			868		303			
1877		1866	154		15 405	917		322			
1878		1869	156	139	15 546	921		324			
1879		1887	166	127	15 634	925		336			
1880		1914	162	135	14 507	924		339			

Table D2: Continued

	WMC		*MNC*	*BCs*	*PMC*		*WMA*	*UMFCs*	*UMC*	*MC*	
	LPs	Mins	Mins	Mins	LPs	Mins	Mins	Mins	Mins	LPs	Mins
1881		1910	168	136		924		341			
1882		1909	172	137		918		339			
1883	14 183	1920	173	141	15 982	910		335			
1884	14 453	1955	174	140	15 883	904		318			
1885	14 721	1947	171	140	15 785	891		323			
1886	15 009	1970	171	143	16 120	891		320			
1887	15 299	1988	178	145		873		318			
1888	15 557	1982	175	146		866		312			
1889	15 841	1975	181	147		850		307			
1890	16 038	2004	186	150	16 317	859		311			
1891	16 334	2018	186	155		883		310			
1892	16 491	2017	183	158		904		309			
1893	16 739	2101	183	159		922		308			
1894	16 981	2107	184	164		921		308			
1895	17 095	2137	187	166	16 728	930		317			
1896	17 224	2127	185	165		926		318			
1897	17 504	2128	188	162		930		331			
1898	17 708	2135	190	165		930		341			
1899	18 017	2152	193	169	16 617	940		348			
1900	19 956	2202	195	168	16 459	955		355			
1901	18 323	2238	195	168	16 497	962		356			
1902	18 473	2238	193	171	16 016	996		355			
1903	18 644	2260	194	172	16 074	1024		353			
1904	18 900	2303	197	176	15 821	1051		359			
1905	19 304	2303	196	177	16 262	1059		366			
1906	19 519	2399	204	177	15 963	1079		370			
1907	19 672	2445	204	181	16 007	1088		377			
1908	19 804	2455			16 189	1067			833		
1909	19 826	2454			16 158	1083			843		
1910	19 578	2455			16 241	1093			849		
1911	19 715	2478			16 139	1094			845		
1912	19 594	2494			16 110	1091			837		
1913	18 823	2509			15 802	1084			838		
1914	19 463	2513			15 718	1092			825		
1915	19 418	2576			15 537	1085			817		
1916	19 211	2603			15 335	1116			789		
1917	19 012	2618			14 976	1113			763		
1918	18 818	2596			14 832	1126			735		
1919	18 618	2594			14 602	1047[1]			709		
1920	18 457	2520			14 383	1044			709		
1921	18 409	2474			14 211	1059			715		
1922	18 414	2472			14 056	1040			709		
1923	18 452	2502			13 939	1034			712		
1924	18 425	2523			13 701	1037[1]			710		
1925	18 651	2537			13 634	1107			713		
1926	18 850	2451			13 636	1089			714		
1927	19 024	2500			13 456	1087			713		
1928	19 082	2540			13 284	1090			708		
1929	18 992	2557			13 110	1092			703		
1930	18 870	2562			12 909	1092			695		

Table D2: Continued

	WMC		MNC	BCs	PMC		WMA	UMFCs	UMC	MC	
	LPs	Mins	Mins	Mins	LPs	Mins	Mins	Mins	Mins	LPs	Mins
1931	18 844	2568				1092			691		
1932	18 785	2510			12 896	1092			689		
1933										34 948	4357
1934										34 694	4376
1935										34 412	4674
1936										34 032	4671
1937										33 465	4635
1938										32 821	4680
1939										31 990	4680
1940										31 307	4645
1941										30 549	
1942											
1943											4668
1944										28 781	4637
1945										28 144	4514
1946										27 560	4514
1947										26 856	4370
1948										26 230	4413
1949										25 817	4424
1950										25 159	4658
1951										24 701	4661
1952										24 387	4628
1953										24 094	4643
1954										23 934	4613
1955										23 605	4518
1956										23 369	4634
1957										23 093	4635
1958										22 806	4634
1959										22 612	4617
1960										22 304	4551
1961										22 063	4517
1962										21 788	4467
1963										21 439	4454
1964										21 217	4438
1965										20 991	4377
1966										20 666	4296
1967										20 244	4226
1968											4167
1969											
1970											

NOTES AND SOURCES

1. The series for Primitive Methodist ministers is discontinuous between 1918–19 and 1924–5. About fifty ministers would have to be added to the totals for 1919-24 to make them approximately comparable with the rest of the series.

2. The Table contains no data for local preachers in the United Methodist Church or its constituent churches. The United Methodist Church had about 6000 local preachers in 1908 and about 3000 in 1932.

3. For the sources of this Table see the first paragraph of note 1, Table A3.

D3 THE PROFESSIONALS: OTHER CHURCHES

	C of S[1]	Free C of S[2]	UP C of S[3]	UF C of S[4]	Baptists[5] Pastors	Baptists[5] LPs	Congregationalists[6] Mins	Congregationalists[6] Lay Ps	Pres C of W[7]	Assemblies of God[8]	Chrstn Science[9]	Salv Army[10]	Unitns[11]	Catholics[12] Sec Clergy	Catholics[12] Reg Clergy
1790	938														
1835	1072														
1836															
1837															
1838															
1839															
1840															
1841															
1842	1229														
1843	759														
1844		583													
1845		627													759
1846		672													781
1847		673													813
1848		684													814
1849		705													883
1850		720													906
1851	1124	736													950
1852		745													968
1853		759													1010
1854		765													1056
1855		786													1059
1856		790											261		1074
1857		811													1124
1858		825													1147
1859		827	555												1190
1860		846	562												1242
1861	1486	859	573												1350
1862		872	577										261		1390
1863		885				2198							320		1420
1864		894	607			2236							336		1450
1865		903	620			2281							339		1526

Table D3: Continued

	C of S[1]	Free C of S[2]	UP C of S[3]	UF C of S[4]	Baptists[5] Pastors	LPs	Congregationalists[6] Mins	Lay Ps	Pres C of W[7]	Assemblies of God[8]	Chrstn Science[9]	Salv Army[10]	Unitns[11]	Catholics[12] Sec Clergy	Reg Clergy
1866		902	623				2338							1574	
1867		917	626				2393		757				337	1616	
1868		923	630				2410		791				348	1639	
1869		942	632				2368		798				311	1688	
1870		947	639				2443		773			12	336	1735	
1871	1540	948	640				2503		793				348	1776	
1872		957	641				2523		801				355	1825	
1873		969	647				2518		798				353	1873	
1874		975	649				2563		830				350	1900	
1875		997	657				2590		827				348	1972	
			....												
1876		1014	564[3]				2614		841				357	2040	
1877		1059	568				2633		872			36	361	2093	
1878		1075	583				2595		897			127	357	2170	
1879		1094	584				2693		920			195		2206	
1880		1095	587				2623		957			363		2249	
1881	1558	1097	587				2830		981			533		2280	
1882		1106	589				2782		970			1067		2362	
1883		1105	594						973			1340		2450	
1884		1116	594						971			1644		2522	
1885		1126	598						989			1780		2541	
1886		1131	610						989			2260		2605	
1887		1141	614						999					2670	
1888		1137	611						987					2635	
1889		1146	615						1003					2748	
1890		1147	605						1012				350	2852	
1891	1684	1169	606						1027					2952	
1892		1165	615						1065				351	2971	
1893		1165	615						1077			3135		3001	
1894		1158	610						1123				357	3000	
														....	....
1895		1165	613						1141				362	2090	924

Table D3: Continued

	C of S[1]	Free C of S[2]	UP C of S[3]	UF C of S[4]	Baptists[5] Pastors	Baptists[5] LPs	Congregationalists[6] Mins	Congregationalists[6] Lay Ps	Pres C of W[7]	Assemblies of God[8]	Chrstn Science[9]	Salv Army[10]	Unitns[11]	Catholics[12] Sec Clergy	Catholics[12] Reg Clergy
1896		1163	615						1166			2935	365	2143	947
1897		1154	620						1193			3054	371	2181	938
1898		1149	631					5117	1200			4170	364	2247	965
1899		1144						5445	1229				370	2286	985
1900				1772	1963	5436	3086	5131	1231				366	2308	990
1901	1828			1764	2000	5271	3083	5143	1224				361	2393	1107
1902					2042	5477	3090	5261	1270		50	....	366	2424	1141
1903					2082	5708	3110	5216	1262				371	2489	1222
1904					2081	5654	3116	5273	1261			2783	373	2514	1280
1905					2074	5436	3095	4981	1248			2730	364	2580	1359
1906					2102	5619	3150	5084	1239		74	2868	362	2636	1388
1907					2101	5551	3164	5221	1333		109		365	2654	1421
1908							3168	5438	1306				370	2699	1467
1909					2087	5502	3129	5282	1320		182		365	2724	1514
1910					2098	5564	3104	5155	1310		193		373	2758	1544
1911	1765				2107	5398	3093	5193	1320		219		378	2804	1709
1912					2125	5319	3089	5056	1270			2555	372	2824	1577
1913				1602	2090	5384	3060	4907	1270				365	....	....
1914				1602	2082	5257	3057	4891					360	2881	1569
1915				1604	2080	5136	3091	4935	1230				359	2949	1616
1916				1596	2038	5053	3048	4680	1216		296	3049	365	2964	1515
1917				1566					1209				356	2955	1486
1918				1545							311	3128	356	3028	1515
1919				1566	2182	4805			1175			3197	350	3022	1481
1920				1563	2046	5026			1156			3290	343	2998	1533
1921	1560			1578	2049	5015					346	3302	338	3000	1577
1922				1562	2010	5031			1161			5399[10]	341	3002	1579
1923				1545	2039	5305						5468	330	2997	1541
1924				1511	2036	5352			1151		416	5650	327	3096	1526
1925				1492	2020	5366			1156			5871	324	3114	1522
1926				1485	2039	5228					585	5772	322	3167	1546
1927				1466	2071	5347		4377	1148			5524	317	3206	1557
1928				1442	2075	5388		4313	1140			5746	306	3205	1602
1929					2051	5288		3494	1147			5923	299	3308	1664
1930					2017	5333	2857					6110	294	3325	1686

Table D3: Continued

	C of S[1]	*Free C of S*[2]	*UP C of S*[3]	*UF C of S*[4]	*Baptists*[5]		*Congregationalists*[6]		*Pres C of W*[7]	*Assemblies of God*[8]	*Chrstn Science*[9]	*Salv Army*[10]	*Unitns*[11]	*Catholics*[12]	
					Pastors	LPs	Mins	Lay Ps						Sec Clergy	Reg Clergy
1931	2751				2000	5261	2843	3750	1150		785	6062	291	3487	1692
1932					2016	5311	2841	3838				6204	296	3568	1722
1933					2018	5488	2853	3824				6216	297	3658	1767
1934					2042	5332	2852	3770	1133			6061	301	3836	1764
1935					2020	5272	2846	3802	1120			6135	304	3909	1806
1936					2026	5243	2843	3911	1116		1000		297	4017	1856
1937					1996	5137	2822	3810	1124			6135	302	4113	1982
1938					2008	5143	2831	3811				6293	302	4238	2049
1939					2035	5065	2804	3729	1075			6691	299	4347	2127
1940											1104	6606	306	4468	2157
1941									1068		979	6580	305	4553	2171
1942										344		6248	300		
1943									1068			6212	290	4642	2148
1944					1886	4453			1043	352		6287	286	4740	2206
1945							2638	3348	970			6093	274	4891	2218
1946					1887	4430	2575	3343		384	1072	6116		4887	2317
1947					1924	4400	2566	3341	932	379		5905	258	4955	2316
1948					1917	4383	2553	3305	934	379		6201	253		
1949					1921	4453	2555	3256	937	383		6126	246		
1950					1907	4424	2591	3192	913	381		6209	243	5078	2589
1951	2485				1895	4309	2528	3204	875	381	876	6118	239	5166	2585
1952					1924	4419	2534	3212	882	388		6041	231	5050	2672
1953					1921	4381	2499	3278	866	401	898	5986	230	5110	2680
1954					1976	4384	2490	3326	861	416		5939	227	5179	2707
1955					1945	4490	2475	3322	839	427		5943	228	5317	2747
1956					1979	4398	2463		814	427	746	5907	222	5352	2830
1957					2036	4485			835			5782		5599	2858
1958					2056	4387			793	430		5656	217		
1959					2041	4410			775	425		5672	221	5566	3219
1960					2049	4382			759	434		5630	228	5637	2959
1961					2017	4174			726	435	735	5618	229		
1962					2057	4250			699	443		5876	224	5771	3023
1963					2085	4257			705	448		5450	228	5831	3024
1964					2090	4251			693	474		5432	226		
1965					2088	4220			664	488	650	5086	229		

Table D3: Continued

	C of S[1]	*Free C of S*[2]	*UP C of S*[3]	*UF C of S*[4]	*Baptists*[5] Pastors	LPs	*Congregationalists*[6] Mins	Lay Ps	*Pres C of W*[7]	*Assemblies of God*[8]	*Chrstn Science*[9]	*Salv Army*[10]	*Unitns*[11]	*Catholics*[12] Sec Clergy	Reg Clergy
1966					2055	4280			641	486		5032	223	6117	3075
1967					2057	4267			623	482		4995		5972	3133
1968					2010	4197				500		4919		5980	3019
1969					2028	4269		2308		507	581	4798	190	5996	3044
1970					2039	4219				518		4976	184	5942	2980

NOTES AND SOURCES:

1. The series refers to clergymen. The figure for 1790, which is assumed to be total clergy, is derived from Sir John Sinclair, *Analysis of the Statistical Account of Scotland*, Edinburgh, 1825, p. 80; the 1835 figure (total clergy) is from *Pp.* 1839 (XXVI), p. 612; the 1842-43 figures are from James Rankin, *A Handbook of the Church of Scotland*, Edinburgh, 1888.

Because the *Church of Scotland Yearbook* does not generally include statistics on the Ministry, we have given Census of Occupations figures for the years 1851-1951. The 1851 census does not distinguish between Church of Scotland and Free Church ministers; and the Church of Scotland *General Report* cites *Oliver and Boyd's Edinburgh Almanack* as its source in estimating that 1124 out of a total of 2725 British Presbyterian ministers belonged to the Church of Scotland. From 1861 onwards, separate Scottish returns were published and occupation tables were more detailed, until 1961, when only total clergy is given.

The census returns appear to accord quite well with figures which the *Church of Scotland Yearbook* printed during 1919-28. The *Yearbook* states that at 1 Nov. 1921 the total number of established Church ministers working in Scotland was 1561, not including ministers wholly retired or serving in England or overseas. In 1928, the year before Union, the comparable total was 1455.

2. The figures refer to the number of clergymen participating in the General Sustentation Fund, as given by *Proceedings and Debates of the Free Church of Scotland.*

3. The series, which refers to ministers, is taken from the *Proceedings of the Synod of the United Presbyterian Church.* For the years 1859-75, figures given include between 70 and 115 ministers of English congregations. From 1876, the year of English Union, figures refer to Scotland only.

4. The series, which refers to ministers, is taken from *United Free Church of Scotland Reports to the General Assembly*, 1900-29. Annual statistics on ministers begin in 1913.

5. Source: *Baptist Hand-Book.* Both series refer to Great Britain.

6. Sources: *Congregational Yearbook of England and Wales* and *Year-Book of the Congregational Union of Scotland.* Both series refer to Great Britain: that is, to the Congregational Union of England and Wales; the Union of Welsh Independents; and the Congregational Union of Scotland. No Union of Welsh Independents statistics have been available since 1956. The ministerial manpower of the Congregational Union of England and Wales in recent years has changed as follows:

	Ministers	Lay Preachers
1962	1809	3035
1964	1774	2891
1966	1747	2735

7. The series, which refers to ministers and preachers, is taken from *Y Blwyddiadur, neu, Lyfr swyddogol y Methodistiaid Calfinaidd;* and *Whitaker's Almanack.*

8. The series, which refers to ministers, is taken from *Assemblies of God . . . Constitutional Minutes,* 1924-43; *Assemblies of God Yearbook,* 1944-63; and the *General Council Report,* 1964-71. The total given includes ministers on probation (42 in 1942, 51 in 1971) and retired ministers (21 in 1960 and 46 in 1971). All figures refer to the United Kingdom and Ireland.

9. The series refers to practitioners. Most of the figures given were obtained by summing the practitioners listed in the *Christian Science Journal;* a few others have been taken from Bryan R. Wilson, *Sects and Society, a Sociological Study of Three Religious Groups in Britain,* London, 1961, and from *Whitaker's Almanack.* Figures for 1921, 1941, 1951, and 1956 refer to England only, all other figures refer to the United Kingdom. In 1925 there were 6 practitioners in Wales, 18 in Scotland, and 12 in Ireland; in 1965, 18 in Wales, 22 in Scotland, and 10 in Ireland.

10. The series, which refers to officers and employees, is taken from William Booth (ed.), *The East London Evangelist... and Organ of the East London Christian Mission,* Vols. I-XI, 1868-79; Robert Sandall, *The History of the Salvation Army,* Vol. II, London, 1950; *Salvation Army Yearbook;* and annual Salvation Army publications for the years 1893-9. Except for the years 1904-21 figures for 'officers and employees' include full-time workers not only in British Territory corps and societies but in Men's Social Services, Women's Social Services, the Reliance Bank Limited, the Migration and Travel Service, the Salvationist Publishing and Supplies Limited, etc. From 1922 onwards, the totals given are taken from maps published in the *Salvation Army Yearbook.* This 'grand total' of full-time workers in the United Kingdom and Ireland is the longest consistent series available for the period, and does appear to be comparable with available nineteenth-century statistics. In the first quarter of the twentieth century, the only statistics published were those showing full-time workers in British Territory corps and societies. These refer to the United Kingdom and Ireland but do *not* include the large number of officers and employees attached to subsidiary Salvation Army organizations such as those mentioned above. For comparison, British Territory statistics on 'officers and employees' since 1956 are:

1956	3682
1961	3412
1966	3327

11. The series, which refers to ministers, is derived from the *Unitarian Almanac,* 1856-64; *Unitarian Pocket Almanac,* 1863-79; *Unitarian Yearbook,* 1892-1923; and the General Assembly of Unitarian and Free Christian Churches. The figures refer to the United Kingdom and Ireland. There are five or ten Unitarian places of worship in Scotland, thirty to forty congregations in Wales, and a similar number in Ireland. The figures given for 1856 and 1862 show only ministers having charge of congregations; all subsequent figures include ministers without congregations. In addition, until 1915, a small number of lay workers (generally ten or twelve) is included in the total.

12. Sources: the *Catholic Directory* and the *Catholic Directory for the Clergy and Laity in Scotland.* Separate statistics for secular and regular clergy were not published until 1895, but occasional notes in earlier volumes indicate that they constituted roughly the same proportion of the total as they did in 1895. Archbishops and bishops, numbering twenty-four in 1895, are not included in the series from 1895 onwards. All figures refer to Great Britain.

From 1845 to 1912 statistics have been assumed to relate to the year before that in which each *Directory* was published; from 1914 onwards, figures for England and Wales are identified as relating to the year of the volume in which they are published, whereas the *Catholic Directory for the Clergy and Laity of Scotland* continued to print statistics relating to the previous year.

E CHURCH BUILDING[1]

	C of E[2]	*C of S*[3]	*Free C of S*[4]	*UP C of S*[5]	*Baptist*[7] Ches	*Baptist*[7] Chpls	*Congregationalist*[8]	*Pres C of E*[9]	*Pres C of W*[10]	*Assemblies of God*[11]	*Chrstn Science*[12]	*Salvn Army*[13]	*Unitns*[14]	*Catholics*[15]
1801	11 379	893[3]											202	
1806		......											207	
1811	11 444												208	
1816													213	
1821	11 555												216	
1826													221	
1831	11 883	1067[3]											225	
1836													234	
1841	12 668	1210											246	
1846			621[4]	453									251	626
			......											
1851	14 077	1183	837										253	737
1856			852	449									260	872
1861	14 731		882	474	2082		2337[8]						276	993
1866		1250	920	500	2364		2811		2032				290	1180
1871	15 522		942	503	2531		2981		2196			22	298	1169
1876	15 867		984	526			2597	258	2355			29	307	1300
1881	16 300		1052	551	2539		2884	273	2522			251	314	1461
							....							
1886	16 686	1625	1060	563			4417[8]	286	2622			1006	326	1599
1891	16 956	1696	1089	571	2777		4587	289	2730			1213	340	1700
													......	
1896	17 205	1755	1107	580			4593	305	2866			1375	354	1812
			UF C of S[6]											
1901	17 468	1828	1630		2710	3972	4876	326	2953		5	....	368	1886
1906	17 817	1679	1623		2944	3977	4890	345	3069			1431	365	2021
1911	18 026	1643	1545		3047	4120	4910	354	3128		65	1316	374	2179
1916	18 236	1701	1516		3110	4177	4861	355	3231			1244	372	2323
1921	18 270	1704	1482		3019	4124		352	3264		113	1221	361	2377
												....		
1926	18 318	1714	1449		3073	4129	4585	350	3265	188[11]	169	1610	352	2443
		....												
1931	18 417[2]	2920			3122	4100	4671	353	3201		206		348	2685
1936	18 550	2588			3139	4081	4576	345	3219	293	289	1837	340	2859
1941	18 666	2483			3203	4138	4615	333	3195	359	313	1660	340	3061
1946	....	2410			3215	4077	4516	334	3133	403	328	1656	337	3242
1951		2340			3277	4004	4280	333	3039	440	341	1638	334	3419[15]
1956	17 980[2]	2280			3200	3743	4188	326	3036	493	349	1610	318	
1961	17 973	2093			3215	3757		318	3010	512	336	1597	313	
1966	17 761	2166			3211	3686		312		535	330	1571	313	
1971										534		1326		

NOTES AND SOURCES

1. The Table gives quinquennial church-building series, but in many instances indicated in the following footnotes it has not been possible to provide data at exact quinquennial intervals. In these cases the Table uses the nearest year for which data is available.

2. The series refers to churches and chapels. Decennial estimates of the number of Church of England buildings, 1801-51, were published by Horace Mann in the *Report of the Census of Religious Worship,* 1851, *Pp.* 1852-3, LXXXIX. Mann stated that the 14 077 churches, chapels, and other buildings belonging to the Church of England in 1851 were built as follows:

Before 1801	9667
Between 1801 and 1811	55
” 1811 and 1821	97
” 1821 and 1831	276
” 1831 and 1841	667
” 1841 and 1851	1197
Unknown	2118

Mann assumed that the greater portion of the 2118 churches ‘of which the dates of erection are not specified’ were built before 1801, leaving perhaps sixty or seventy built in the period 1801-31. Hence he estimated that ‘above 500’ new churches were built between 1801 and 1831.

The figures for 1861 and 1871 are from the *Convocation of Canterbury Report,* 1876, p. 9. Those for 1876-1941 are based on the annual series for ‘New Churches, Built or Rebuilt and Consecrated’ published in the *Church of England Yearbook.* These figures take no account of dilapidations. Since 1957, the *Church of England Yearbook* has given ‘Total numbers of Parochial Churches and Chapels’. The figure printed here for 1956 refers to 1957. The series refers to churches and chapels in the provinces of Canterbury and York.

3. The series refers to churches and chapels. The figure given here for 1801 is for 1790 and refers only to the number of parish churches. See Sir John Sinclair, *Analysis of the Statistical Account of Scotland,* Edinburgh, 1825. The statistics for 1831-1926 are for parish churches, chapels, and preaching or mission stations. The 1831 figure is taken from ‘Comparative Numbers of Churchmen and Dissenters’, *Church of Scotland Magazine,* June 1834 (and refers to 1833), and that for 1841 from the *Scottish Ecclesiastical Register, and National Almanac,* 1843. The 1851 figure is from the *Report of the Census of Religious Worship,* 1851, *Pp.* 1852-3, LXXXIX. All subsequent figures are taken from the *Church of Scotland Yearbook.* From 1931 onwards, the series refers to the number of congregations.

4. The 1846 figure is taken from the ‘Returns [of churches], now completed and occupied’, in the *Free Church Proceedings and Debates.* All subsequent figures are from R. Howie, *The Churches and Churchless in Scotland: Facts and Figures,* Glasgow, 1893, and refer to the number of *congregations.*

5. Source: *Proceedings of the Synod of the United Presbyterian Church.* The figures refer to Scottish congregations only.

6. The series, which refers to congregations, is taken from *United Free Church of Scotland Reports to the General Assembly,* 1900-29.

7. Source: *Baptist Hand-book.* See also *Baptist Magazine; Record,* 26 September 1839; *General Baptist Handbooks;* and the *Protestant Dissenters' Almanack.* There were 1042 English Baptist Churches in 1832 and 1426 Baptist churches in England and Wales in 1838. In 1861, England had 1593 churches and Wales 399. All figures given in the table refer to Great Britain.

8. The series, which refers to places of worship, is taken from the *Congregational Yearbook of England and Wales* and the *Year-Book of the Congregational Union of Scotland.* Up to 1881

the series refers to self-supporting congregations only; but from 1886 onwards the series includes both those congregations and branch and mission churches. The 1871 figure refers to 1872; the 1876 figure refers to 1875; and the 1881 figure refers to 1880. All figures refer to Great Britain: that is, to the Congregational Union of England and Wales, the Union of Welsh Independents, and the Congregational Union of Scotland. No Union of Welsh Independents statistics have been available since 1956. The Congregational Union of England and Wales had 2941 places of worship in 1961 and 2747 in 1966.

9. The series, which refers to congregations, is taken from the *Minutes of the Synod of the Presbyterian Church of England;* and *Minutes of the General Assembly of the Presbyterian Church of England.*

10. The series, which refers to churches, chapels, and other buildings, is taken from *Y Blwyddiadur, neu, Lyfr swyddogol y Methodistiaid Calfinaidd;* and *Whitaker's Almanack.*

11. The series, which refers to assemblies, is taken from *Assemblies of God . . . Constitutional Minutes,* 1924-43; *Assemblies of God Yearbook,* 1944-63; *General Council Report,* 1964-71. There were 70 Assemblies in 1924. The figure given for 1926 refers to 1927. All figures refer to the United Kingdom and Ireland. In 1927 there were 62 assemblies in Wales and Monmouthshire, 5 in Scotland, and 4 in Ireland; in 1966 there were 78 in Wales, 20 in Scotland, and 9 in Ireland.

12. The series, which refers to churches and societies, is taken from the *Christian Science Journal;* and *Whitaker's Almanack.* All figures refer to Great Britain.

13. The series, which refers to centres of work, is taken from William Booth (ed.), *The East London Evangelist...and Organ of the East London Christian Mission,* Vols. I-XI, 1868-79; Robert Sandall, *The History of the Salvation Army,* Vol. II, 1878-86, London, 1950; *Salvation Army Yearbook;* and annual Salvation Army publications for the years 1893-9. The figures for 1871-96 refer to 'preaching stations' or 'corps' (that is companies of soldiers, recruits, and junior soldiers). Figures for 1906-71 refer to British Territory 'corps, outposts, and societies'; but from 1926 onwards, auxiliary centres of work are included in the totals given. All figures refer to the United Kingdom and Ireland.

14. The series, which refers to congregations, is derived from the *Unitarian Year Book,* 1892-1923; and the General Assembly of Unitarian and Free Christian Churches. The figures for the years 1801-91 are derived from the 1897 edition of the *Yearbook* which lists the years in which all then extant congregations were founded. These figures understate the actual number of congregations in existence at any one time, since some congregations, founded before 1897, did not survive till that year. The 1897 *Yearbook* states that at least fifty of the 378 places of worship listed in an 1878 summary were not in 1897 'living centres of worship'; and the *Unitarian Almanac* of 1864 stated that, of a total of 362 'places at which chapels are situated', 28 were vacant and 70-80 kept open by support from other chapels. All figures refer to the United Kingdom and Ireland.

15. The series, which refers to churches, chapels, and stations, is taken from the *Catholic Directory* and the *Directory for the Clergy and Laity in Scotland.* The figures given are for Great Britain and include a certain number of private chapels: in England and Wales 503 in 1911, and 1196 in 1966. No Scottish statistics on churches, chapels, and stations have been published since 1950, when there were 506 places of worship (here included in the 1951 total). The number of churches, chapels, and stations in England and Wales in 1970 was 4797.

F1 THE CENSUS OF RELIGIOUS WORSHIP 1851 : ENGLAND AND WALES

	Number of Places of Worship	*Number of Sittings*	*Number of attendants*			
			Morning	Afternoon	Evening	Total
BRITISH						
CHURCH OF ENGLAND	14 077	5 317 915	2 541 244	1 890 764	860 543	5 292 551
SCOTTISH PRESBYTERIANS:						
Church of Scotland	18	13 789	6949	960	3849	11 758
United Presbyterian Church	66	31 351	17 725	5085	8818	31 628
Presbyterian Church in England	76	41 552	22 908	3390	10 826	37 124
REFORMED IRISH PRESBYTERIANS	1	120	....	....	....	....
INDEPENDENTS, OR CONGREGATIONALISTS	3244	1 067 760	524 612	232 285	457 162	1 214 059
BAPTISTS:						
General	93	20 539	5404	8130	8562	22 096
Particular	1947	582 953	292 656	175 572	272 524	740 752
Seventh-Day	2	390	27	40	16	83
Scotch	15	2547	649	986	312	1947
New Connexion, General	182	52 604	23 951	15 718	24 652	64 321
Undefined	550	93 310	38 119	23 822	39 050	100 991
SOCIETY OF FRIENDS	371	91 599	14 364	6619	1495	22 478
UNITARIANS	229	68 554	28 483	8881	12 697	50 061
MORAVIANS	32	9305	4993	2466	3415	10 874
WESLEYAN METHODIST:						
Original Connexion	6579	1 447 580	492 714	383 964	667 859	1 544 528
New Connexion	297	96 964	36 801	22 620	39 624	98 045
Primitive Methodists	2871	414 030	100 125	176 435	234 635	511 195
Bible Christians	482	66 834	14 902	24 345	34 612	73 859
Wesleyan Methodist Association	419	98 813	32 308	21 140	40 655	94 103
Independent Methodists	20	2263	601	1311	1208	3120
Wesleyan Reformers	339	67 814	30 470	16 080	44 953	91 503
CALVINISTIC METHODISTS:						
Welsh Calvinistic Methodists	828	211 951	79 728	59 140	125 244	264 112
Lady Huntingdon's Connexion	109	38 727	21 103	4380	19 159	44 642
SANDEMANIANS	6	956	439	256	61	756
NEW CHURCH	50	12 107	4846	2404	3102	10 352
BRETHREN	132	18 529	5699	4509	7384	17 592
ISOLATED CONGREGATIONS	539	104 481	36 969	24 208	43 498	104 675

Table F1: Continued

	Number of Places of Worship	Number of Sittings	Number of attendants: Morning	Afternoon	Evening	Total
FOREIGN:						
LUTHERANS	6	2606	1152	264	......	1416
FRENCH PROTESTANTS	3	560	225	32	150	407
REFORMED CHURCH OF THE NETHERLANDS	1	350	70	....	......	70
GERMAN PROTESTANT REFORMERS	1	200	120	....	60	180
OTHER CHRISTIAN CHURCHES:						
ROMAN CATHOLICS	570	186 111	252 783	53 967	76 880	383 630
GREEK CHURCH	3	291	240	....	....	240
GERMAN CATHOLICS	1	300	500	....	200	700
ITALIAN REFORMERS	1	150	....	20	......	20
CATHOLIC AND APOSTOLIC CHURCH	32	7437	3176	1659	2707	7542
LATTER DAY SAINTS	222	30 783	7517	11 481	16 628	35 626
JEWS	53	8438	2910	1202	1918	6030

NOTES AND SOURCES

1. Source: *Pp.* 1852-3, LXXXIX. This Table reproduces the arrangement and titles of the Census Table.

2. In 1851 the census enumerators were required to obtain returns relating to public worship and this undertaking was organized by Horace Mann. Mann described the 'mode of procuring and digesting the returns' as follows (*Pp.* 1852-3, LXXXIX, clxix-clxxi):

> The first proceeding was to obtain a correct account of all existing edifices or apartments where religious services were customarily performed. The enumerators, therefore, were directed to prepare . . . a list of all such placed within their districts . . . . To each [minister or other official party] was delivered . . . a schedule of inquiries – chiefly respecting the accommodation furnished in the building, and the number of the congregation upon Sunday, March the 30th . . . .
>
> The schedules were collected by the enumerators in the course of their rounds upon the Census day, viz., March 31st, 1851. They were then transmitted to the registrars; who, having previously received the lists above referred to, would compare the number of returns collected with the number mentioned in the lists, and would take measures to procure, if possible, the returns, if any, which were missing.

After considerable efforts to obtain information about places of worship which made no return, 'a return was ultimately . . . procured from . . . 14 077 places belonging to the Established Church, and from 20 390 places belonging to the various dissenting bodies, making 34 467 in all.' There were still, however, 2524 returns which failed to mention sittings or attendants, or both. The Census provides both the original, authenticated figures and totals which included estimates for the defective returns. *It is these estimated or 'corrected' totals which are reproduced in this Table* (*Pp.* 1852-3, LXXXIX, clxxxii-clxxxiii, and 1854, LIX, 317).

The estimates were made by assuming that each place of worship making defective returns had as many attendants as the average of places of worship making complete returns; and that the number of sittings was one-fourth more than the number of attendants.

Mann's attendance figures make no distinction between the 'general congregation' and Sunday-school scholars, because, since many of the returns gave total numbers only, Mann decided it was 'the better course in every instance to include them in one total'. The category of 'total attendants' includes an unknown number of persons who attended more than one service.

For further discussion of the census, see K. S. Inglis, 'Patterns of Religious Worship' in *Journal of Ecclesiastical History*, April 1960, and D. M. Thompson, 'The 1851 Census: Problems and Possibilities', *Victorian Studies*, September 1967.

3. The following summary shows, for the larger religious bodies, the original 'uncorrected' figures given for North and South Wales (Table C, *Pp.* 1852-3, LXXXIX, ccxxxiii-ccxxxiv). For the purposes of comparison, the comparable *uncorrected* England and Wales figures for total attendances are given.

	Wales						England and Wales
	Number of places of Worship	*Number of Sittings*	*Attendances*				*Total Attendances*
			Morning	Afternoon	Evening	Total	
Church of England	979	236 650	83 089	40 525	31 452	155 066	4 939 514
Congregationalists	640	153 945	79 069	31 911	86 730	197 710	1 191 978
All Baptists	440	98 035	50 550	20 843	64 324	135 717	900 085
All Methodists	533	89 167	25 115	21 039	50 296	96 450	2 370 460
Calvinistic Methodists	780	183 095	73 188	56 396	116 416	246 000	264 112
Catholics	12	2823	3302	718	546	4566	365 430

The number of attendants in each case refers to attendants in places of worship making complete returns.

F2. THE CENSUS OF RELIGIOUS WORSHIP 1851: SCOTLAND

	Number of Places of Worship	Number of Sittings	Number of Attendants			
			Morning	Afternoon	Evening	Total
PROTESTANT CHURCHES:						
PRESBYTERIAN:						
Established Church	1183	767 088	351 454	184 192	30 763	566 409
Reformed Presbyterian Church	39	16 969	8739	7460	2180	18 379
Original Secession Church	36	16 424	6562	5724	1629	13 915
Relief Church	2	1020	220	250	275	745
United Presbyterian Church	465	288 100	159 191	146 411	30 810	336 412
Free Church	889	495 335	292 308	198 583	64 811	555 702
EPISCOPAL CHURCH	134	40 022	26 966	11 578	5360	43 904
INDEPENDENTS, OR CONGREGATIONALISTS	192	76 342	26 392	24 866	17 273	68 531
BAPTISTS	119	26 086	9208	7735	4015	20 958
SOCIETY OF FRIENDS	7	2152	196	142	....	338
UNITARIANS	5	2437	863	130	855	1848
UNITED BRETHREN OR MORAVIANS	1	200	16	......	55	71
WESLEYAN METHODISTS:						
Original Connexion	70	19 951	8409	2669	8610	19 688
Primitive Methodists	10	1890	327	404	715	1446
Independent Methodists	1	600	190	150	180	520
Wesleyan Reformers	1	......	11	......	11	22
GLASSITES OR SANDEMANIANS	6	1068	429	554	100	1083
NEW CHURCH	5	710	211	67	120	398
CAMPBELLITES	1	80	11	14	......	25
EVANGELICAL UNION	28	10 319	3895	4504	2171	10 570
ISOLATED CONGREGATIONS	50	11 322	2871	2046	3053	7970
OTHER CHRISTIAN CHURCHES:						
ROMAN CATHOLICS	117	52 766	43 878	21 032	14 813	79 723
CATHOLIC AND APOSTOLIC CHURCH	3	675	272	126	190	588
LATTER DAY SAINTS	20	3182	1304	1225	878	3407
JEWS	1	67	28	....	7	35

NOTES AND SOURCES

1. Source: *Pp*. 1854, LIX. This Table reproduces the arrangement and titles of the Census table.
2. Note 1 to Table F1 applies to this Table also.

G1 REPUBLIC OF IRELAND[1]

	Total Population	Catholics	Percentage[2]	All Other Denominations	Protestant Episcopalians[3]	Percentage	Presbyterians	Percentage	Methodists	Jews	Baptists	Others
1861	4 402 111	3 933 575	89.4	468 536	372 723	8.5	66 172	1.5	17 480	341	943	10 877
1871	4 053 187	3 616 426	89.2	436 761	338 719	8.4	61 917	1.5	16 905	230	801	18 189
1881	3 870 020	3 465 332	89.5	404 688	317 576	8.2	56 498	1.5	17 660	394	734	11 826
1891	3 468 694	3 099 003	89.3	369 691	286 804	8.3	51 469	1.5	18 513	1506	1139	10 260
1901	3 221 823	2 878 271	89.3	343 552	264 264	8.2	46 714	1.5	17 872	3006	1159	10 106
1911	3 139 688	2 812 509	89.6	327 179	249 535	7.9	45 486	1.5	16 440	3805	1588	10 325
1926	2 971 992	2 751 269	92.6	220 723	164 215	5.5	32 429	1.1	10 663	3686	717	9013
1936	2 968 420	2 773 920	93.4	194 500	145 030	4.9	28 067	0.9	9649	3749	715	7290
1946	2 955 107	2 786 033	94.3	169 074	124 829	4.2	23 870	0.8	8355	3907	462	7651
1961	2 818 341	2 673 473	94.9	144 868	104 016	3.7	18 953	0.7	6676	3255	481	11 487
1971	2 978 248	2 795 596	93.9	128 319	97 791	3.3	16 054	0.5	5646	2635	591	54 333

NOTES AND SOURCES

1. The series refer to the twenty-six counties that formed the Irish Free State, and later the Republic of Ireland. It has been estimated that the population of the *whole* of Ireland in 1834 was 7 954 100, of which 6 436 060 (or 80·9) were Catholics, while 1 518 040 were affiliated to other denominations. Protestant Episcopalians were calculated to number 853 160 or 10·7 per cent of the whole; and Presbyterians 643 058 or 8·1 per cent of the whole. See 'Report on Religion and Education' in *Pp*. 1861, LIX. The only earlier enumerations of the Irish people according to religion were in 1672 and 1732–3.

Sir William Petty's *Political Anatomy of Ireland* (published in 1691 but apparently referring to December 1672) divided the inhabitants of Ireland according to national origin and religion as follows:

Total Population:			1 100 000	
Irish–	Catholics:		800 000	
English–	Established Church:	above	100 000	200 000
	Protestant Dissenters:	under	100 000	
Scots–	Presbyterians:		100 000	

The 1861 'Report on Religion and Education' (from which this summary is taken) suggests that Petty's estimates are not wholly reliable. He does not give the basis of his calculations and the 'Report' states that, 'even if we allow his figures to have approximated somewhat closely to the real numbers, his ethnological distribution of the people, according to religions, is not historically accurate': for example, not all the Irish were Catholics, nor all the Catholics Irish.

The second attempt to gather statistics on religious affiliations in Ireland was made in 1736 in connection with the returns to the Hearth-Money Office in Dublin in 1732 and 1733: see *An Abstract of the Number of Protestant and Popish families in the several Counties and Provinces of Ireland, taken from the returns made by the Hearth-Money Collectors . . .* , Dublin, 1736. These returns are also discussed in the Report on the 1861 Census, which states that the population returned for all Ireland was 527 505 Protestants and 1 407 005 Catholics. The 1861 Report adjusts these returns 'in order to represent with some accuracy, the total population of the island',

and gives the following 'corrected' estimate for 1732:

Protestants of all denominations:	562 805
Catholics	1 417 005
Total	1 979 810

In 1971 the religious affiliation question in the Census became optional; and this may account for much of the increase in the column for 'Others', which includes those giving no answer to this question.

2. All percentages refer to total population.

3. For the definition of Protestant Episcopalians see Table G2, note 3.

4. Sources: *Censuses* of Ireland, and Republic of Ireland; *Catholic Directory of Ireland*.

G2 NORTHERN IRELAND

	Total Population	*Catholics*	*Percentage*[2]	*All other Denominations*	*Protestant Episcopalians*[3]	*Percentage*	*Presby-terians*	*Percentage*	*Methodists*	*Others*
1861	1 396 453	571 690	40.9	824 763	320 634	23.0	457 119	32.7	27 919	19 091
1871	1 359 190	534 441	39.3	824 749	329 279	24.2	435 731	32.1	26 536	33 203
1881	1 304 816	495 559	38.0	809 257	321 998	24.7	414 236	31.7	31 179	41 844
1891	1 236 056	448 304	36.3	787 752	313 299	25.3	393 505	31.8	36 987	43 961
1901	1 236 952	430 390	34.8	806 562	316 825	25.6	396 562	32.0	44 134	49 041
1911	1 250 531	430 161	34.4	820 370	327 076	26.1	395 039	31.6	45 942	52 313
1926	1 256.561	420 428	33.5	836 133	338 724	27.0	393 374	31.3	49 554	54 481
1937	1 279 745	428 290	33.5	851 455	345 474	27.0	390 931	30.5	55 135	59 915
1951	1 370 921	471 460	34.4.	899 461	353 245	25.8	410 215	29.9	66 639	69 362
1961	1 425 042	497 547	34.9	927 495	344 800	24.2	413 113	29.0	71 865	97 717
1971	1 519 640	477 919	31.4	899 210	334 318	22.0	405 719	26.7	71 235	87 938

NOTES AND SOURCES

1. The series refer to the six counties that form Northern Ireland. For religious affiliations in the whole of Ireland before 1861, see Table G1, note 1. In 1971 the religious affiliation question in the Census became optional.

2. All percentages refer to total population.

3. Most but not all Protestant Episcopalians belong to the Church of Ireland as the following figures for Northern Ireland show:

	Church of Ireland	Church of England	Episcopal Church in Scotland
1926	320 001	18 682	41
1961	329 920	14 834	46

4. 'Others' include those who state no denomination in their census returns.

5. Sources: *Censuses* of Ireland, and Northern Ireland.

H1 MARRIAGES BY MANNER OF SOLEMNIZATION: ENGLAND AND WALES

	All	*Religious*	*C of E*[1]	*Catholics*[2]	*Other Denominations*	*Jews*	*Civil*
1838	111 481	110 388	107 201		2976	135	1093
1839	121 083	119 519	114 632		4654	160	1564
1840	124 329	122 391	117 018		5140	152	1938
1841	122 482	120 446	114 448		5816	116	2036
1842	118 825	116 468	110 047		6200	163	2357
1843	123 818	121 001	113 637		7152	151	2817
1844	132 249	128 803	120 009	2280	6284	175	3446
1845	143 743	139 766	129 515	2816	7181	180	3977
1846	145 664	141 497	130 509	3027	7669	224	4167
1847	135 845	131 587	120 876	2961	7483	184	4258
1848	138 230	133 440	121 469	3658	8060	186	4790
1849	141 883	136 325	123 182	4199	8662	229	5558
1850	152 744	146 537	130 959	5623	9626	260	6207
1851	154 206	147 393	130 958	6570	9540	260	6813
1852	158 782	151 682	133 882	7479	10 017	247	7100
1853	164 520	156 922	138 042	8375	10 149	288	7598
1854	159 727	152 134	134 109	7813	9873	287	7593
1855	152 113	144 672	127 751	7344	9296	224	7441
1856	159 337	151 240	133 619	7527	9710	312	8097
1857	159 097	149 455	131 031	7360	10 686	311	9642
1858	156 070	146 118	128 082	6643	11 094	220	9952
1859	167 723	156 879	136 210	7756	12 519	324	10 844
1860	170 156	158 899	137 370	7800	13 342	312	11 257
1861	163 706	151 981	130 697	7782	13 182	262	11 725
1862	164 030	151 307	129 733	7345	13 870	300	12 723
1863	173 510	159 921	136 743	8095	14 714	318	13 589
1864	180 387	165 776	141 083	8659	15 627	349	14 611
1865	185 474	170 682	145 104	8742	16 429	353	14 792
1866	187 776	172 530	146 040	8911	17 215	301	15 246
1867	179 154	164 096	138 930	7918	16 865	315	15 058
1868	176 962	161 084	136 038	7517	17 150	306	15 878
1869	176 970	160 225	135 082	7231	17 526	336	16 745
1870	181 655	163 807	137 986	7391	18 024	358	17 848
1871	190 112	171 734	144 663	7647	18 975	396	18 378
1872	201 267	181 272	152 364	8427	20 009	428	19 995
1873	205 615	184 437	154 581	8222	21 071	484	21 178
1874	202 010	180 754	150 819	8179	21 253	456	21 256
1875	201 212	180 210	149 685	8411	21 562	492	21 002
1876	201 874	180 165	148 910	8577	22 164	459	21 709
1877	194 352	173 083	142 396	8277	21 905	427	21 269
1878	190 054	167 998	137 969	7980	21 484	505	22 056
1879	182 082	160 313	131 689	7437	20 673	460	21 769
1880	191 965	167 785	137 661	8210	21 394	463	24 180
1881	197 290	172 235	140 995	8784	21 922	484	25 055
1882	204 405	178 688	146 102	9235	22 768	513	25 717
1883	206 384	179 837	147 000	8980	23 260	539	26 547
1884	204 301	177 515	144 344	8783	23 726	601	26 786
1885	197 745	171 894	139 913	8162	23 130	640	25 851

Table H1: Continued

	All	*Religious*	*C of E*[1]	*Catholics*[2]	*Other Denominations*				*Jews*	*Civil*
1886	196 071	170 481	138 571	8220	22 969				674	25 590
1887	200 518	173 183	140 607	8611	23 259				649	27 335
1888	203 821	176 012	142 863	8632	23 667				799	27 809
1889	213 865	184 086	149 356	8988	24 802				867	29 779
1890	223 028	192 652	156 371	9596	25 703				905	30 376
1891	226 526	195 717	158 439	9517	26 642				1045	30 809
1892	227 135	195 719	158 632	9133	26 837				1048	31 416
1893	218 689	187 310	151 309	9019	25 788				1113	31 379
1894	226 449	192 899	155 352	9453	26 907				1129	33 550
1895	228 204	194 455	156 469	9405	27 293				1214	33 749
1896	242 764	207 325	166 871	10 042	29 059				1252	35 439
1897	249 145	212 519	170 806	10 095	30 098				1429	36 626
1898	255 379	217 441	174 826	10 164	30 900				1445	37 938
1899	262 334	222 931	177 896	10 686	32 603				1666	39 403
1900	257 480	218 009	173 060	10 267	32 936				1669	39 471
1901	259 400	218 333	172 679	10 624	33 135				1813	41 067
1902	261 750	218 989	173 011	10 606	33 337				1944	42 761
1903	261 103	216 583	170 044	10 621	33 918				1894	44 520
1904	257 856	211 609	165 519	10 450	33 745				1815	46 247
1905	260 742	212 974	165 747	10 812	34 355				1980	47 768
1906	270 038	219 356	170 579	11 455	35 094				2139	50 682
1907	276 421	222 395	172 497	11 700	36 094				1997	54 026
1908	264 940	210 892	163 086	10 940	35 003				1756	54 048
1909	260 544	207 039	159 991	10 962	34 233				1760	53 505
1910	267 721	213 043	164 945	11 312	34 866				1811	54 678
1911	274 943	217 508	167 925	12 002	35 658				1820	57 435
1912	283 834	225 467	174 357	12 715	36 399				1904	58 367
1913	286 583	224 255	172 640	13 349	36 241				1934	62 328
1914[4]	294 401	223 521	171 700	13 729	36 021				1973	70 880
					Baptists	*Congregationalists*[2]	*Methodists*	*Others*		
1919	369 411	284 081	220 557	19 078	7176	8657	20 804	5811	1861	85 330
1924	296 416	225 812	171 480	16 286	5950	7335	17 757	4956	1972	70 604
1929	313 316	232 841	176 113	18 711	5801	7189	17 606	5252	2088	80 475
1934	342 307	245 187	183 123	22 323	6056	7276	17 979	6061	2233	97 120
1952	349 308	242 531	173 282	33 050	5277	6952	16 640	5378	1876	106 777
1957	346 903	249 819	172 010	39 960	5897	6632	17 182	6345	1713	97 084
9162	347 732	244 630	164 707	42 788	5991	6479	16 927	6098	1549	103 102
1962	386 052	254 476	173 278	43 305	5523	6632	17 468	6588	1557	131 576
1972	426 241	232 107	155 538	39 694	5152	5419	16 792	7855	1656	194 134

NOTES AND SOURCES

1. Marriages according to the rites of the Church in Wales are included in the total for marriages according to the rites of the Church of England.

2. The Catholic Education Council for England and Wales has supplied the following figures for the number of 'Catholic' and 'Mixed' marriages according to the rites of the Catholic Church, that is, marriages between two Catholics and between a Catholic and a non-Catholic.

	Catholic	Mixed	Total
1959	23 318	22 079	45 397
1960	23 217	23 263	46 480
1961	23 701	23 392	47 093
1962	22 705	23 305	46 010
1963	21 839	23 558	45 397
1964	21 431	24 161	45 592
1965	20 808	25 304	46 112
1966	19 893	26 650	46 543
1967	19 123	26 942	46 065
1968	18 647	28 827	47 474
1969	17 263	28 148	45 411
1970	17 251	28 854	46 105

The figures are not comparable with those published by the Registrar-General.

3. On 5 October 1972 the Congregational Union of England and Wales and the Presbyterian Church of England united to form the United Reformed Church. Between 1 January 1972 and 5 October 1972 there were 1500 Presbyterian Church of England marriages; and between 5 October 1972 and 31 December 1972 there were 1102 United Reformed Church marriages.

4. Society of Friends marriages have been omitted from the column for 'Other Denominations', but included in the columns for 'Religious Marriages' and 'All Marriages'. The number of Society of Friends marriages in England and Wales has fluctuated as follows:

		1870	48	1919	137
		1880	57	1929	81
1840	81	1890	77	1952	76
1850	69	1900	77	1962	91
1860	75	1910	109	1967	125

5. Between 1914 and 1972 the Registrar-General for England and Wales has published data on the manner of solemnization of marriages only for the years given here.

6. Source: *Annual Reports* of the Registrar-General for England and Wales.

H2 MARRIAGES BY MANNER OF SOLEMNIZATION: SCOTLAND

	All	Religious	C of S	Free C of S	UP C of S	UF C of S	Catholics	Ep C in S	Other Denoms	Civil and Irregular[2]
1855	19 680	19 671	8879	4665	2952		1826	350	923	9
1856	20 740	20 704	9863	4645	2875		1953	360	984	36
1857	21 369	21 362	10 194	4789	2926		1919	416	1017	7
1858	19 655	19 628	9104	4650	2707		1697	379	1034	27
1859	21 201	21 184	9769	4861	2936		1822	378	1175	17
1860	21 225	21 209	9705	4870	2837		1857	414	1217	16
1861	20 896	20 871	9332	4969	2925		1806	386	1290	25
1862	20 597	20 570	9307	4930	2846		1778	371	990	27
1863	22 234	22 215	9929	5242	3249		2119	487	1113	19
1864	22 725	22 703	9907	5507	3198		2276	459	1231	22
1865	23 611	23 579	10 177	5636	3345		2399	476	1516	32
1866	23 688	23 646	10 392	5570	3385		2259	516	1483	42
1867	22 618	22 575	10 066	5347	3247		2039	488	1323	43
1868	21 855	21 795	9736	5015	3244		1872	467	1403	60
1869	22 144	22 075	9761	5095	3277		2043	450	1393	69
1870	23 854	23 780	10 678	5465	3422		2121	538	1496	74
1871	24 019	23 914	10 985	5404	3325		2087	551	1498	105
1872	25 641	25 493	11 794	5661	3312		2461	579	1681	148
1873	26 748	26 551	12 187	5806	3596		2451	648	1853	197
1874	26 390	26 174	11 820	5922	3586		2267	643	1923	216
1875	25 974	25 739	11 587	5889	3443		2254	658	1899	235
1876	26 579	26 281	11 996	5944	3603		2279	719	1703	298
1877	25 817	25 462	11 773	5833	3313		2368	651	1477	355
1878	24 358	23 970	11 330	5431	3013		2181	653	1350	388
1879	23 519	23 193	10 744	5314	2878		2171	653	1415	326
1880	24 505	24 142	11 275	5287	2981		2337	700	1529	363
1881	26 004	25 585	12 179	5402	3088		2537	695	1638	419
1882	26 596	26 145	12 356	5481	3128		2697	746	1678	451
1883	26 869	26 278	12 384	5478	3252		2726	728	1699	591
1884	26 106	25 489	12 000	5499	3001		2606	705	1678	617
1885	25 304	24 736	11 692	5344	2915		2443	700	1642	568
1886	24 515	23 925	11 507	5036	2812		2241	723	1597	590
1887	24 876	24 247	11 689	4866	2928		2422	685	1655	629
1888	25 305	24 546	11 647	5052	2876		2464	783	1724	759
1889	26 344	25 503	11 846	5263	3004		2653	791	1943	841
1890	27 469	26 436	12 408	5347	3097		2791	768	2025	1033

Table H2: Continued

	All	*Religious*	*C of S*	*Free C of S*	*UP C of S*	*UF C of S*	*Catholics*	*Ep C in S*	*Other Denoms*	*Civil and Irregular*[2]
1891	27 969	26 850	12 698	5415	3207		2692	788	2050	1119
1892	28 670	27 466	12 865	5677	3284		2850	809	1981	1204
1893	27 145	25 900	12 371	5259	3048		2489	813	1920	1245
1894	27 604	26 438	12 650	5313	3074		2608	801	1992	1166
1895	28 422	27 179	12 832	5496	3051		2855	870	2075	1243
1896	30 270	28 802	13 694	5552	3316		2991	981	2268	1468
1897	31 050	29 520	14 002	5729	3467		3026	980	2316	1530
1898	32 112	30 544	14 567	6033	3486		3091	949	2418	1568
1899	32 978	31 158	14 687	6080	3567		3419	1033	2372	1820
1900	32 444	30 530	14 600			9242	3322	964	2402	1914
1901	31 387	29 435	14 167			8669	3184	942	2473	1952
1902	31 913	29 822	14 267			8803	3337	969	2446	2091
1903	32 351	30 425	14 692			8778	3487	876	2592	1926
1904	32 271	30 409	14 803			8776	3328	925	2577	1862
1905	31 270	29 408	14 245			8240	3376	946	2601	1762
1906	33 142	31 157	14 983			8634	3644	983	2913	1985
1907	33 298	31 074	15 116			8667	3536	1005	2750	2224
1908	31 606	29 360	14 238			8271	3272	934	2645	2246
1909	30 108	28 093	13 753			7821	2975	908	2636	2015
1910	30 902	28 722	13 871			8110	3171	867	2703	2180
1911	31 844	29 237	14 032			8083	3404	984	2734	2607
1912	32 506	29 951	14 168			8440	3607	964	2772	2555
1913	33 676	30 625	14 328			8480	3960	1111	2746	3051
1914	35 028	30 629	14 644			8260	3951	1032	2742	4399
1915	36 233	28 812	13 414			7901	3907	1155	2436	7420
1916	31 419	25 457	11 632			7037	3612	985	2191	5962
1917	30 421	25 439	11 922			6858	3429	1070	2160	4982
1918	34 529	28 586	13 299			7790	3789	1243	2465	5943
1919	44 060	35 709	16 709			9808	4663	1429	3100	8351
1920	46 754	38 906	18 157			10 739	5318	1346	3346	7848
1921	39 243	33 108	15 976			9082	4220	1076	2754	6135
1922	34 375	29 700	14 329			8022	3730	1031	2588	4675
1923	35 200	30 904	14 757			8411	4034	1005	2697	4296
1924	32 328	28 393	13 488			7657	3849	974	2425	3935
1925	32 456	28 424	13 548			7531	3865	951	2529	4032

Table H2: Continued

	All	Religious	C of S	Free C of S	UP C of S	UF C of S	Catholics	Ep C in S	Other Denoms	Civil and Irregular[2]
1926	31 244	27 532	13 203			7403	3580	964	2382	3712
1927	32 553	28 615	13 858			7534	3804	945	2474	3938
1928	32 948	29 041	13 942			7607	3937	941	2587	3934
1929	32 967	28 816	15 503			5849	3925	930	2609	4151
1930	33 315	29 250	21 328				4162	897	2863	4065
1931	32 652	28 555	20 765				4115	870	2805	4097
1932	33 157	29 134	21 034				4346	917	2837	4023
1933	34 201	30 190	21 687				4577	925	3001	4011
1934	36 934	32 633	23 476				4888	1040	3229	4301
1935	37 988	33 626	24 069				5069	1018	3470	4362
1936	37 896	33 393	23 791				4925	1026	3651	4503
1937	38 334	33 620	24 219				4874	1004	3523	4714
1938	38 716	33 232	24 012				4760	1033	3427	5484
1939	46 236	38 596	27 779				5729	1212	3849	7667
1940	53 522	47 182	33 756				7230	1715	4481	6340[2]
1941	47 620	42 218	30 017				6282	1705	4214	5402
1942	47 402	41 674	29 827				6103	1671	4073	5728
1943	38 177	32 987	23 377				4891	1489	3230	5190
1944	37 017	31 882	22 554				4831	1334	3163	5135
1945	48 642	41 790	30 107				6025	1745	3913	6852
1946	45 785	38 249	27 599				5770	1390	3490	7536
1947	44 360	36 416	26 189				5714	1176	3337	7944
1948	43 718	36 233	25 798				5879	1243	3313	7485
1949	41 708	34 526	24 590				5694	1065	3177	7182
1950	40 459	33 208	23 579				5660	1009	2960	7251
1951	41 361	34 429	24 259				6062	1122	2986	6932
1952	41 154	33 687	23 671				6033	1022	2961	7467
1953	40 902	33 715	23 597				6284	935	2899	7187
1954	41 974	34 127	23 802				6425	988	2912	7847
1955	43 199	34 883	24 213				6734	1017	2919	8316
1956	43 963	36 086	24 915				7235	950	2986	7877
1957	42 661	35 231	24 325				7093	939	2874	7430
1958	41 186	33 684	23 118				6904	868	2794	7502
1959	40 442	33 190	22 773				6785	910	2722	7252
1960	40 103	32 926	22 709				6789	820	2608	7177

Table H3: Continued

	All	*Religious*	*C of S*	*Free C of S*	*UP C of S*	*UF C of S*	*Catholics*	*Ep C in S*	*Other Denoms*	*Civil and Irregular*[2]
1961	40 562	32 989	22 580				6940	831	2638	7573
1962	40 244	32 131	21 843				6858	846	2584	8113
1963	39 653	31 582	21 519				6715	806	2542	8071
1964	40 242	31 631	21 568				6702	847	2514	8611
1965	40 475	31 200	21 297				6687	845	2371	9275
1966	41 851	31 591	21 572				6756	875	2388	10 260
1967	42 116	31 522	21 284				6940	920	2378	10 594
1968	43 696	32 223	21 938				6949	935	2401	11 473
1969	43 294	31 234	21 046				6875	878	2435	12 060
1970	43 203	30 885	20 664				7099	857	2265	12 318

NOTES AND SOURCES

1. Between 1855 and 1889 a number of returns for religious marriages did not state denomination. These marriages, never more than 350 in one year, are included in the totals for religious marriages.

2. Irregular marriages by declaration were abolished on 1 July 1940.

3. Source: *Annual Reports* of the Registrar-General for Scotland.

H3 MARRIAGES BY MANNER OF SOLEMNIZATION: IRELAND

	All	*Religious*	*Catholics*	*C of I*	*Presby-terians*	*Other Denoms*	*Civil*
1846				5760	2712	67	797
1847				4321	1777	62	772
1848				5313	2313	87	1320
1849				5324	2440	67	1647
1850				5387	2504	85	1789
1851				5201	2517	80	1527
1852				5365	2547	92	1475
1853				5562	2890	100	1626
1854				5188	2701	77	1447
1855				4922	2435	79	1316
1856				5319	2551	83	1580
1857				5343	2847	75	1660
1858				4941	2477	86	1444
1859				4979	2686	90	1498
1860				4956	2680	109	1427
1861				4779	2621	95	1403
1862				4564	2489	79	1287
1863				4514	2362	101	1200
1864	27 406	26 297	18 819	4761	2514	192	1109
1865	30 802	29 740	21 782	5064	2709	165	1062
1866	30 121	29 175	21 211	5006	2697	245	946
1867	29 742	28 865	20 977	4992	2674	206	877
1868	27 699	26 919	19 521	4678	2457	243	780
1869	27 277	26 485	18 986	4739	2515	230	792
1870	28 667	27 930	20 454	4704	2528	235	737
1871	28 960	28 263	20 942	4205	2805	294	697
1872	26 943	26 382	18 932	4374	2773	291	561
1873	25 730	25 164	18 129	4210	2484	324	566
1874	24 481	23 934	17 348	3914	2365	299	547
1875	24 037	23 515	16 589	4088	2495	326	522
1876	26 388	25 848	18 930	4033	2528	347	540
1877	24 722	24 216	17 458	3912	2493	344	506
1878	25 284	24 772	17 898	3900	2571	390	512
1879	23 254	22 747	16 528	3646	2214	338	507
1880	20 363	19 814	13 494	3709	2283	312	549
1881	21 826	21 336	14 981	3690	2318	341	490
1882	22 029	21 536	15 181	3688	2312	349	493
1883	21 368	20 869	14 616	3649	2233	359	499
1884	22 585	22 088	15 873	3617	2224	362	497
1885	21 177	20 720	14 591	3540	2233	343	457
1886	20 594	20 151	14 248	3383	2118	379	443
1887	20 945	20 481	14 224	3640	2237	363	464
1888	20 060	19 623	13 361	3601	2247	394	437
1889	21 521	21 101	14 787	3644	2268	393	420
1890	20 990	20 545	14 297	3556	2251	432	445

Table H2: Continued

	All	*Religious*	*Catholics*	*C of I*	*Presby-terians*	*Other Denoms*	*Civil*
1891	21 475	21 076	14 697	3570	2353	442	399
1892	21 530	21 158	14 757	3553	2352	481	372
1893	21 714	21 339	15 092	3546	2295	385	375
1894	21 602	21 240	14 795	3582	2373	470	362
1895	23 120	22 720	15 938	3817	2461	489	400
1896	23 055	22 667	15 733	3980	2436	492	388
1897	22 891	22 507	15 638	3831	2492	529	384
1898	22 580	22 190	15 526	3625	2509	511	390
1899	22 311	21 938	15 256	3665	2403	587	373
1900	21 330	20 954	14 795	3297	2295	549	376
1901	22 564	22 196	15 603	3542	2480	555	368
1902	22 949	22 564	15 913	3633	2441	565	382
1903	22 992	22 642	16 095	3669	2358	499	350
1904	22 961	22 586	16 165	3590	2267	549	375
1905	23 078	22 691	16 128	3678	2361	509	387
1906	22 662	22 262	15 818	3604	2330	485	400
1907	22 509	22 078	15 571	3668	2347	479	422
1908	22 734	22 313	16 069	3474	2306	446	421
1909	22 650	22 252	16 057	3427	2296	462	398
1910	22 112	21 597	15 527	3474	2214	457	415
1911	23 473	23 038	16 729	3627	2211	461	435
1912	23 283	22 878	16 577	3494	2331	454	405
1913	22 266	21 935	15 738	3447	2279	452	331
1914	23 695	23 318	17 014	3601	2252	428	377
1915	24 154	23 762	17 334	3521	2412	479	392
1916	22 245	21 907	16 393	3011	2049	441	338
1917	21 073	20 739	15 049	3099	2101	468	334
1918	22 570	22 158	15 733	3566	2319	522	412
1919	27 193	26 679	18 756	4247	3008	643	514
1920	26 826	26 148	18 290	3937	3215	678	678

NOTES AND SOURCES

1. Jewish and Society of Friends marriages have been omitted from the column of 'Other Denominations', but included in the columns for 'Religious Marriages' and 'All Marriages'.

2. Source: *Annual Reports* of the Registrar-General for Ireland.

H4 MARRIAGES BY MANNER OF SOLEMNIZATION: REPUBLIC OF IRELAND

	All	*Religious*	*Catholics*	*C of I*	*Presbyterians*	*Methodists*	*Other Denoms*	*Civil*
1920	17 276	17 115	15 655	1140	205		96	161
1921	15 102	14 947	13 700	970	180		88	155
1922	15 141	15 014	13 915	856	154		78	127
1923	15 632	15 549	14 576	752	154		53	83
1924	14 822	14 757	13 835	709	143		54	65
1925	13 820	13 766	12 897	671	112		70	54
1926	13 570	13 483	12 600	672	144		48	87
1927	13 418	13 345	12 501	612	163		52	73
1928	13 716	13 631	12 782	653	122		61	85
1929	13 593	13 519	12 670	660	116		60	74
1930	13 631	13 548	12 670	667	131		66	83
1931	13 133	13 068	12 228	652	126		56	65
1932	13 029	12 958	12 177	584	121		65	71
1933	13 992	13 922	13 093	646	119		51	70
1934	14 251	14 195	13 431	562	125		65	56
1935	14 336	14 264	13 454	636	118		47	72
1936	14 763	14 699	13 834	660	134		59	64
1937	14 780	14 721	13 808	718	139		46	59
1938	14 893	14 844	13 969	680	128		54	49
1939	15 204	15 152	14 282	660	132		59	52
1940	15 212	15 163	14 252	681	147		75	49
1941	15 021	14 966	14 061	668	160		66	55
1942	17 470	17 413	16 466	720	153		64	57
1943	17 328	17 276	16 386	677	152		49	52
1944	16 772	16 709	15 882	645	128		49	63
1945	17 301	17 244	16 425	632	124		51	57
1946	17 525	17 494	16 705	639	108		36	31
1947	16 290	16 236	15 379	623	160		58	54
1948	16 115	16 065	15 293	559	127		68	50
1949	16 009	15 961	15 205	578	105		60	48
1950	16 018	15 948	15 049	671	145		64	70
1951	16 017	15 954	15 195	570	131		50	63
1952	15 876	15 778	14 985	582	147		32	98
1953	15 888	15 834	15 118	534	121		46	54
1954	15 831	15 767	15 000	582	121		41	64
1955	16 443	16 376	15 594	605	107		42	67
1956	16 761	16 686	16 041	483	95		51	75
1957	14 657	14 605	13 948	509	97		30	52
1958	15 061	15 016	14 483	389	91	32	4	45
1959	15 420	14 344	14 748	444	97	35	4	76
1960	15 465	15 408	14 866	371	115	34	4	57
1961	15 329	15 290	14 772	375	92	29	5	39
1962	15 627	15 580	14 977	438	120	28	3	47
1963	15 556	15 478	14 888	430	112	30	6	78
1964	16 128	16 062	15 506	412	103	31	3	66
1965	16 946	16 890	16 329	429	83	33	7	56

Table H4: Continued

	All	*Religious*	*Catholics*	*C of I*	*Presby-terians*	*Methodists*	*Other Denoms*	*Civil*
1966	16 849	16 770	16 164	444	117	33	4	79
1967	17 788	17 714	17 097	475	103	30	6	74
1968	18 993	18 897	18 260	465	120	31	13	96
1969	20 304	20 180	19 441	567	116	36	5	124
1970	20 778	20 657	19 989	518	104	29	10	121

NOTES AND SOURCES

1. Jewish and Society of Friends marriages have been omitted from the column for 'Other Denominations', but included in the columns for 'Religious Marriages' and 'All Marriages'.

2. Source: *Annual Reports* of the Registrar-General for the Republic of Ireland.

H5 MARRIAGES BY MANNER OF SOLEMNIZATION: NORTHERN IRELAND

	All	*Religious*	*Catholics*	*C of I*	*Presby-terians*	*Methodists*	*Other Denoms*	*Civil*
1920	9550	9033	2635	2797	3010		582	517
1921	8121	7746	2487	2337	2471		442	375
1922	8072	7683	2267	2503	2458		445	389
1923	7974	7576	2231	2515	2349		475	398
1924	7514	7111	1999	2401	2189		516	403
1925	7682	7265	2231	2266	2280		480	417
1926	7228	6789	2020	2222	2073		467	439
1927	7175	6787	2091	2150	2074	235	231	388
1928	7264	6809	2073	2111	2087		519	455
1929	7426	6947	2126	2201	2084		523	479
1930	7547	7040	2095	2245	2164		532	507
1931	7369	6843	2249	2138	1933		515	526
1932	6959	6435	1964	2027	1947		491	524
1933	7630	7039	2350	2209	1952		513	591
1934	8230	7549	2375	2390	2281		592	581
1935	8844	8224	2413	2586	2474		742	620
1936	9144	8466	2566	2586	2662		644	678
1937	8623	7976	2396	2426	2473	426	244	647
1938	8617	7986	2422	2377	2534		645	631
1939	9185	8546	2465	2545	2822		707	639
1940	9795	9177	2554	2729	2990	480	361	678
1941	11 966	11 093	3101	3349	3651	587	397	873
1942	11 673	10 814	3366	2968	3533	582	360	859
1943	10 155	9343	2928	2528	3100	495	281	807
1944	9508	8782	2828	2273	2877	474	307	726
1945	10 452	9615	3027	2576	3168	547	289	837
1946	9801	9006	2693	2493	3046	491	276	795
1947	9517	8781	2613	2359	3003	479	318	736
1948	9360	8651	2624	2314	2927	494	285	709
1949	9216	8486	2617	2295	2812	475	278	730
1950	9084	8440	2638	2278	2815	460	242	644

Table H5: Continued

	All	*Religious*	*Catholics*	*C of I*	*Presby-terians*	*Methodists*	*Other Denoms*	*Civil*
1951	9414	8720	2723	2270	2975	446	304	694
1952	9300	8624	2731	2244	2845	487	314	676
1953	9416	8760	2887	2261	2880	462	266	656
1954	9154	8539	2847	2195	2739	448	305	615
1955	9153	8896	3032	2219	2897	455	286	617
1956	9359	8832	2986	2255	2817	452	315	527
1957	9391	8852	2811	2377	2809	507	346	539
1958	9257	8804	2959	2234	2807	466	336	453
1959	9610	9131	3108	2291	2920	472	340	479
1960	9881	9406	3312	2308	2930	509	341	475
1961	9861	9341	3285	2258	2942	517	334	520
1962	9842	9361	3249	2285	2987	486	354	481
1963	10 155	9591	3405	2247	3031	534	381	557
1964	10 614	9961	3672	2343	3130	522	294	653
1965	10 452	9905	3574	2264	3165	533	369	547
1966	10 735	10 190	3707	2338	3207	582	356	545
1967	10 924	10 455	3913	2328	3204	566	444	469
1968	11 240	10 720	4107	2410	3178	587	438	520
1969	11 587	10 969	4325	2399	3217	582	446	618
1970	12 297	11 416	4678	2497	3194	596	451	881

NOTES AND SOURCES

1. Jewish and Society of Friends marriages have been omitted from the column for 'Other Denominations', but included in the columns for 'Religious Marriages' and 'All Marriages'.

2. Source: *Annual Reports* of the Registrar-General for Northern Ireland.

I1 ESTIMATES OF LISTENING AND VIEWING AUDIENCES (Per cent)[1]

	Radio[2]					*Television*[3]		
	Daily Service (Home)	Sunday Morning Service (Home)	People's Service (Light)	Sunday Evening Service (Home)	Sunday Half Hour (Light)	Morning Service	Meeting Point[4]	Songs of Praise
1940	8.20	10.15		11.17				
1941	8.95	12.93		10.30				
1942	6.08	9.10		6.65				
1943	5.50	12.95		9.03				
1944	6.56	13.53		10.53				
1945	6.00	12.98	5.91	10.68				
1946	6.79	10.25	9.25	9.25	20.50			
1947	4.33	9.00	12.50	8.50	24.00			
1948	3.75	4.00	16.60	6.80	24.80			
1949	3.29	3.75	13.75	6.25	23.75			
1950	2.17	3.25	13.00	3.75	26.50			
1951	1.91	2.50	14.75	3.75	21.75			
1952	1.70	2.50	13.75	4.00	19.25			
1953	1.38	3.50	14.00	3.75	18.00			
1954	1.62	4.25	11.75	2.75	15.25			
1955	1.08	3.00	15.25	3.00	13.75			
1956	1.08	2.50	13.75	3.50	11.00		5.75	
1957	1.04	2.75	10.50	2.50	9.75		7.00	
1958	1.17	3.50	10.50	1.75	8.25		6.75	
1959	1.08	2.25	10.00	1.00	7.00		4.75	
1960	0.85	2.45	9.55	1.20	4.65		4.25	
1961[5]	0.61	1.68	9.78	0.65	3.80'		4.25	
1962	0.52	1.58	11.13	0.63	3.23		7.00	9.25
1963	0.53	1.63	11.93	0.60	2.83	0.75	8.75	11.25
1964	0.55	1.73	11.33	0.35	2.30	0.50	6.25	9.25
1965	0.40	1.98	9.65	0.28	1.85	0.50	7.50	10.75
1966	0.51	1.70	7.98	0.08	1.53	0.38	7.15	11.28
1967[6]	0.50	2.00	8.20		1.20	0.30	6.30	10.70
1968	0.40	2.20	4.30		1.10	0.20	5.80	9.50
1969	0.60	1.70	4.10		1.30	0.40	4.60	10.10
1970	0.50	1.70	4.40		1.00	0.30	5.30	8.00

NOTES AND SOURCES

1. The estimates are derived from the British Broadcasting Corporation's daily surveys of the listening and viewing habits of random samples of 2000–4000 people in the United Kingdom. Until 1961, percentages of the population aged sixteen and over are given; thereafter, percentages of the population aged five and over. There is little discontinuity between the series. For example, the percentages of those surveyed claiming to watch 'Songs of Praise' in 1967–70 were:

	Percentage of population aged 5 and over	*Percentage of population aged 15 and over*
1967	10.7	11.1
1968	9.5	10.4
1969	10.1	10.9
1970	8.0	8.8

The percentages refer to February of each year and have been supplied by the British Broadcasting Corporation. The figures for 1967–70 were obtained from audience research analyses.

2. The approximate times of the radio programmes included in the table are:

Daily Service	10.15 – 10.30 a.m.
Sunday Morning Service	9.30 – 10.15 a.m.
People's Service (Sunday)	11.30 – 12.00 a.m.
Sunday Evening Service	7.45 – 8.25 p.m.
Sunday Half-Hour (hymns)	8.30 – 9.00 p.m.

The Sunday Evening Service was discontinued in 1967.

3. The approximate times of the Sunday television programmes included in the table are:

Morning Service	10.30 – 11.00 (or 11.30 a.m.)
Meeting Point (and later discussion programmes)	6.20 – 6.45 p.m.
Songs of Praise	6.50 – 7.25 p.m.

4. From 1967 onwards, the series for 'Meeting Point' includes other discussion programmes such as 'A Chance to Meet'.

12 INDEPENDENT TELEVISION WEEKLY AUDIENCE REPORTS (Percent)[1]

	Religious Music	*Discussion/ Didactic*	*All 'Religious Slot' Programmes*[2]
1957		10	10
1958		20	22
1959[3]			
1960		24	24
1961		24	24
1962		23	23
1963		17	17
1964	13	16	16
1965	17	17	18
1966	15	13	15
1967	17	13	19
1968	16	14	16
1969[3]	20	19	20
1970	26	21	22

NOTES AND SOURCES

1. The table gives TAMratings and JICTAR estimates of the proportion of homes receiving independent television switched on to specified transmissions. These estimates have been supplied by the Independent Broadcasting Authority. The table gives averages for each *type* of programme. Religious music programmes include, e.g., both 'Choirs on Sunday', and 'Stars on Sunday', a variety programme which caused marked increases in the audiences for Independent Television religious broadcasts. 'Discussion/didactic' programmes include 'Sunday Break', 'About Religion' and 'Living Your Life' (the three main Independent Television religious programmes during the period 1957–63), 'Food for Thought', 'Looking for an Answer', 'Round House', and 'Got the Message?'.

2. Both religious music and discussion/didactic programmes are broadcast in the Sunday 'religious slot', that is 6.15 – 7.25 p.m. The religious-slot average includes these programmes, children's religious programmes and series such as 'Adam Smith', a dramatic serial with a religious theme. Religious-slot averages are not directly comparable with British Broadcasting Corporation estimates. The British Broadcasting Corporation gives the following percentages of the total population as the audiences for Independent Television religious music and discussion programmes in February of each year:

	Religious Music	*Religious Discussion*
1967	6.1	2.0
1968	2.6	3.6
1969	8.9	8.0
1970	8.4	4.5

TAMratings and JICTAR estimates for the Independent Television religious slot may be compared with the following TAM ratings and JICTAR estimates for Independent Television variety programmes broadcast between 7.30 and 8.00 p.m.:

1961	43
1966	35
1971	40

3. No TAMratings are available for 1959. TAMratings were replaced by JICTAR data in 1968; and there is some discontinuity for the years 1967–9.

Index